THE CONSTANT ART OF BEING A WRITER

The Life, Art & Business of Fiction

N.M. Kelby

WRITER'S DIGEST BOOKS
Cincinnati, Ohio
www.writersdigest.com

For more resources for writers, visit www.writersdigest.com/books.

To receive a free weekly e-mail newsletter delivering tips and updates about writing and about Writer's Digest products, register directly at http://news letters.fwpublications.com.

13 12 11 10 09   5 4 3 2 1

Distributed in Canada by Fraser Direct
100 Armstrong Avenue
Georgetown, Ontario, Canada L7G 5S4
Tel: (905) 877-4411
Distributed in the U.K. and Europe by David & Charles
Brunel House, Newton Abbot, Devon, TQ12 4PU, England
Tel: (+44) 1626-323200, Fax: (+44) 1626-323319
E-mail: postmaster@davidandcharles.co.uk
Distributed in Australia by Capricorn Link
P.O. Box 704, Windsor, NSW 2756 Australia
Tel: (02) 4577-3555

Library of Congress Cataloging-in-Publication Data
Kelby, N.M.
    The constant art of being a writer : the life, art & business of fiction / N.M.
Kelby. -- 1st ed.
      p. cm.
    Includes index.
    ISBN 978-1-58297-575-7 (pbk. : alk. paper)
    1. Fiction--Authorship. 2. Fiction--Technique. 3. Authorship--Marketing. I.
Title.
    PN3355.K42 2009
    808.3--dc22   2009013370

Edited by Kelly Nickell
Designed by Terri Woesner
Production coordinated by Mark Griffin
Cover image ©gettyimages/Christine Balderas

Dedication

To Steven, always.

About the Author

© chrisbottphoto.com

N.M.Kelby is the author of *A Travel Guide for Restless Hearts*, *In the Company of Angels*, *Murder at the Bad Girl's Bar and Grill*, *Whale Season*, and *Theater of the Stars* (Theia/Hyperion). Named "Outstanding Southern Artist" by The Southern Arts Federation, Kelby's work has been translated into several languages and offered by The Literary Guild, Doubleday Book Club, and Quality Paperback Book Club.

Her short stories have appeared in many publications including *One Story*, *Zoetrope ASE*, and the audio magazine *Verb*. Her story "Jubilation, Florida" was selected for National Public Radio's Selected Shorts, and later recorded by actress Joanne Woodward for the NPR CD *Travel Tales*, and included in *New Stories from the South: Best of 2006* (Algonquin Books).

She is the recipient of a Bush Artist Fellowship in Literature, an NEA Inter-Arts grant, the Heekin Group Foundation's James Fellowship for the Novel, both a Florida and Minnesota State Arts Board Fellowship in fiction, two Jerome Travel Study Grants, a Jewish Arts Endowment Fellowship and numerous prizes.

She is currently working on the film version of *Whale Season* along with Actor/Singer Dwight Yoakam.

Acknowledgments

If you've read this book already and you're here trying to figure out who my agent is I'll make it easy—Lisa Bankoff at ICM. She is wise, funny, and loyal beyond all good reason. She also doesn't like chocolate, so she can't be bribed. If you want to query her, bring your best work and your most professional attitude, and she'll do the same.

You should also know that not only did my editor, Kelly Nickell, make this book possible, she also made it an exciting and enriching project to do. She is a joy to work with.

If you're reading this because you're looking for a place to get a lot of work done, a bulk of this book was written while in residence at the Santa Fe Art Institute. Staff members Gabe Gomez and Michelle Laflamme-Childs worked hard to make our time there productive and also convivial. They know where to get the best margaritas in town.

Of course, as is standard in most acknowledgment sections, I do want to thank my family who gives new meaning to the term "patron of the arts," in addition to all my friends and mentors who helped me with this book and with my journey in the world.

This simple line of thanks doesn't make up for all the ruined dinners and last-minute cancellations, but it's all I've got. Besides, they all know how much they mean to me. Books come and go, as does fame, but their love keeps me inspired, hopeful, and working.

And finally, I thank the readers. Without readers, I would be just another madman typing away in the dark.

table OF CONTENTS

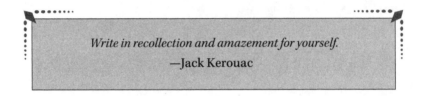

Write in recollection and amazement for yourself.
—Jack Kerouac

INTRODUCTION:
A Life in Words

At twelve thousand square feet, Kincaid's Billiards is larger than any nearby church, but it's just as filled with prayer, desire, and the need for one or another type of salvation.

This is where I come when words logjam in my brain. I play for the need of the perfect moment, and that perfect sound—the clack—that pure note of ball on ball. I play because the game reminds me that hard work and practice do pay off. I play because the distraction of the sport, which is similar to the process of writing, makes me see my work in a new light. I play because I like to win.

I tell my family I'm doing research.

The back room of Kincaid's is where the real players are found. They circle the table silently. Calculate the angle. Consider the calibration. Lean in. Show no mercy.

To me, it's just like a writer facing the page.

Billiards is not a gentleman's game. Mark Twain once said it "destroyed my naturally sweet disposition." Still, many writers are drawn to it. George Plimpton was so obsessed that every party at his apartment ended with a game. The next morning, he had the staff of his *Paris Review* analyze maps of shots taken before magazine business could begin. Even Shakespeare had Cleopatra try to roust up a game. (Act 2, Scene 5: "[L]et's to billiards: come, Charmian.")

I can understand. Pool is a game of nerve and bone. Of geometry and architecture. And lies. Lies you tell yourself, lies you tell others. And you must always practice. Always.

How is this not like writing?

With a story, or a novel, you begin with what is crucial. When you break the rack, it's the same. You are setting the tone, establishing a style. Then you have choices, so many angles to play. You have to be careful and choose the one you are the most able to capitalize on, the most crucial one. You have to make each shot count. As in writing, everything you do matters.

When I break the rack, I never go head-on. I always angle the rack, like I angle a story. I like to begin a little off-kilter, make it look impossible; it gives you more leverage. I always try to hit the cue ball as hard as I can, with authority and power. If I can put some English on it, a slight sidespin, I do it. Like an opening paragraph, how you break announces who you are, what your game is, what's at stake.

I ignore the easy shots. Any variation on a tricky pattern—hitting the rail first and then caroming back into the same rail—I try. I have to because it's all about the thrills, after all. The only problem is that I'm not very good at pool. I'm taking a huge risk with this style of play. And so, as with style in a story, I have to pay off the fancy shots. Always. The ball better end up in the pocket. Or, at the very least, create a problem cluster of balls that will be impossible for my opponent to overcome.

I try never to waste a shot. Never waste a word on the page.

Robert Byrne, a master player and teacher, has written twenty-three books about the game. He tells me that billiards, like writing, takes a certain mindfulness: "Philip Roth, in dismissing writers who talk about the mystical elements in writing, claimed that writing is an act of controlled intelligence. The writer is always in conscious control—as is the player."

So when I lean across the felt and let the possible trajectories play out in my head, I think of Roth, of his writer in conscious control. I think about how to shape whatever story or novel I'm working on at the moment, how to see it from all different angles, as I see the shot from all angles.

All I want is that perfect peal of ball on ball. The perfect clack.

So I try to go big, try to make the impossible seem easy. More often than not, I learn a lesson in humility. But I keep on despite all my failures, as I keep writing. Pool reminds me that a passive defense is avoiding defeat, but an aggressive one improves your chances of winning.

The same is true of writing. So, in the silence of my office, I face the empty page. Lean in. Show no mercy.

PART ONE

The Life

Above all, in the most silent hour of your night, ask yourself this: Must I write? Dig deep into yourself for a true answer. And if it should ring its assent, if you can confidently meet this serious question with a simple, "I must," then build your life upon it. ... Your life, in even the most mundane and least significant hour, must become a sign, a testimony to this urge.

—*Letters to a Young Poet,* Rainer Maria Rilke

1

EMBRACING
THE PROFESSION

The most difficult part of being a writer is living the life. There are no guarantees that you will be a success, and, if you are, there are no guarantees that you will continue to succeed. But you just keep on working. You have no choice; it's as if being a writer is encoded in your DNA.

Lorrie Moore writes in her short story "How to Become a Writer": "First, try to be something, anything, else."

But you can't. You're here for the duration.

Surviving as a writer is a constant art. You balance your desire to work, which is often overwhelming, and your work, which is often consuming, with your desire to have a full life with the people you love. That isn't easy.

A writer's life is focused in a way that others can't really understand. Most people go to work every day, take a paycheck home at the end of the week, and have time to see a movie or take in a ball game. Their lives are divided into the time that they work and the time they relax.

Writers are different: They're always working. Even when they're having fun, their minds are still working, recording the world around them. It's an occupational hazard. From the moment you wake up in the morning until you sleep at night, there's something about the particular sound of jaded laughter, the scent of a vanilla orchid, or the sight of an older woman carefully, painfully, walking across the street with a slight tremble in her gait that you can't turn away from. You take it all in, and it becomes a part of how you see the world, how you write.

Writing is not a profession—it's a way of being.

And so you travel, you inquire, you imagine—you write it all down. You're always in the process of learning and evolving. In order to survive, you need to understand that change is the only constant and you need to be careful not to get caught in the undertow of it.

You change your style as you mature in your craft: Issues that were of interest to you when you were in your twenties no longer captivate when you're thirty-five years old. You change your work habits when you have children, and it's more difficult to find time. You change how you go about your work when you suddenly find you have arthritis and need to use voice-activated software to write. Sometimes you even re-create yourself, changing both your name and style.

You are your own co-workers, your own office romance. You are given no safety net, no company 401K, and no health insurance benefits. Everything you have you've received through your own hard work, skill, and vision.

And while you're changing, the world changes around you. Your audience comes and goes. The society you live in gets more complex and your writing must always reflect that. We are now a society of visual creatures raised on the Internet, television, and film. We are messy thinkers with messy lives, and so our stories need to provide levels of truth and chaos with equal measure. There are no easy solutions any-more, no simple happy endings. Normal is never the norm. These days our mysteries don't even need a detective to solve them.

Even the method for the simple act of recording words has evolved from ink and paper to computers, and with that evolution, how you think and write changes: Your process can be much more fluid because you correct your text as you go. There are other forms of evolution, too. Some genres, like Westerns, fall out of favor, and their bones are incor-porated into other genres or forms, such as literary fiction.

The constant art of being a writer is not without peril.

You have to be fluid if you want to continue to have an audience. And you have to be patient to find one. And you never can lose hope. Being a writer is about giving yourself over to a long process of building and rebuilding: You build your career one book, one reader, at a time. It's a never-ending process because even when you do publish, even when you do write that bestseller, it doesn't get easier.

Philip Roth once said, "Each time you begin a book, you're an ama-teur. You're different from the doctor who's been at it for fifty years. I don't have the confidence the doctor has when he opens the door to the waiting room. It's a doubt-ridden profession."

At some point in your life, you may ask yourself if all the sacrifice and struggle is worth it, but you already know the answer in your heart. Writing is a journey filled with great joy. The sheer pleasure of spending every day of your life creating whole worlds is a gift unto itself—as is that first fan letter, or the moment that you pull up to a bookstore for a reading and people are lined up outside, all holding your books, all happy to see you.

Until Tony Hillerman died at the age of eighty-three, he had lived through two heart attacks, as well as prostate and bladder cancer. He still kept writing even though his eyesight was nearly gone, his hearing faded, and rheumatoid arthritis gnarled his hands.

"I'm getting old," he said before his death, "but I still like to write." It's that simple. We write until we can no longer write again.

The life of a writer is a blessed and sometimes a difficult one, but it's the only life most of us are suited for. We are public dreamers, after all. We have no choice.

·······• 2 •·······

SETTING UP PRACTICE

In the nonfiction book *Outliers*, an analytical look at how people excel in their given fields, author Malcolm Gladwell suggests that the difference between a professional and a talented amateur is ten thousand hours of practice. "There is a threshold of preparation for greatness," he says. "Nobody has been a chess grandmaster without having played for ten years, or composed great classical music without having composed for ten years."

Aspire to greatness. Begin now.

Writing is real work, and you need a real place to do it. Don't write all over your house. Pick one place that you feel comfortable in and set it up with a chair, something to write at like a desk or a table, and something to write with. Once it's furnished, always refer to it as your office.

The importance of having a place to call your office can't be underestimated. It's vital. It gives you a sense of validity that encourages you to set the bar high. That said, finding a space is always a problem. Some writers' organizations, like The Loft in Minneapolis, rent writing rooms at a low rate. You may even find a community center or a business that has an extra room they can rent.

If you don't have the money or don't want to drive to an office every day, a spare room or the corner of your bedroom will make a great office. Any place that you can call your own will work—even if it's the dining room table set aside for your use from 8 P.M. to midnight. Some writers work in bed.

The key to using common spaces is to work when no one else is around. That makes it easier to have some time alone with your thoughts. John O'Hara worked at night. He began at midnight, after his family was asleep.

Jon Hassler, a college professor, would get up before dawn and write while the entire household was still asleep. He'd begin by rereading the work he'd done the day before, giving it a quick edit, and then moving on. He'd do that every weekday, putting in at least two hours of work before going to work. On the weekends and holidays, he'd spend time with his family. He found that by using this schedule he could get at least three good pages written every day, sometimes more. It would take about six months to write the first draft. When he was done, he'd start at the beginning and rewrite until he was finished.

Some people write in cafés or public places. It's difficult to imagine being so public during such an intimate act. Most feel quite naked when they write and are often overwhelmed by an idea or made uneasy by the discomfort that truth brings. Some cry. Some shout. Some reread paragraphs aloud to test their buoyancy. Some laugh until they can't breathe. To the casual observer, writers often seem quite mad (and probably are).

These coffeehouse writers are a brave lot to work in the fray of life like that; playwrights David Mamet and August Wilson are two of the most memorable practitioners. Still, Mamet says he doesn't polish his work that way.

So before you settle into writing in cafés, rather than setting up an office, ask yourself why you're doing it. If you find that you gather inspiration from being in a crowd and can actually get work done, then that's great. But if you suspect that you write in public because it makes you feel more like a writer, because people see you writing and you feel a sense of pride from that, you may want to set up that office in your home and save café writing for times when you're lonely or frustrated.

You really don't want to get tied up in living the writer's mystique. Having to play the role of the writer takes energy and takes away from your work.

Many years ago, I studied with the Nobel Prize-winning poet Derek Walcott at Boston University. "Your body is a tool, take care of it," he said. "Go to bed early, get up early, and be ready to work. Keep regular hours. Do not drink or eat too much. You must be serious about the work."

Countless others talk about how drinking interferes with their work and reduces their ability to produce. Barry Hannah once told a group at Sewanee Writers' Conference that he used to try to drink and write but when he was sober couldn't make sense of the work that he'd done. "And you can't write well with a hangover," he added. John Cheever's lifelong struggle with alcoholism makes you wonder how much work he could have done if things had been different.

So don't worry about being the next best thing—just work on the next sentence and let the rest take care of itself.

Keep consistent hours. Writing is a job, after all. It gives you a sense of purpose to be at your desk by a specific time every day—five, six, or seven days a week.

How many hours you spend at your desk and how you divide that time is totally up to you. Many people who write full time will write in the morning and then, after lunch, work on the business end of things or research new work. Any schedule that fits your lifestyle is perfectly appropriate. There are many variations to consider.

Ernest Hemingway kept to a strict schedule while writing in Key West, waking at dawn and walking to his pool house, where he wrote 500 words a day at an old wooden desk. After work, he met his circle of friends every afternoon at 3:30 P.M. at Sloppy Joe's Bar.

Carl Hiaasen divides his week into two parts. He'll spend about two days writing his column for the *Miami Herald* and the rest of his time working on his own projects. In an effort to have his office perfectly quiet, he often wears a pair of ear muffs—like the ones you wear at a rifle range to protect your hearing. And when he wants things loud, his guitar collection is close at hand.

Sartorial decisions can also be important; surprisingly, writers are often concerned about what they wear to the office. Many never get out of their pajamas. Some only wear yoga pants. Some write buck naked.

John Cheever wore his only suit when he went to his studio in the morning. When he arrived, he undressed, hung it up, and worked in his underwear. After his day was done, he dressed and returned home.

Allan Gurganus says he wears a moving man's zip-up uniform because "I perspire so freely that I sweat my way through the fiction."

The options, as you can see, are endless.

The most important part of setting up your practice is creating a set of goals. No matter if you write in the morning, afternoon, or late at night, if you are clothed or naked, it's always good to aim to write a number of words or pages every day and never leave your desk until you're done.

Three pages a day, about 600 to 700 words, is a doable amount. Multiply that by five days a week and it's approximately 3,000 a week, which is 12,000 a month. In four months, you'll have about 50,000 words, which is a nice start for a book.

That's not to say that the 50,000 words you pound out in that short amount of time will be publishable as is, that's just to say that if you followed this course you'd have a good-sized manuscript to work on. Begin each writing day by going over the previous day's work. Edit the pages so they will be fresh in your mind and then move on. This method really helps with continuity.

Of course, everybody has an individual style. Woody Allen once said that he would just stop working when he was at his peak, even if it was in the middle of a scene, so that he wouldn't face a blank page the next day.

Like many things about this profession, you have to do what feels right for you. It's up to you to decide what brings your most efficient and creative self to the game. If you don't want to sit for several hours, you can be like Thomas Wolfe and write standing up. Again, it's your choice.

Many writers find that music often helps stimulate creative energy, but stay away from anything that engages you too much. Music should be more of a white noise to stimulate you. If you find you're paying more attention to the words of a song, you might switch to classical or jazz. Or you can listen to the same song over and over again; it's amazing how quickly you stop hearing the words and just use the energy of the music to move you along through the workday.

Of course, music doesn't have to be white noise; it can also inspire you. I often listen to the blues when writing about the South, for example. Something about the depth of pain in the music informs my work.

If you're using a radio, be careful not to turn to talk radio unless you're doing research—again, you want your white noise to be part of the background and not to engage you.

There are other ways to create white noise. Some people run a fan. Some use a sound machine. While the sound of an electronic surf doesn't much resemble the real surf, it does provide a predictable noise that somehow focuses your mind.

Try to discover what makes you comfortable enough to write from that deep place in your heart; what makes you unafraid to take risks, and what makes you willing to write until you lose yourself in the work and all sense of time slips away.

Then write. Write every maddening moment you can. The more you work with words, the less afraid you are to be playful—or truthful—with them. Writing should be the one thing that makes you happy in the day. It should be your refuge and your joy. You should need to write every day. A friend of mine who is a motivational speaker once told me that it takes three weeks to form a habit. Those three weeks could begin right now.

So figure out what's right for you and do it. Do it now, because you can't be a writer by wishing to be one. If you don't work every day at it, then you're just not being serious enough. Writing, even if you approach it as a hobby, is a highly competitive field that takes every ounce of focus and talent that you can bring to the table. If you don't work at it, you have no right to complain that others are more successful than you are. This is not a job for the lazy. Writing has to be your number one priority.

And, yes, all this focus and drive will make you crazy. It will also make your family crazy and your pets a little unhinged. It will make you wear your only suit to your office and then, Cheever-like, force you to sit in your underwear and work until you create a world that is more beautiful, more lively, and more complex than you ever thought possible. And then you will put your suit back on and join the rest of the world until tomorrow, when you will start the process all over again.

The real truth of the matter is that the writing life is not a life of grace, but insanity. So take good care of yourself and get some sleep because you're going to need your strength.

······ 3 ······

READING AS A WRITER

Once you become a writer, reading is one of the most important things that you'll do.

The excuse of not reading because you don't want other books to influence your work is wrong-headed. You *do* want books to influence your style, to make you think about how you go about your own work, to challenge you to raise the bar higher, and to teach you how others approach the page. Books provide you an education: the ability to hone your skills and sensibility. If you're not willing to learn to read as a writer, you have no realistic chance of having a career as one. You may publish a book, or two, but you'll soon begin to stagnate and write the same book over and over again. Eventually, you'll lose your readership. It's a trap that many writers fall into; that's why being a writer is a constant art in itself. You must always be willing to grow and evolve.

When you read as a writer, you stop reading for pleasure, stop allowing the writer to lure you in, and begin to see how he or she wields the craft. Just like a chef analyzing a well-made stew, you are trying to figure out how the work is put together—how words work on the page. Is it grammatically complicated? What are the word choices made? Once you determine what has been done, then you have to ask yourself *why* it was done.

While this sounds easy, it isn't really. People often read quickly, skimming as they go. But when you read as a writer, you need to pay close attention and read every word in a sentence. Not only does that take more time, it's also a lot more difficult than it seems. It's not your fault: It's your brain.

When you read, your brain skips over words and gives you a general idea of what is being said. That's just a fact of living in a modern world. We don't read every "the" and "he said"—there just isn't enough time. So your brain makes assumptions about what the author has written.

Unfortunately, some of these assumptions are based on your experience, and not often on the writer's intent.

It's sort of like that old parlor game, Telephone—you know the one. You begin with a sentence that one person will whisper to another until finally everyone in the room has heard it. The last person then repeats what he's heard and everyone laughs because the sentence began as "Mary Jane has a new pair of shoes" and ends up as "May you never be in the position to choose."

So try to read every word. It's important to know when an author used the protagonist's name and when he was just referred to as "he." You'll find some patterns that you can learn from. For example, many writers will use the protagonist's name more frequently in the front of the book than in the back. This is usually done to firmly establish the character and his ticks. Once you can identify the protagonist, you really don't need to say his name quite so often—unless you want to.

A good place to begin your analysis of form is to pick several books and take a close look at the first page. Note how a writer introduces the work. In the opening page, he'll usually give you an idea of his worldview, set the tone for the story he's telling, and begin to set the factual groundwork of his story—the who, what, and where of it.

Consider this sentence from Garrison Keillor's *Lake Wobegon Days*:

> From the south, the highway aims for the lake, bends hard left
> by the magnificent concrete Grecian grain silos, and eases
> over a leg of the hill past the SLOW CHILDREN sign, bringing the
> traveler in on Main Street toward the town's one traffic light,
> which is almost always green.

Keillor has chosen to use a long rolling sentence with a comfortable cadence and a Midwestern worldview. The "magnificent concrete Grecian grain silos" and the perpetual welcoming of travelers with "the town's one traffic light, which is almost always green" is solidly Midwestern and that makes sense because Keillor's territory as a writer is the mythical Lake Wobegon, which is set somewhere in the state of Minnesota.

The warm conversational tone of this sentence is an earmark of Keillor's style; he is, after all, a radio-based storyteller. He writes this as a friend who wants to tell you a story. And, given the length and cadence of the sentence, it's going to take a while, so you might as well get comfortable.

The next thing that's the most obvious is how Keillor uses personification. This device of making an inanimate object seem human helps the reader identify with the subject. When Carl Sandburg wrote, "Show me another city with lifted head singing / so proud to be alive and coarse and strong and cunning," you understand Chicago in the same way that you understand yourself. Keillor begins with "the highway aims for the lake," and then builds with "bends hard left" and "eases over a leg" and ends with bringing the traveler into the welcoming town.

At the other extreme is Chuck Palahniuk. Here's his opening for *Choke*:

> If you're going to read this, don't bother.
> After a couple of pages, you won't want to be here. So forget it. Go away. Get out while you're still in one piece.

Keillor and Palahniuk obviously represent two wildly different styles of storytelling. Palahniuk spends a good deal of his opening salvo warding you off. You have to read quite a bit more of *Choke* to understand that this book is a dark and humorous meditation on sexual addiction and salvation, but that's Palahniuk's way. He speaks directly to the audience in an absurd fashion.

And he is correct. As the book progresses, there are times that you really don't want to be "here," in the world of the book. It's a scary place that proves that things can't get better until they get horribly worse. And they do get horribly worse. But he did warn you going in, just as a friend would, which is charming. So you say with him. It's a very interesting ploy.

As you notice, Palahniuk uses short, quick sentences. Those sentences attempt to build a sense of impending dread. He begins with the fair warning of "After a couple of pages, you won't want to be here" and moves on to "Get out while you're still in one piece."

Speaking directly to the reader is an approach that other writers have used with a great deal of success. Italo Calvino began his novel *If on a winter's night a traveler* in a similar, although more welcoming, manner.

> You are about to begin reading Italo Calvino's new novel, *If on a winter's night a traveler.* Relax. Concentrate. Dispel every other thought. Let the world around you fade. It's best to close the door; the TV is always on in the next room.

The self-referential direction of this paragraph speaks to the reader directly, makes you feel as if Calvino knows you. He at least knows what you're doing—you're reading his book. From the start, Calvino creates a work where the reader identifies with the writer and a bond is formed.

Even though there are some similarities of form between Palahniuk and Calvino, the two differ greatly in their approach. In the first paragraph, Palahniuk sets the tone and style of his novel, but not much else. Calvino does the same but also uses this first paragraph to signal to the reader what the book is about—reading. *Traveler* is an inventive work that is not one novel, but ten. Each novel-within-a-novel is very different in style and content, but all are interrupted at its climax. The main characters of the story are a man and woman, two unnamed readers, who work their way through the literary labyrinth and towards each other. One is called "you" and you, of course, are the reader.

--- *Exercise* ---

Appropriating Style

Take the opening paragraph of *A Christmas Carol*, Charles Dickens's "ghostly little book," as he called it, and retool it in the style of Palahniuk, Calvino, or Keillor. Expand it to one page, taking it in any direction that you wish, even if that means you re-create the story.

Marley's Ghost

Marley was dead: to begin with. There is no doubt whatever about that. The register of his burial was signed by the clergyman, the clerk, the undertaker, and the chief mourner. Scrooge signed it: and Scrooge's name was good upon 'change, for anything he chose to put his hand to. Old Marley was as dead as a door-nail.

When you're finished rewriting this paragraph, evaluate your version by asking:

1. How does the textual shift change the outcome of the story?

2. What do the stylistic changes add to the work? How do they detract from it?

3. Why did you take the work in the direction that you did?

4. What about your reworking made you feel this was the right choice? Or, the wrong choice?

Now look at a current project that you're working on. How does your first page read when examined with this same scrutiny? Are you using form and language in a manner appropriate to the story you want to tell and how you want to tell it? If not, think of a book that you feel your work is similar to and read it carefully; read it as a writer. Take what you learn from it and apply it to your own work.

CULTIVATING A CRITICAL EYE

While dissecting a piece of writing will tell you how it was put together, critical thinking also is an important tool for writers because you need to understand why something is considered good. It helps you have a deeper understanding of your own work. Many graduate school writing programs focus on teaching you how to cultivate a critical eye, but if you haven't been to graduate school, you can certainly learn to do this on your own. (Even if you have been, you should always be honing your skills.)

First, buy a notebook. All writers need a notebook to keep their thoughts and inspirations in. Make sure it's a sturdy notebook, because you'll want to save your thoughts and refer back to them for years to come. It should be rugged enough so that you can carry it at all times to jot down ideas. I put postcards and pictures in mine, things that inspire me or make me laugh. Sometimes, I'll write down interesting names I come across. Don't forget to put your name and contact information in it, just in case it gets lost. Date it, too. It's fun to go back and dig though old ideas. You never know what's in there that you can reuse.

After you get your notebook, find a current novel to read. It can be either a paperback or hardback. Something your friend told you about, or something that caught your eye in *The New York Times Book Review*. Keep in mind that while you want to work with something that's current to the marketplace, not all great books sell well. According to Bookscan, Jhumpa Lahiri's Pulitzer Prize-winning *Interpreter of Maladies* only sold about ten thousand copies in hardcover—and that was a great book.

It's often instructive to read a book that the critics either love or hate, something they are not neutral about. Do *you* need to love it? No. Love is good, but blind. Sometimes you can learn a great deal from what you despise. What if you are indifferent to it? That's interesting, too.

When you're done reading, you should gather enough information to form your own independent review. Write down the answers to these questions in your notebook.

1. What does the author do that impresses you the most? The language? The rhythm of the text? The message? The grit of the world that is presented? Supply passages to illustrate your observations.

2. What does the author do that least impresses you? Too many literary ticks? The overuse of vulgar language? Why do you feel these elements are ineffective? Is it a matter of personal style, or do you feel the elements detract from the storytelling? Explain why.

3. Has the work enriched you? Provide passages that strike you as meaningful. If not, provide passages that strike you as most meaningless.

4. How does it relate to your own work in style? In theme? If it doesn't, explain why.

5. Even if the book is not funny, does the writer use humor? If so, how? Choose a few passages where you believe humor was used.

6. What makes this work feel authentic? Or not? Give examples.

7. What makes this work feel universal? Or not? Give examples.

8. Is there a traditional protagonist? What is the most important thing about him/her?

9. Which passages did you love? Why?

10. Which did you dislike? Why?

Once you've answered these questions, go through the list and choose the most important things about the book that you'd want to tell the public. Now, write your own review. Limit yourself to about three typewritten pages, or a maximum of 600 words.

When you finish your review, gather other reviews and compare your findings to those of the critics. See where they differ from yours and where they are alike. You can learn a great deal from what is said by others. If a review seems totally off base, you need to ask yourself how the reviewer came to that conclusion and try to understand why he might read the text that way.

If you're having a difficult time finding reviews, both Amazon.com and Barnes & Noble's Web site (bn.com) publish the complete reviews of newer books.

While you don't want to do this exercise in such great detail for every book you read, it's good to get in the habit of making extensive notes on what you read and comparing your ideas to those of critics. This will not only help you get a deeper understanding of the marketplace, it will also help you shape your own work and give you a sense of what the review process should be.

Not every reviewer is good, however. Sometimes the critic doesn't pay close attention to the work; it's a sad truth. Some get names wrong, confuse plot points—the list goes on. By creating your own reviews, you can gain insight into how deeply the critics should read the work, and, if they don't, you know what weight you should give their opinions and not get too discouraged if someday they pan your own work.

The most interesting thing about reading work with a critical eye is looking at how things are interpreted. Hemingway always spoke of what the reader brings to the page and how that was even more important than what the writer actually intended. When you read a work that's been reviewed, and form your own critical response, you really begin to understand what he was talking about. The good reviewer makes a case for his opinion of the work, which gives you a baseline to compare your opinion to. It also allows you to understand how different readers see things differently—and that skill alone will serve you well as you put your own words to paper.

A Note About Reading Reviews of Your Work

It's good practice to attempt to make sense of every review you get, good or bad. Weigh the veracity of each concern. If you take the good from a review, you can't edit out the bad, even though that's what the marketing department does. No professional critic is usually totally off base, and there's always a little bit of truth, or confusion, in even the most painful things.

If a critic didn't understand what you were going for with a story, you may consider taking a different approach next time, or not. It depends on how professional the critic is and what his prejudices are (which you can easily find out by doing a Google search) and how committed you are to the choice that you made.

In the end, you need to trust your gut and skill because you're the writer and the final judge of your own work—and perhaps the toughest. If you feel secure in your own understanding of the critical process, responding to criticism will be a lot easier and slightly less painful; but only slightly.

········ 5 ········
JOINING A WRITING
COMMUNITY

No matter where you live, thanks to the Internet, you live in a community of writers. There are many online communities to work with, and they certainly have a place in the writer's life, but you really may not need anything that formal. It's often enough just to e-mail friends you met in writing classes or at book festivals. Many people exchange work with classmates from college or graduate school. With the Internet, getting feedback is easier than ever, and very valuable. It's always good to have a trusted second opinion.

But, if you like to get out of the house, there are several organizations around the country geared to helping writers grow. For example, in Minneapolis, there's SASE: The Write Place and The Loft—both do a fine job of bringing writers together.

Many towns, even small ones, have writers' groups. You can usually find their meetings listed in the newspaper, especially the weekly or community publications. If you don't find anything there, try the library or bookstores, as both often hold meetings. Many independent booksellers like I Love a Mystery in Mission, Kansas (just across the state line from Kansas City, Missouri), invite writers' organizations such as Sisters in Crime to meet at the store.

If working within a community of local writers is not of interest to you and you'd like more of a national perspective without a large time commitment, join The Association of Writers and Writing Programs (AWP, awpwriter.org). While primarily focused on the academic side of the profession (graduate programs and their students), it's a great organization for writers. Not only do they publish *The Writer's Chronicle*, a good resource for publishing opportunities and trends in writing, they hold a yearly conference where many writers not associated with graduate programs can talk shop both in public lectures and at the conference hotel lobby, bar, or cafés. There are writers in every corner. It's a great chance to hear the finest talent in America and catch up with old friends and make new ones. Plus, the dances are fun.

There are also national organizations for each writing genre, including Romance Writers of America (rwanational.org), Mystery Writers of America (mysterywriters.org), Science Fiction & Fantasy Writers of America (sfwa.org), the Horror Writers Association (horror.org), and the Society of Children's Book Writers and Illustrators (scbwi.org). All offer information on writing and getting published, a community of writers with like-minded goals, and a variety of support services.

While being part of a community is important for a writer, before you venture into communal waters you should think about your expectations. Identifying yourself as part of a writing community is a worthwhile thing; it gives you perspective and a sense of pride. It can also drive you crazy if it's not the right situation. Make a list of your needs. For example, do you just want someone to bounce a manuscript off of? Or, are you more interested in general shoptalk? If you're not sure, sample a few options before you commit your heart and your work.

COLLABORATIVE WRITING

If you do become part of a community and make friends with people you'd like to work with, don't be afraid to try to give some time over to collaborative writing. It's good every now and then to do a project with someone else—it shakes things up, demystifies words, and, if you're lucky, a sense of play is instilled. Playing with words always leads to discovery, and it's certainly more fun to play with somebody else. There's great energy when two people work together.

The biggest problem with collaboration is the same as with finding the right community—it has to be the right match. A couple of basic elements are necessary to make these relationships work: You must have comparable, or at least compatible, work ethics and the ability to clearly communicate.

If somebody tells you they will get back to you next week, and three months later you hear from them, it's best not to get involved. They're either too busy to work on a new project or maybe don't share your sense of urgency; when you're working with deadlines, that's always a stressful situation.

Of course it's fine to collaborate on work just for fun and personal writing development, but you and your potential writing partner may want to try collaborative writing for publication. Before you commit to any project, it's always good to create a timeline and find a lawyer to set up a simple agreement that makes it clear that you are in a partnership and what each is expected to do in terms of writing and promotion. Keep in mind that a fifty-fifty split of the advance and royalties should never be assumed. Once all these details are settled, then the real work, and real fun, can comfortably begin.

Right at the start it's also good to set goals for the project (like to write and edit 500 words a week) and create a schedule of writing meetings. The meetings don't have to be face-to-face, a volley of Internet exchanges will do, as long as the meetings are on some sort of schedule, like Tuesdays and Thursdays from 10 A.M. to noon. Whatever you do, try not to make it over lunch. As well intended as working lunches are, food often interferes with the process. Yes, you will get some things done, but not as much as if you weren't hungry or chewing, and had both hands free to write.

INTERNET OPTIONS

If you'd like to be part of a community but really don't have the time or energy to deal with people face-to-face, you may look into joining a cyber community of writers. There certainly are a lot of choices these days. But before you log on, there are a few things you should consider before signing up.

1. What kind of work does the site deal with? Some sites are geared to genre writers and some are more literary. It's really important to understand what kind of writing the site deals with because when you post your stories for people to read they're going to come to your work with expectations.

Some sites do say that they accept all kinds of writing, but you should really lurk awhile to be sure. Nothing is more frustrating than posting a first chapter to a site and having it misread by people who think *The Catcher in the Rye* is a novel about an alien who abducts farmers by hiding out in fields.

2. Get a feeling for the site's intent. Read the Frequently Asked Questions (FAQs) and make sure you understand what posting means for your work. For example, at Zoetrope.com, the film rights to your story, or chapters, are actually offered to the site for a set fee when you post. That's something you might want to talk over with an intellectual property lawyer or your agent, if you have one.

3. Read the work of others before you post your own. Some sites make you critique a set number of stories before you can post, others don't. Still, it's a good idea to read at least five stories and present critiques. First, you'll get a sense of how others write and what they write. And, perhaps more importantly, you'll get a keen understanding of how they take criticism.

4. Evaluate your time. Since the best way to get critiques is to give them, you have to make sure you have time to read the work of others and write helpful critiques. If you can read critiques from other writers, that would be good, too. Workshops all have some sense of etiquette, and you want to make sure that you understand what exactly can and can't be done *before* you start posting. For example, some places hate it when you solicit reviews—others are okay with it.

If you read the site board and see lots of flame wars (that lovely Internet phrase for "insane pointless screaming arguments") over how people critiqued a work, then take good notes. Nothing makes people angrier than to be read by a reviewer who obviously didn't care enough to give a thoughtful review and yet expects one back.

In order to join an online community, you really have to have the time to be thoughtful and mindful of what you say. Because the Internet is all about text, and the human element of vocal inflection is gone, it's easy to joke and be misunderstood. Sometimes the most innocent comment can lead to a bitter confrontation. You just have to be able to take the time and think about what you write before you write it.

5. Edit with a professional eye. Don't slam the work, no matter how awful it is. Remember, a critique is about what works and doesn't work. If you don't like the treatment of a subject, or the type of story being told, it's often better to walk away. If you can't, then you should be clear about that right at the beginning. Always point out the work's strengths. Then pick one or two things that you think need work, like point of view, and give specific examples of what's wrong. Line edits are great, if they are just about grammar issues. Don't say, "Fred is an awful name for a character; try Jonas." But do mark the name if it isn't capitalized. Always use proofreader's marks when editing text so your intent is clear.

6. Always send private e-mails to thank people for their critiques, even if you disagree or think they did a bad job. They did take the time to go over your work, which, given how busy people are, is a very kind thing. And, no matter how wrong you think they were, don't "critique" their critique. Don't argue with them. If you do, you may find your e-mail posted all over the Internet.

7. Not all critiques are equal. While most people really try to be helpful, some will be more helpful than others; it all depends on people's experience and temperament. These communities are a mixed bag of participants. Some are professionals just looking for another outlet for feedback, while some can be children posing as adults. You can even run across people who are out of their minds and totally raving or editing drunk. That's the problem with cyberspace: You never know whom you're really dealing with and what state of mind they're in.

You can, however, meet some great editors at workshops. The best way to increase your odds of that happening is to always check the bio and see if the person has any publication credits or any teaching experience. It really makes a difference.

You have to have a thick skin when working with Internet communities because sometimes you'll get scathing reviews, and maybe even several of them, and not know what to do with that information. Whenever you get an awful review, you have to weigh what's being said. (See "A Note About Reading Reviews of Your Work" on page 19.) Does the writer have a valid point or is she ranting for no good reason? If your review is peppered with foul language, strange suggestions, or ranting, it's a pretty good bet that the reviewer is not worth listening to.

It does pay to post your work, though. The funny thing about having your work on the Internet is that there's a certain consistency in people's remarks. The mistakes that you've made usually become evident after the first five reviews. By the tenth review, you'll begin to notice similar themes. Some people will like this element, while others won't. Once you begin to notice patterns, you can decide what you want to do about these criticisms.

8. Use your real name. I know this seems unsafe, but not using your real name causes many more problems. Sometimes people will actually call you out and claim that you're trying to hide behind a fake identity or say that you're using multiple identities—and that causes a lot more drama than you want. Or, they may just feel that if you're being sincere with your criticism, and your interest in the group, why would you use another name? So, it's best to keep your life as uncomplicated as possible and use your real name. Besides, if you're doing good work, and helping others, don't you want people to know that? It certainly helps build a fan base.

9. Resubmit the edited piece. If you've made changes, not just fixing the grammar or spelling, but real substantive changes, it's time to resubmit. People want to see how you responded to their suggestions.

10. If you do submit to a publisher and it's accepted, thank everyone who critiqued your work. Always send a private e-mail and then thank your reviewers publicly. If there's a "new publication" thread, post the specifics. While some may be jealous, those who helped you will feel honored. I know your mother told you this already, but it's true: People always remember good manners, and saying "thank you" for people's time, concern, and efforts will serve you well.

11. Be a good community member. Even when you don't have something to critique, spend some time critiquing the work of others.

12. Always critique people who have critiqued you—and not just at the time that they did it. Try to cultivate a few online reviewers as friends; that's why you're there, after all.

Online Writing Communities

Just to get you started, here's a list of writing communities from cyberspace. As you can see, many of them are quite niche-oriented.

- **Thewritingbridge.org** is a membership-based site looking for writers serious about the craft and interested in working in small groups. Everybody fills out an application, so they're careful about whom they admit.

- **Momwriterslitmag.com** is a site for "mom writers who have something to say." It features supportive articles geared to women writers with children.

- **Newbie-writers.com** is for writers of all genres. It's a great support group for those just starting out and includes tips on how to get started and how not to get discouraged.

- **Thefrontlist.com** is designed to fast-track your writing to several publishers and agents who are looking for work. It's an Internet slush pile, of sorts. If you join, you critique several manuscripts, then you submit your own. If the work meets the community standards, it's passed along to people who can help you get published.

- **Zoetrope.writingclasses.com** is the online writing workshop sponsored by Francis Ford Coppola. It is an international community of writers and lurkers. You take your chances when you post work on the general board, but there are lots of great readers so it can be worth it. And, while the discussion board on the short-story site is always filled with tiresome melodrama, there are also quite a few good publication leads. Most of the real workshopping is done in private offices. If you see an office that you like, you can just ask to join in.

- **Internetwritingworkshop.org** is a manuscript exchange service that allows writers to critique and be critiqued through e-mail. There are monthly minimum participation requirements that vary given the discipline. Fiction requires two submissions or criticisms a month and does not allow for discussions. Poetry requires eight e-mails with more criticisms than submissions and discussions on theory only.

Of course, this is just a sample of your options. For a current list, do a search for "online writing communities" and there will be hundreds more—and probably the right one for you.

•••••••• 6 ••••••••
CREATING YOUR OWN COMMUNITY

If you're not interested in joining an existing community, and you have some time to spare, you may want to start one of your own. You could take a classified ad out in the newspaper or on your local Craigslist.com page or post a meeting notice at the local bookstores or college asking other writers to join you in a writers' group. You'll get a mixed bag of people that way, but some may be worth working with.

The biggest problem with creating a writers' group is that you may spend all of your time workshopping writing and none of it talking about literary issues and great works. After a while, it starts to feel like an endless homework assignment.

A more interesting approach is to create a salon that's a mix of writers and readers. It's a great way to meet people, sort of like a book club without the reading assignment—or with it. It's your choice. Salons are incredibly flexible; they're just a way for people to get together and discuss ideas.

The Algonquin Round Table, a decade-long salon of writers, actors, and editors, met each day at The Algonquin Hotel to have lunch and make history through their wit and wisecracks, which ended up in members' columns in newspapers across America. The Vicious Circle (as they called themselves) was made up of a core group of members including critic, writer, and screenwriter Dorothy Parker; *New York Times* drama critic Alexander Woollcott; humorist and actor Robert Benchley; and the play-wright and director George S. Kaufman. They were often joined by many others, including actress Tallulah Bankhead and Harpo Marx.

While traditionally salons are not exactly writing groups, they can focus on writing and invite guest writers to read and sell their work. Again, it's your salon; if you want to invite just writers who wish to workshop, you should. Just keep in mind that all work and no play will limit the group dynamic and its effectiveness. People will get bored. Maybe you could workshop one month, and then the next month you could have a local poet swing by and give a lecture on concise language and read from his latest book. Like everything in life, a sense of balance always works the best.

While hosting salons is a wonderful way to create your own community, it does take some work. Most salons are closed groups of friends inviting friends to someone's house, although they are also held in the back rooms of bars and cafes. They usually take place on the same day, like the first Wednesday of each month, and they run about four hours. Here are some tips.

GUESTS

A great salon starts with great people. You'll want to invite people from all over the writing spectrum and mix it up politically and socially because that's what makes a lively salon—one you can learn from. Try not to get it too polarized, however. If you have a group that's composed of extremes on both sides, there'll be endless arguing and rabid posturing— and that's not fun.

Salons usually have a core of regulars who feel that they have some investment because they've come since the beginning. So, your first meeting is the most important. Choose those people wisely and engage them in helping you organize, host, promote, and moderate future events. Make sure that they're always invited personally, but don't forget to grow the group. The same guests tend to make an evening dull.

Don't worry about attrition too much. It happens. People lose interest or get busy. But, even if you haven't seen someone in a while, unless they ask to be taken off the mailing list, don't remove them. Always send everyone, including those who seem MIA, an e-mail (or snail mail) notice about the topic, location, and time. They may come back.

Of course, if you *do* start losing people at a rapid rate, there maybe a group dynamic that is really not working or a member who is driving everyone away. Unfortunately, as host, it's your job to fix the problem.

While it isn't easy to ask people to leave a salon, when it has to be done, it really *has* to be done. The mean and the condescending have no place in a genial group dynamic, nor do the conversation hoggers or constant interrupters. Some salons also kick out people who don't contribute to the conversation and freeloaders who just come to drink wine and eat whatever they can get their hands on.

A salon is to be a civil and lively exchange about ideas. Anyone who doesn't contribute is taking up valuable space. If you find you have a member that you'd rather do without, it's important to have a private, non-threatening conversation with him. After your chat, you may decide that he deserves a second chance. But, whatever you do, don't e-mail them about it. While e-mail is great for invitations, it's not a very respectful way to deal with someone who's creating a problem for you. Just pick up the phone. You may find that the problem is easily solved once you talk it through.

MECHANICS

There are two basic salon models you can work from: open houses or invitation only. Most salons are open houses. They're usually held in someone's house, and while core invitations are sent to people you really want to come, most of the inviting is done through word of mouth. Your friends invite other friends. The downside is that you never know who is coming.

If you do an invitation-only event, it's a little more time-intensive. To get a lively group, get recommendations from your friends and colleagues, and then call those people to see if they're interested in coming. During your phone call, you should try to interview them. This is all about chemistry, after all. Even though this method takes more time, it can be worth it because you get a clear idea about how many you'll have at the salon and what the dynamic will be.

As mentioned earlier, always send out an invitation before the event. The invitation needs to include the usual particulars (time, place, and date) in addition to the topic (such as the relevance of the Civil War in Southern literature) or the nature of the event (like a poetry reading). E-mails are very handy for this and should be sent out about two weeks before the event.

Keep in mind that you don't want to send out too much e-mail, as people are very sensitive about being spammed. However, if you want the group to read an essay to discuss, or for them to pass along the invite to friends, e-mails are the most affordable and convenient way to do this.

One thing to consider is that you may not want to have everyone's e-mail visible when you send the invites. Sometimes you'll get people who will take the mailing list and use it for their own group mailings and that's not good at all. If you choose to set some ground rules in the beginning, not using the salon mailing list should be one of them. Nothing is worse than being copied on a variety of lame jokes or "special offers" from people you barely know.

Before the night of the salon arrives, you need to figure out if you want to be both host and moderator, or allow someone else to moderate. Both duties are time-intensive, and I think it's always better to separate the two. As host, your job will be to make your guests feel welcome by feeding and watering them: bread, cheese, and wine will usually do the trick. But the moderator's job is to be the tough guy. He makes sure that the salon stays on-topic and no one gets unruly. Since it's very difficult to show someone where the bathroom is while trying to keep a discussion going, it's really best to find someone to take over this role—or, to be host. Doing both jobs is just too much for one person.

The topic of the salon is, of course, important, but how you chose it is up to you. If you want a salon for and about writers, you'd probably do well to enlist the group in making decisions, since they are trying to learn something too and everyone's skill set is different.

Most of these events start after dinner, usually about 7 or 8 P.M., depending on where you live. Cocktails or refreshments are served for about an hour and then the discussion begins. It can run up to three hours, with a fifteen-minute break somewhere at the halfway point.

And while most salons are held in homes, as long as the space isn't too large for the group, they can really be held anywhere. The key is that the space needs to be set up so that the salon members are comfortable and can easily hear and be heard.

Group size varies, but a salon can be as small as five or as large as twenty to twenty-five. Once people have to raise hands, it seems a little too much like school and spontaneity is lost. So smaller really is better.

While all this seems like a lot of work, the point is to make a community. You write because you love books, but you can get stale writing alone all the time. The power of community can't be underestimated. Your fellow writers, and your readers, can share in your journey, enlighten you, sharpen your vision, and, if you're lucky, bring fellowship and a rather nice Cabernet to your table.

There's really no need to make the journey of writing alone.

········ 7 ········

UNDERSTANDING
THE READER

Writing is a powerful act. Since most people read in bed before they go to sleep at night, it's as if you're whispering in the dark to a stranger who is naked in many ways. They're tired and vulnerable. They may not be wearing their jammies. When they read your work, you are inside their head. They think the words you want them to think because you've written them on the page.

The relationship between writer and reader is an intimate bond, a commitment. It's all about trust. Readers trust that you won't waste their time. You trust that they'll try to understand what you're saying, and why.

If you keep this is mind when you write, you will make more thoughtful choices. You may take a moment before you write a particularly graphic scene and ask yourself if you really need it. You probably do. And if you do, your reader will accept it because they trust you.

For example, when you write a murder mystery, it's going to be shocking because people die. A writer must deliver that shock to his readers because you just can't have a successful murder mystery where nobody dies. How characters die and how much you tell the audience about the details of their death is up to you and should be based on what your story needs to be the story you want to tell and what your audience needs to completely understand and be compelled by the work.

Extremely graphic work does pay off. Chuck Palahniuk's novels are quite graphic, but it's always in keeping with his themes. Take, for example, the novel *Snuff.* Anyone who picks up a book with that title, by the very nature of the title, is going to expect it to be graphic.

When you write, you enter into a conversation with the reader. You've defined the genre in which you're writing and its themes, and, therefore, the reader has certain expectations. If you've written a romance, you need to put enough of the traditional formula of "boy meets girl, boy loses girl, boy gets girl," even if you play against those expectations by writing an atypical romance. You need, at least on some minimal level, to fulfill their expectations of the type of book that you appear to be writing.

Once you do that, you can decide if you're going to play to their tastes or against them, but you need to set up the framework. As long as you give readers an interesting tale that meets certain expectations of the genre, or literature in general, you can get away with taking risks. However, books that are graphic, vulgar, or shocking, just for shock value, will let some readers' expectations down and they will abandon the book before they get to the last page.

To write a good book, you need to respect the reader, and to do that, you need to understand how your work will be welcomed into the world. Read widely—and outside your field of interest. Examine both the standards and expectations of each work. Allow yourself to be sparked by the words of others. Study the work of genre writers, Nobel Laureates, National Book Award recipients, and Pulitzer Prize winners. Read books from all cultures, races, and religions. You will not only learn about the standards of form, you will discover the surprising beauty of an unexpected phrase, the lyrical cadence of a sentence, and the elegant worlds mapped by literary vision. You will also come to understand what it is like to be "the other" and to accept "the other" in yourself. Once you understand the other, your work will take a more inclusive scope.

Another good way to understand your readers is to try to imagine who they are. Pick somebody who you think might be interested in what you have to say and write to them. Since it's someone you know, you'll try harder to surprise and amaze. It's often fun to scare them, too. If you imagine your reader as a real person with feelings and expectations, it's difficult to go wrong, and you'll often find that it makes the writing process more pleasurable.

Of course, who you imagine your reader to be will change your end product. There's understandably a huge difference in content, form, and style between telling a story about a hot date to your best friend and telling that same story to your father.

On some level, your work decides who your audience is. Your voice in the world, no matter what story you tell, doesn't change. You just need to find people who will be interested in hearing it.

Engaging Your Reader(s)

Take the first chapter of your novel, or a short story that you're working on, and rewrite it twice. First, rework it in an effort to engage a family member, like a parent. Second, rework it to engage a friend, a coworker, or anyone else you feel could be your reader. Be careful to use real people and not a composite of a demographic, like women between the ages of thirty-five and fifty-one. Although that's the market most likely to buy books, it's much more effective to put a real face and name to your rewrite.

When you're finished with the rewrites, compare and contrast your work. Look for places where you've shifted the outcome of a scene based on each reader. For example, consider whether you made the lovers reunite because your mother likes happy endings, or you cleaned up the language because you know your good friend doesn't like vulgarity. Evaluate if these people are the best people to tell your story to. Some stories need to end badly; people often need to curse.

The purpose of this exercise is not to teach you to write to please people, but to help you recognize that real people will read your work and will interpret it based on their own history, personality, and sensibility. While you don't want to shape your fiction for one person, you do want to understand how to tell your story in a way that will be true to it—and reach the most readers possible. After all, that is the point of writing.

······· 8 ·······
OVERCOMING WRITER'S BLOCK

Don't buy into the idea of writer's block; it's just a term that speaks to fear. Words are nothing to be afraid of. Yes, they shape our existence. But they are glorious tools. They are dangerous. They define. They elevate. They destroy. And yet words are breathtakingly simple. At their essence, they are comprised of one or more sounds that, in combination, have a specific meaning assigned by the structure of what we call language. They are noise. We make the rules. Certain words may define us, or destroy us, but we're the ones who give words their power.

So sit down and write. Write your heart out, because it's your heart that guides you. The heart allows you to be human and to see your humanity in others—that's the secret to being a good writer. No matter what you write, you must always go out of your way to show the humanity in your characters, or readers will not believe in them and will lose interest.

Don't let anything scare you away from the page. Too many writers in mid-career find themselves lost. Maybe they've had a bestseller and their other books didn't sell as well so their editor is unhappy and they just can't write because they're afraid of losing their contract. Maybe they have had a gradual build of audience book after book but never really developed strong numbers. Whatever brought them to this point, they now feel blocked. They try to write but can't concentrate or start and stop project after project until they finally can't face the page anymore.

While "story starters" and other devices seem to keep some people writing, although often not for publication, that really isn't effective for people who can't write because they are profoundly frightened to fail.

It's no wonder that they are blocked. Always thinking about numbers and your book's "market" can destroy you, if you let it. You can't write to sell. You just have to write. Don't let anybody tell you how you should write or what you should write. Only you know what you want to write, and you have to trust that.

There really is, always, a market for good storytelling. You have to believe that because it's true.

Writer's block usually manifests out of anxiety. This is simple to say, but when you're a writer, anxiety is a way of life. So don't be hard on yourself. There are just too many variables (such as book sales) that are out of your control, and it's normal for you to be anxious. The key is not to let it overwhelm you. According to the Mayo Clinic, general anxiety disorder symptoms can include restlessness, being keyed up or on edge, difficulty concentrating, fatigue, irritability, impatience, being easily distracted, muscle tension, trouble falling or staying asleep, and excessive sweating. If your symptoms are interfering with your life, and you find you can't relax or enjoy yourself, then you need to see your family doctor as soon as possible. Anxiety is easier to treat if it's addressed quickly.

If you just find yourself unable to work because you're having some of the above symptoms, but the doctor says you're fine, here are a few tricks that can help alleviate your stress and get you writing again.

- **Creatively distract yourself.** Yes, the problem *is* that you're too distracted to work, but you can create positive distractions that will help you work again. Get away from your desk for a while. Go to a museum or movie. Or take up a hobby, like playing the guitar.

  Amy Tan, Stephen King, Mitch Albom, Frank McCourt, Carl Hiaasen, and Dave Barry are just some of the writers who use music as an outlet. In fact, they've all been part of the band The Rock Bottom Remainders (rockbottomremainders.com). Their Web site explains: "By day, they're authors. Really famous authors. But once a year they shed their pen-and-pencil clutching personas and become rock stars, complete with roadies, groupies and a wicked cool tour bus."

  If it's good enough for them, you can do it. Engage your mind and do something positive for yourself.

- **Take control of your life.** One of the worst things about being a writer is giving in to the feeling that you're not in control of your life or career. Capriciousness is the nature of the beast, but don't let that eat away at you. Do something that puts you in charge; something that makes you feel valuable. Maybe you could take a day and teach a workshop at your local school or volunteer at a soup kitchen. Or try a hobby that has a defined outcome, like knitting. Derek Walcott paints, as do other writers. You just want to be able to have something concrete to show for your efforts.

- **Get some exercise.** It really is amazing how much better you feel after you get your heart pumping. Talk to your doctor before starting any new activity, and then find something you like to do. Walking, running, yoga, basketball—whatever you chose, try to get your heart rate up for thirty minutes a day and you'll be amazed by how much better you feel about the world.

- **Manage pain before it becomes a problem and an excuse not to work.** It's very easy not to write when you've written so much that you've given yourself a good old-fashioned case of tendonitis. So, at the first sign of numbness in your hands while you're sleeping, go to the doctor to confirm the problem. If you just take ibuprofen to keep the swelling down, you may make matters worse and actually develop a full-blown case of Carpal Tunnel Syndrome, which is no fun at all and can cause permanent damage if you're not careful. In most cases, you'll have to wear wrist braces when you sleep, because we sleep with our wrists flexed, and when you work. If you seek treatment and don't just try to "work through the pain," you can avoid permanent damage to the median nerve.

- **Believe in yourself no matter what.** Sometimes, you just have that feeling. You know what you're working on is the right thing; and it's the right moment for it. Robert Louis Stevenson had a dream and told his family not to bother him while he wrote it down. A week later he'd written *Dr. Jekyll and Mr. Hyde*. When that feeling strikes you, cast any doubt aside. Believe in it. Sit down. Write.

The most important thing to do when writer's block hits is to believe in yourself, stuff the fear back into the corner of your brain, crank up the music, and work. Don't worry about a thing; just write.

Writing is a solace, if you let it be. Pulitzer Prize-winning author Michael Cunningham once said, "I think writing is, by definition, an optimistic art."

So, give in. A little optimism never killed anybody.

GENRE VS. LITERARY WRITING

Some hold fast to the idea that there are two schools of writing—either you are a literary or a genre writer. While many writers work solely in the world of formula fiction, the distinction really doesn't have to be so rigid if you don't want it to be.

Mystery writer Dennis Lehane wrote *Mystic River* as a literary work: It was his graduate thesis for an MFA at Florida International University. Although he dropped out and never received the degree, the work eventually was published, became an Academy Award-winning film, a finalist for the PEN/Winship Award, won the Anthony Award, the Barry Award for Best Novel, and France's Prix Mystère de la Critique.

William Gibson's science-fiction novel *Neuromancer* certainly staked the claim of literary with the opening sentence: "The sky above the port was the color of television, tuned to a dead channel." *Neuromancer* not only launched the cyberpunk generation and coined the word "cyberspace," it was the first novel to win the holy trinity of science fiction: the Hugo Award, the Nebula Award, and the Philip K. Dick Award.

Breaking the rules pays, as long as you know what the rules are. It's crucial that you fully understand how and why things are done and disregard them only because your story demands it, because it can't be told otherwise.

Think of jazz players and their riffs. They know how the Earl Hines Band played *A Night in Tunisia*; they know each and every note that Dizzy Gillespie scored. But the art of jazz is improvisation: bringing to the moment these wild imaginings and explorations of heat and emotion that the composer could not have foreseen. And so every time they play this standard, they bring in elements that are new, fresh.

That's what you should be doing with your writing. You always need to reinvent your own wheel. Don't let the critics shame you into writing in ways that don't suit your voice. If you enjoy writing standard mysteries, you should. If you want to write great literature, give it a go. If you want to combine the two, run with it.

Jean-Paul Sartre felt it was immoral to squander the power writers have to make change, and that unwittingly spawned all these unwritten rules about what's acceptable and not acceptable for writers. A story that's fun, or funny, often has a difficult journey in the literary landscape, even if it strives to make change.

But all stories *are* fun. How can they not be? Think about *The Remains of the Day* by Kazuo Ishiguro. It's such a magical puzzle. On one hand, the novel seems to be about a perfect English butler taking a journey and looking back on his life, a life of service to a "great" man. But, as the tale unfolds, you start to see that maybe this man was not so great. And, just maybe, this story is not a simple story at all. The book surprises you and makes you think—and that's fun.

Tim O'Brien always cautions about what he calls the "LIT-rare-E," which he defines as the ticks with presumed airs that writers fall into. He really gets after students who show off the fact that they can write impressive, and maybe even ponderous, sentences at the expense of the story itself. And when he accuses a work of being "LIT-rare-E," he always has his pinky out, as if he's the Grand Duke at high tea. It's a pretty funny sight, but a point well made.

Since the 1970s, Sartre's ideas have taken root and there's been a lot of fuss made about what is literary (read: superior) and what is genre (read: not superior). It seems as though the reason why we write is lost in all of this posturing: We write to tell stories.

All over the world, the storyteller is revered because he not only entertains, but is the guardian of the history of his people. It's a noble profession that deals with both the profound and the profane—and, it's usually okay to spread some fun around, too. To superimpose a hierarchy of style on a teller, or writer, forces some to make a choice. That may be ill-suited to the veracity of the tale.

In literary circles, Rita Mae Brown may be best known for *Rubyfruit Jungle*, but with mystery fans, she's the beloved author of the Sneaky Pie Brown mystery series, named after her cat. Why she decided to walk away from literary fiction was a practical matter, but now, it seems, it's become an artistic one. She says, "I was in Hollywood making money hand over fist, which is what you do in Hollywood—you starve or you hit it big. The Writers Guild went on strike, and it lasted a year. The bills came in, and the money ran out. Sneaky Pie, my cat, who's incredibly intelligent, said, 'Why don't you write a mystery?' I tried it, and thank God I did because it has taught me so much. All genre fiction is a sonnet."

A mystery novel, like all genre fiction, is written within a very restrictive form. There are expectations that must be met, just like in a sonnet. So, Rita Mae Brown has discovered how to apply her literary mind to fiction that not only sells, but provides growth for herself as an artist.

The word "literary" delineates the field, but it doesn't really tell you much about the type of book it is. It's an ill-defined word. There are no firm rules about what makes something literary. It's generally accepted that the use of poetic language, deep characterizations, and less focus on plot are the elements that provide the framework for literary works. For the most part, literary writers aren't that interested in making things happen, but discovering *why* things happen and the texture of language that shaped it.

That's a very basic description, and for every literary book that fits it, two more will not. The shorter definition is that it's anything that's not formula fiction.

This class war between writers is absurd if you think about it. But, in many ways, having this tension between the two schools is freeing. All this conflict and posturing compels you to break every rule and tell the story that comes from your "white hot center," as Robert Olen Butler always says, in your own way. Redefine the indefinable school of literary writing. Shift the paradigm of genres. It's your work after all; it comes from your heart, your blood, your sweat, and your darkest dreams. Don't let any title co-opt it.

PROFESSIONAL DEVELOPMENT: EDUCATION, AWARDS, AND RESIDENCIES

From the moment you write your first story or novel, you'll be eligible for all manner of grants, fellowships, and awards—many of them targeted to the new writer. Take advantage of every opportunity that you can because every time you need to give an artist statement, or answer questions like, "Why is this project important to your growth as a writer?" you learn something about yourself and your craft that is vital. In addition, it's important to build your résumé—and the money's nice, too.

WRITERS CONFERENCES

Writers conferences are just like summer camps for adults. If you're the kind of person who liked camp, you should try them out. And even if you hated camp, give them a whirl. They really are quite rewarding. You can make good friends and professional contacts, and you really do learn a lot. Some, like Bread Loaf and Sewanee Writers' Conference, also provide fellowships and scholarships that will waive fees and help you get some teaching experience.

Writer's Digest sponsors a lively conference focused on the more commercial aspects of writing, like tuning up your work and getting it published. The BookExpo America/Writer's Digest Books Writers Conference is an all-day event with workshops and panels throughout the morning and afternoon and a two-hour pitch slam session, featuring the largest gathering of agents and editors of any conference. Included in the registration fee is lunch and a copy of the latest edition of *Writer's Market*. And just to make matters more interesting, the conference is held in conjunction with the premier industry gathering for book publishing, BookExpo America. The Expo is massive, and was created to showcase most of the books that are scheduled to come out during the year—which is an amazing amount of books.

Again, there is an application process for many of the conferences, although most are just interested in seeing a manuscript. If you're applying for a scholarship or fellowship, which are forms of financial assistance, you'll probably need references and a copy of your tax returns. However, since all organizations' requirements vary, pay close attention to their guidelines.

To find out more about conferences, fellowships, and grants, you can search the mainstay resources just as you would for residencies, including the writer's magazines *Writer's Digest, The Writer, Poets & Writers,* and *The Writer's Chronicle*—many of them do seasonal features on each topic.

GRADUATE SCHOOL ... OR NOT?

This is always a quandary. On one hand, there's a solid argument to be made that if you're writing and getting published, you should only attend graduate school to get your degree so that you can be accredited to teach. Graduate school is not easy. Even if you get a fellowship, it's expensive and takes anywhere from two to seven years of your life to complete.

If you start later in life—let's say you're forty years old—it's even more difficult to complete your degree because you may have a profession and family commitments that could distract you. And, if you're an older student, it may be difficult for you to find a tenure-track position, and, even if you do, you'll soon discover that many colleges pay entry level professors salaries that are well below what you should be making for your age given how close to retirement you actually are.

In addition, and this is the most important thing to keep in mind, graduate school is about the academic underpinnings of writing. You do write but, at the same time, you're going to be expected to study theory, history, and many other things that will take up time that you may want to spend writing.

On the other hand, if you love learning and enjoy working within a community, graduate school is wonderful. If you think of the title of the degree—Master of Fine Arts in Creative Writing—who doesn't want to be that? No matter where you go, these programs are designed to help you gain a deep understanding of how writing works and what makes as successful story.

The contacts you make in graduate school can be important to your career. From your professors to your fellow students, these are people that form your community and inform your work. After you graduate, you may even continue to keep their company and repeatedly call upon their opinions. And, of course, if you need a letter of recommendation, most organizations would prefer one from someone who helped you get your MFA than from your agent who, eventually, stands to benefit personally from any grant or award you garner.

The graduate school option was once only open to writers willing to work in literary fiction, but that's changed. A number of schools have created low-residency MA and MFA programs that offer an opportunity to write and workshop genre fiction. Seton Hill, a Catholic university in the small town of Greensburg, Pennsylvania, focuses primarily on commercial fiction including fantasy, science fiction, mystery, and romance, in addition to writing for children and adults. They also offer classes in marketing issues, genre trends, and the industry of publishing. Other low-residency programs, such those at Goddard College and Stonecoast at the University of Southern Maine, also offer tracks in the full-gamut of genre writing.

What's interesting about these programs is that their approach is academic; they don't see genre writing as plugging words into a set format and calling it a book. They approach the craft with an artistic aesthetic. While focusing on plot, because plot is crucial to all popular fiction, they also place emphasis on helping students develop an approach to the work that takes into account how language is used as well as other elements that one would find in literary fiction.

There are all sorts of graduate schools for all sorts of learners. If you feel you'd like to go back to school, there's a program out there and a community of writers for you to join. And if you don't, you still won't be alone. As Junot Díaz says, "What we do might be done in solitude and with great desperation, but it tends to produce exactly the opposite. It tends to produce community and in many people hope and joy."

GRANTS

National Endowment for the Arts, Guggenheim, state grants—whatever grant, award, or fellowship that will boost your visibility and give you a sense of accomplishment is worth pursuing at one time or another. The biggest problem is that it takes a huge amount of time to craft artist statements and thoughtfully answer questions about your work—time in which you should be writing. Also, the competition is stiff, so try to get a solid body of work written before you apply. You really want to put your best foot forward.

Here are some tips that will make the process easier.

1. **Don't apply for all the grants at once.** This will just drive you crazy. You should carefully pick the ones you think you have the best chance at.

2. **Rework material.** Once your artist statement and project information is written, you can reuse it over and over again—not just for awards but to garner residencies and other professional opportunities that might arise.

3. **Follow the instructions and be neat.** This is the most common mistake writers make. You'd be surprised how many talented people can't follow directions.

4. **More is not better.** Another common mistake is sending in a writing sample that is not exactly what the grant guidelines requested. Avoid mortal sins such as sending more than the requested number of pages, printing on both sides of the paper, using a typeface that's less than twelve points in size, using tiny margins, or single-spacing your pages. You have to look at this from the reader's point of view. He's going through hundreds of writing samples, and by the time he gets to you he's nearly blind.

5. **Send the right sample.** Always send your strongest work. If you don't catch the judge's attention in the first paragraph or the first page at the latest, you're going in the "no" pile. Novel chapters should be inclusive and read like a short stories. Short stories often are better received.

6. **Don't be whiney.** Your artist statement should be factual, businesslike, and passionate, but never whiney or self-indulgent. Don't talk about how you were passed over for a publication, or how you can never get a break. Just present your work and it will speak volumes.

7. **Don't name-drop.** Saying how much other people liked your work doesn't make it with the judges; they want to make up their own minds. However, if you were given another grant, do mention it. Most funders like to award grants to writers who already have received one because it makes you look like a good investment.

8. **Make everything legible.** Always type (and spell check) your work. Handwriting strains the eyes.

9. **Be accurate.** Never inflate your résumé. Everything needs to be the truth—no half-truths allowed. Someone will eventually find you out. The Internet makes the world a very small place.

10. **Don't apply for the wrong grant.** It's a waste of time to try to shape yourself into someone else for money. If you don't write about history, don't fake it. Leave that grant for people who need those funds.

11. **Don't apply for grants you don't need.** A few years back, there was a writer who made a lot of money off a book, and it won many awards, and so the writer applied for an NEA and got it. People were very angry because they felt he didn't "need" the money and should have left those funds for struggling writers. He said all he wanted was the NEA on his resume, and he tried to return the funds but found he couldn't. And so there were more hard feelings. While grants are a way to reward artists and good work, they are mostly designed to help the artist continue her work. The etiquette is that if you're a bestseller, you shouldn't apply.

12. **Don't send photos.** While you may be as cute as a bug, if the grant doesn't call for a photo, don't send one. Don't send anything that's not called for because you'll look like an amateur, and you don't want that.

Besides awards, there are other ways writers can use institutions to further develop their career, including fellowships and residencies.

FELLOWSHIPS

There are several types of fellowships available, and they're worth looking into. Like residencies, fellowships provide a change of scenery, and that can stir the creative juices. They also are a good source of income to keep you going between books.

Some fellowships are community-based like the Writer-in-Residence program at the Arts Branch of the YMCA of Greater Syracuse. But, if you have your MFA and some teaching experience, you might want to think about applying for fellowships at universities and colleges. There are many positions for those who want to teach but aren't sure they want a teaching job. They're also perfect for someone who wants to teach but can't find a job. Either way, you'll find that fellowships are offered to writers at all levels of their careers. Some pay quite well and provide housing.

If you'd like a life-changing fellowship experience, you should also check out the Fulbright Programs at the Institute for International Education (iie.org). Established in 1946, this State Department program funds all sorts of applicants, including educators and writers, who wish to study and live in foreign countries. You can even bring your family; there's a stipend provided for them. As you can imagine, the English language-based countries are the most competitive.

If you don't want to go the government route, there are several private foundations that provide support, including the Gladys Krieble Delmas Foundation, which offers a grant (delmas.org/guidelines/v_ir_a.html) for individuals who want to live in Venice and study its culture, and The Camargo Foundation (camargofoundation.org), which maintains a study center in Cassis, France.

If it's early in your career and you just want a place to write for an extended period of time, The Fine Arts Work Center in Provincetown, Massachusetts (fawc.org) offers seven-month fellowships. It's like a residency that pays you to be there, but there's no teaching involved. Every year, they select twenty fellows to be in residence and provide them with a modest monthly stipend. No pets, but family is allowed. Residencies run from October 1 through May 1, which includes the dead of winter, but don't let that dissuade you. Many fine writers are alumni of Provincetown, so there must be something about being isolated on this beautiful tip of the Cape that tends to inspire.

Another consideration is Stanford University's Stegner Fellowship (named after Wallace Stegner). The program offers ten two-year fellowships each year, five in fiction and five in poetry. All the fellows meet once a week in a three-hour workshop, but it isn't a degree program. The fellowship comes with a $26,000 stipend and health insurance.

Keep in mind that all fellowships have applications that will remind you of grants because they have many of the same concerns and requirements. For example, most fellowships will often require a work plan, and you still don't want to send that "cute as a bug" photo unless it's asked for. Fellowships are as competitive as grants, but, again, if you don't give it a try, you can't win.

RESIDENCIES

Artist residencies can be a great way to start, or even complete, an entire project without the distractions of your real life. When Mark Winegardner wrote *The Godfather Returns,* the sequel to *The Godfather,* he spent every other month for a year traveling away from his teaching at FSU and his wife and young children to work in artist colonies across the country. He had to. The book was a daunting project with a quick turnaround date, so he couldn't afford to be distracted.

Surprisingly, it's not uncommon for writers to spend an entire year or more moving from one residency to the next. Besides getting a lot of work done, it's a great way to travel because you have the interesting distinction of being a tourist and not being a tourist at the same time. The settings for artist colonies are often inviting, and even exotic. Plus, you learn a lot about yourself when you're thrust into a foreign environment with a dozen or more strangers who love the process of making art as much as you do.

But there are some things to consider when thinking about doing a residency; the first is the facility itself. Worldwide there are several hundred places you can go to work and live. While they all provide the basics of shelter, that's about the only thing they have in common. For example, some places don't serve meals, or just provide limited food that you must prepare yourself. Most avoid breakfast, but will provide lunch and dinner.

Again, this is a matter of choice on your part. You have to know what you can and can't tolerate. For some, shared bathrooms are another consideration. Private bathrooms are a luxury when you're on residency. And if you need a handicapped-accessible space, you should mention that up front. In fact, any special needs you have you need to mention before you fill out an application.

There are other, more subtle, elements of residencies that you also may need to consider. If you live in a humid climate or at sea level, you should take a moment and check out what physical issues you may encounter before considering a residency in the desert or the mountains. If you live in a tropical climate, Vermont in the winter is a huge shock to the system. And, if you suffer from allergies, you may want to try to find out what time of the year has the worst pollen count.

While all these details may seem insignificant—after all, life is an adventure and it's often good just to dive into the moment—in a residency situation, you really want to make sure you understand what you're getting into. The entire point of a residency is to work, sometimes in an exotic location, but you are still trying to get work done. So, if you're at Ragdale in Lake Forest, Illinois, in spring, and you suffer from allergies, you're going to be pretty miserable because it's surrounded by gardens and has no central air conditioning. And, as we all know, you just don't get a lot of work done when you're miserable.

It's also important to keep in mind that these places are not like hotels, or even like home. They really are designed for you to "camp" awhile in a community of kindred spirits. The rule of thumb is that if you want a mint on your pillow, you're going to have to buy it at the corner store.

Read all the information the sponsoring organization's site provides, and read it carefully. There's lots of fine print that you really need to consider. If you have a question, write the residency director; every site has one. The following are some other basic but important considerations.

1. Finances

Every dollar you spend adds up quickly. So, if money is an issue, you have to make sure you understand exactly what you're getting into. For example, The Santa Fe Art Institute has a wonderful residency program. The space is beautiful. You have a private room and bathroom. They do a good job of screening applicants, so it's a very lively community. It's a great place to work.

On the other hand, they only provide limited breakfast foods (bulk cereal, milk, eggs, bread, honey, butter, and oils.) Since it is Santa Fe, a very fashionable and costly city, it's expensive to eat out, and groceries, which you have to buy yourself, are very pricey.

Even getting around is expensive. The Institute is slightly out of town, so when you get groceries, you have to either walk a few miles or bike, and both are difficult because of all the tourist traffic and desert sun. Since refrigerator space is limited, you find yourself needing to buy food nearly every day.

However, if you're an American citizen and a licensed driver, you can borrow one of the donated cars—but you have to top them off with gas every time you use them. And when you add $5 on top of every grocery purchase, it adds up quickly.

Does that mean the SFAI isn't a good place to be? No. Not at all. It's wonderful. The staff, the space, the office dog, and the well-picked residents make it memorable. When I was there, I found that because residents had to provide their own food, they did so with great flourish. On Mother's Day, we threw each other a massive brunch with food bought from the local farmers' market. We also had a series of cookouts and communal dinners, which often ended up with everyone dancing to Rumanian rock and roll music until deep in the night.

So, even though it was expensive, it was worth it. It's just good to know how much you may be spending before you sign up.

2. Temperament

It does take a particular kind of temperament to do this.

You have to be able to leave your family and pets behind and turn off your cell phone. It's tough to do, and it takes a while to let go of the guilt and concern. But it can be done. The key to making a residency work is not to turn a deaf ear on your life, but to understand that whatever problems are happening at home are temporary. They will solve themselves one way or another without you. You've left all the people and things that you love to go to work, and your family needs to understand that the more work you get done, the quicker you'll get your project done. And once your project is done you can chase those snakes out of the laundry room, find the nutmeg, and maybe even have some time to make a homemade pizza.

A residency is not about sacrifice, and should never be thought of in that way—not even by the people you leave behind. It's an honor to be chosen; most residencies are very competitive. It says that your work is valuable and exciting and other people want to be a part of it. The experience should not only be about working but about recharging and refocusing yourself as a writer—and that's important if you're going to be a productive and happy person.

Family issues aside, the group dynamic of a residency can be, well, dynamic. Artists often come from all over the world, certainly all over the United States, and bring with them their own cultural mores. You have to be able to adjust and open your heart to a myriad of ways of seeing things and doing things.

And when you have a dozen or so passionate people madly working on their art during the day, on occasion, that passion often spills over onto the dinner table. Friendships, love affairs, bitter rivalries—you may see all the possibilities that human nature has to offer germinate at the evening meal. Residencies can sometimes be a little like high school with a lot of hormone-driven drama, but that's just the extreme. I say "sometimes," because most places are quite convivial and welcoming and the assembled artists are a well-chosen mix and more than professional—and often fun.

I've made lifelong friends while on residency and have only had a couple of problems in more than a decade of doing this. But if you do find yourself in one of those odd situations, it's not really a problem. Just go back to your studio and work. If you're really concerned, talk to the residency director—that's why he's there.

One thing that's great about residencies, no matter what's going on, is that people always make it a point to respect each other's privacy. If a bedroom or studio door is closed, that means the person doesn't want to be disturbed, and won't be.

So despite the cost, craziness, and inconvenience, a residency can be a boon to your work life. The freedom it gives you is amazing. You can stay up all night. You can skip meals. You can even dance all night. You can catch up on some sleep, or just spend the day thinking. And, most of all, without taking care of every detail in your life, you can write as much as you want. You can sometimes work so much you complete your project early and go home before your time is up.

3. Discipline

Before you send an application away, you need to ask yourself how disciplined you are, how disciplined do you need to be to get your project finished, and how much time will you actually need to complete the work.

These considerations all rest upon two factors—how big your project is and how many distractions you'll have at the residency campus. For example, if you're thinking about spending a month in the south of France, you should figure in time for goofing off. Most people like to explore their surroundings. They go into town and check out how people live. Eat in a few cafés. Play tourist for a while.

In general, it's always good to give the first two days of any residency over to the idea of "settling in." In a fun or exotic environment, two weeks can slip by before you know it. Try to judge how much time you need based on how much work you need to get done.

When on a tight deadline, it's better to go to a place that you've been to before, or a place that's a lot like where you live. In a sense it's like home; there's no mystery there. You can just hunker down and write. In a situation like that, you may only need two weeks, instead of a month, because you can get a lot done.

At the beginning of a project, it's often good to go someplace exotic. You may not get lot of work done, but it's a good way to kick-start your creativity and celebrate a new literary adventure.

4. Paperwork

A residency isn't like checking into a hotel. Because it's competitive, and sometimes extremely competitive, the application form is much like a grant. The more venerated the campus is, the more accomplished the residents are, the tougher the screening process is.

One of the campuses at the top of the list is Yaddo, which sits on more than forty acres of land in Saratoga Springs, New York. Artists who've worked there have won sixty-three Pulitzer Prizes, twenty-five MacArthur Fellowships, fifty-eight National Book Awards, and a Nobel Prize (Saul Bellow in 1976). The roster of past artists include James Baldwin, Leonard Bernstein, Truman Capote, Langston Hughes, Sylvia Plath, Katherine Anne Porter, and Mario Puzo—so not everybody who applies gets in.

Yaddo's application form requires that you have two written recommendations by professionals who can speak to your work and your ability to be a good resident, a work sample, a work plan that details your project and what it means to be able to complete it at this point in your career, a professional summary that highlights your most important professional achievements, and a two-page résumé.

After your application is received, a group of former residents will review and rate your request based on your talent, what your recommenders say about you, and the feasibility of your plan.

Most residencies require more or less the same information and have the same process. Some, however, are much less competitive.

If you're not much for paperwork, you may just decide to rent a studio space in another city or country. You can find ads for these in the back of both *Poets & Writers* and *Writer's Digest.*

Resources for Residencies

There are many places where you can learn about the hundreds of residency offerings both here and abroad. This list should get you stated.

- *Writer's Digest* lists residency opportunities. On their Web site, they're listed both through the magazine at writers digest.com/conferences and in conjunction with Shaw Guides, which can be linked through the site or found at writing.shaw guides.com.

- *Poets & Writers* magazine (pw.org) also features a wide range of residency opportunities and, in their classifieds, rental spaces for those who want to get away but would rather not be in a nonprofit environment.

- Res Artis (resartis.org) is a worldwide network of artist-residencies and residential art centers, representing more than two hundred centers and organizations in forty-nine countries. It began in 1993 as a volunteer organization and includes information for residencies all over the world, from Argentina to the USA and Vietnam.

- Trans Artists (transartists.nl) is an independent foundation that informs artists of all disciplines about international artist-in-residence programs and other opportunities for artists to stay and work elsewhere "for art's sake." The Web site offers a newsletter and features information on funding, fellowships, and continuing education.

······• 11 ········

YOUR DAY JOB

Many famous writers had day jobs. When Wallace Stevens won the Pulitzer Prize in 1955, he was offered a faculty position at Harvard but turned it down because he would have had to give up his position as Vice President of The Hartford Accident and Indemnity Company. It's a big job, and yet he still managed to write. William Carlos Williams was a doctor and poet who wrote every chance he could find—in his office and while making house calls. He always found a way to work the work in.

On the other hand, some writers have been able to focus on the practice of writing because they've had some financial backing. Edith Wharton was born into a wealthy family but in later years became so popular that money from her book sales greatly outweighed her family money. At the pinnacle of her career, she was America's highest paid novelist.

If you're not rich, haven't married into wealth, or don't have a loved one who makes enough to support you, you still can quit your day job and live off grants and advances, but it isn't easy. Poet and novelist Charles Bukowski worked for the post office for more than a decade until John Martin, the publisher of Black Sparrow Press (now HarperCollins/ECCO), paid him to leave and write full time. It was a big risk on the part of both men. Bukowski was a relative unknown at the time, but given the chance to just write, he did, and had a very successful career as a cult writer. However, despite his success, he really was quite poor.

Novelist Stewart O'Nan was a structural engineer for Grumman Aerospace when he left it all to write: "I quit only when my wife encouraged me, saying I wasn't paying any attention to her, or the kids, or the house—all I was doing was going to work and coming home and reading and writing. She said if that's what I wanted to do, I should try doing it full time. Five years later, we were broke, I was unemployed, and we had two kids and a mortgage. So I wouldn't recommend quitting your day job to anyone, unless they were utterly obsessed, and ready to give all their time to their work. And have the total support and understanding of those closest to them.

"Of course I miss engineering, and being on the shop floor and working with planes, but I'd rather read and write than do anything else in the world, so I'm crazily happy, even when the writing isn't going well."

Quitting your day job to become a writer is a modern concept, and one that's not entirely financially feasible if you're the sole provider for your family—unless you hit the bestseller list and stay there awhile. The problem is not just having enough money to live on, it's being able to make enough money to have an excess so that you can be comfortable through retirement. Today's millionaire needs ten million to be considered wealthy enough to live well through retirement. In order to achieve that goal, he has to invest a substantial part of those funds with high-paying yields, live off the interest alone, and not touch the principle.

So what hope do you have?

To be able to put away $100,000 or even $10,000 a year for twenty years is pretty difficult unless you're a consistent bestseller. The average writer with a major publisher can make an advance of anywhere from $20,000 to $50,000 for a book that takes about three years from the time the first word is set to the page to the point where the book is unboxed and set on the shelf. That's about $16,666 a year. According to the United States Department of Health and Human Services, the 2008 poverty guidelines for those living in the forty-eight contiguous states are $10,400 for one person and $17,600 for a three-person household. Some writers get paid much less.

That's why it's always important to start a new book as soon as you finish the old one. It will reengage you, take your mind off of the stress of sales, and, as soon as you get fifty pages and an outline, your agent can present it to your editor and try to sell it. Cash flow is the key to survival.

If you happen to get a six-figure advance, you still really need to be careful about money. If your book doesn't make it back or, at the very least, come close to making it back, then you could be facing a drastic pay cut for your next book. Most writers are paid based on marketability, and your marketability is based on the fickleness of taste and fashion.

If you're in this just for the money, it's enough to give you an ulcer.

And even though you may find yourself building a core of readers and becoming more and more bankable with each book, that's still no guarantee that you can completely survive off your writing.

Cash flow is always a problem because advances don't come when they're supposed to. Contracts get stalled, and when the advances are finally agreed upon, they're often late, or in the mail somewhere, or on someone's desk. It's especially difficult during summer and the holidays, when publishing tends to shut down completely. Despite the fact that people will do their best to rush things through, since your check has to be signed off on by dozens of people both at the publisher's office and your representative's agency, there's a lot of room for mishap.

So even though you're supposed to get your final check in August, you may see it in September—which isn't good when you're trying to make a car payment.

I was once having lunch with an editor who asked me what I did for a living besides writing. "I just write," I said. "Nothing else."

She looked crestfallen and said, "That's too bad. We'd rather not publish people who don't have other jobs. Writers who just write often go crazy on us."

I would have laughed, but that seemed like too true of a statement.

Quitting your day job is a risky thing to do considering that there are many professions well-suited to writers, with medicine, journalism, law, and teaching being some of the most common choices.

Still, some writers, myself included, are primarily writers. We teach sometimes, we write articles sometimes, we get lucky and get a grant or two sometimes, but most of the time we write—but that's not our only income source. Besides fiction, most writers I know balance a variety of other writing projects and have a wide range of revenue streams, so that they don't have to wait for one single check to arrive or be dependent on one editor to buy the next project.

You may even want to redefine how you approach your work. Instead of focusing on longer works of literary criticism, Roland Barthes needed money and so applied his vast knowledge of literary theory to popular culture and began to write about burlesque, toys, and wrestling matches. "I have tried to be as eclectic as I possibly can with my professional life, and it's been pretty fun," he said.

The decision to leave your day job, like many decisions that you'll make as a writer, is really about how you want to live your life. Success makes the decision easy, but how do you define success? Money? Happiness? It's your decision to make.

If you do decide to leave your job, any monies that you receive, like grants and advances, must be treated as income from a business venture—because they are. While it's rather giddy to receive a $100,000 check in the mail, it's not a gift. You earned that money though your hard work and talent—you need to make it work for you. Here are some tips to help you navigate the treacherous financial waters.

1. **Reward yourself.** You worked hard. You deserve a little gift to commemorate the book sale or the grant. But make sure it's a *little* something, like a collectable pen or a new leather briefcase. Whatever you buy, it's always best if it makes you feel more professional and contributes to your life as a writer— plus, depending on what it is, it could be tax deductible. Make whatever money you get work for you.

2. **Reinvest some of your funds into your practice.** This reinvestment can be anything from a workshop on screenwriting to expand your skill base to a new computer with software that will enable you to create your own Web site.

3. **Pay estimated quarterly taxes.** It's always good to pay estimated taxes—if you have to. If you're married, before you set up a pay schedule with the IRS, calculate all the money that's coming into the house that year and take a close look at what's being withheld already. If your spouse can withhold enough for the both of you, there's no need to establish quarterly payments, and that's a lot less paperwork. Just one caution: Make sure you do the math properly. Call the IRS to double check. Two years down the road, you don't want to discover that you've made a mistake and now not only owe taxes, but a hefty penalty.

4. **Set aside 10 percent of your total advance for your tour.** Even if the publisher is picking up the costs for a tour, you'll find that you'll still need to pay for some things—or want to.

For example, for about $300, more or less, you can get five thousand high-quality bookmarks made to leave at stores in an effort keep the PR going after you're gone. Little things like that can increase the effectiveness of a tour and are certainly worth the time, effort, and cost.

5. **Don't let anyone talk you into spending money for your career that doesn't seem to make sense.** This can really be a big problem, especially for new writers. Outside publicists are one of those things that people tell you you need, but it really depends on what you're writing and what publishing house you're with. If you're with a large house, it's a waste of money when you're publishing fiction. While you may not get the attention you feel you need from your assigned publicist, a publishing house has so much more clout than most of the independent PR professionals and many good PR people will not take on novelists. Fancy Web sites are another economic drain with little pay off. These days you can easily create your own site, or hire a college student to do it. You don't need to pay big money for this. Nor do you need a professional photographer to take your headshot. Most author photos are snapshots taken with high-quality digital cameras.

6. **Invest in health insurance.** Yes, you may be in good health, but you could get in an accident and suddenly find yourself with medical bills that you can't cover unless you quit writing and work several jobs. Many writers' organizations like PEN and Mystery Writers of America offer affordable health plans along with membership.

7. **Stay optimistic during times of economic upheaval.** All economic downturns are cyclical: Things will get better eventually. Don't panic. Don't give up writing. Everyone needs writers. If you think about your skill set, there may be some things that you can do that will still be within the field. There are the obvious things like journalism, PR, and technical writing, but there are also some more interesting options. If you like to teach, you could look into the Artists-in-the-Schools program across the nation. The program is designed to place working artists, including writers, in the communities. Many states,

like Ohio, will take non-residents, pay quite well, and provide work time and space for you to write.

Whether you keep your day job or shed it, there will always come a time when you regret your decision. It's human nature. It's not an easy decision to make. Jobs add community and purpose to your life. They are a great distraction when the writing is not going as well as you'd like it to. And who doesn't like the security of a paycheck?

But don't keep your job because of money alone. Don't let money define you. How much you make doesn't matter. Money is just a tool: It's something that you use to create a framework for you to thrive in. Don't be afraid of it, or afraid of losing it. There's always a way to make a living, even in the most catastrophic of times.

During the Depression, the Works Progress Administration (WPA) created what they called the Federal Writers' Project. Roosevelt's vast program employed more than 6,600 writers, editors, and historians to do a variety of tasks, including gathering oral histories, collecting slave narratives, and creating state guidebooks. When asked why he included artists in the work programs, FDR said, "Why not? They are human beings. They have to live."

He never questioned if writers had a right to make a living writing, and neither should you. So keep writing, no matter what—day job, or not. No matter what you choose, you never want to give up writing for "a while" and then try to return. Not only will you have lost momentum and your audience, you may have even lost your way. Roosevelt knew that and wanted artists to continue to develop their craft. The WPA writers included Saul Bellow, Richard Wright, Nelson Algren, Loren Eiseley, and Ralph Ellison. Think how rich our world is today because they didn't give up and get a "real" job. They wrote no matter what—and so should you.

MAKE YOUR OWN MUSE

There's a lot of talk about this muse thing. You can take an entire weekend workshop about coaxing your muse, or flirting with your muse, or dancing with your muse, or just spending time getting to know your muse better. It's as if a muse is some sort of Chia Pet: All you have to do is water her and the next thing you know, you're Norman Mailer.

It's understandable where all this muse-centric chat comes from. There are times when you're writing and your hands type faster than your brain can even think. One moment you've just had breakfast and the next the cat is screaming for dinner. And how many times have you looked at what you've written and thought, *Who came up with that? I'm not that smart.*

If those moments make you wonder if there's some sort of otherworldly creature inhabiting your body that is smarter and more profound than you are, you're not alone. The Greek poet Hesiod (799 B.C.) was the first writer to begin this practice of muse worship and is given credit for naming them. The idea of the muse took hold in 1374 when the English poet Geoffrey Chaucer evoked them and destined all English poets to do the same forevermore.

The word "muse" comes from the Latin *musa,* which is derived from the Greek *mousa* and is a generic term given the sisterhood of goddesses born of Zeus and Mnemosyne (Memory). It's their job to inspire.

Having a muse makes sense. Fiction *is* a magical art. Writers craft paradoxical empires of logic and beauty and the reader lives within them, or at least it feels as if they do, and they do this through the simple act of interpretation—the puzzling out of an assortment of symbols on a page. Yet in their minds the characters are as real to them as that bow-legged man who walks his small nervous dog past their house every evening. How is that not magic?

But waiting for a spirit to inspire you to sit down and write may not be the most prudent course; you could wait for a very long time.

If you do sit down and still feel stuck, you could cruise the Internet for inspiration, but that often leads to shopping, blogging, and generalized goofing off.

If you want to catch the muse, you have to court it.

It's better to let your mind wander in a directed way. You can make yourself a set a flashcards with images you take from magazines, photographs, or postcards, or with evocative phrases like "The language they spoke was iridescent," or "He had eyes darker than any night." Or thumb through your old journals, picking up on ideas you made note of long ago. Or take a walk. Or pick up your guitar and play until the words of a song become secondary to the emotion of it.

Let the world at large be your muse. Be unafraid to walk aimlessly through a city's street at night, through unknown neighborhoods, and search for that part of yourself that is lost there. Embrace the world's sorrow. Linger in the silence of a moment. Learn the language of your own heart.

Don't wait for anything to guide your work. Dig deep inside of yourself. You are the collective memory of your culture. You hold history in your hand. Never ask for permission to write. Just take it. As Charles Simic said, "He who cannot howl will not find his pack." You have to howl until you are heard.

Embrace your muse as the spirit of life that passes through you— and there will be times that something larger than yourself will inspire you, amaze you, and overwhelm you with inspiration. But those moments are few and far between, and you must be ready for them. You must show up for work, put in your time, always have your heart open and your hand outstretched towards the heavens.

But, whatever you do, never confuse those moments of brilliance on the page with the idea that you are brilliant. That's dangerous. It leads to destructive behavior. As does the idea that you are failed as a writer—if you've done your part to succeed, maybe your muse was just having an off day.

Elizabeth Gilbert gave a talk about the idea of genius on TED.com (an amazing Web site filled with lectures on big topics by famous people that you should take a minute to check out). Gilbert's "genius" could also be called the muse, as she defines it as a disembodied spirit that enters artists and allows them to create work that is seemingly divine.

At one point in her lecture, she spoke about the sacred dances in North Africa that went on centuries ago. People would gather in the moonlight, and the dancers, filled with a sense of ecstasy, would dance into the morning. And every now and then one of them would suddenly be filled with this sense of the otherworldly. He would become transcendent. Even though he was doing the same dance he'd done a thousand times before, time stopped, and it suddenly seemed as if he'd stepped through a portal.

"He seemed to be lit from within and lit from below and lit up on fire with divinity," she said. "And when this happened ... people knew it for what it was. Allah! Allah! Allah! They would start to chant. That's God.

"... when the Moors invaded Spain they took this custom with them. However, it changed from over the centuries from Allah! Allah! Allah! to Ole! Ole! Ole!, which is still heard at bullfights."

When you write, you sit in your office and bang away hoping for brilliance, hoping that your genius, your muse, your Allah, comes to you and elevates your work. But you can't wait for it. You have to be there ready to catch it, even on days when it doesn't seem worth the effort of getting out of bed.

Never give up.

PART TWO

The Work

The young man or woman writing today has forgotten the problems of the human heart in conflict with itself, which alone can make good writing, because only that is worth writing about, worth the agony and the sweat. He must learn them again. He must teach himself that the basest of all things is to be afraid; and, teaching himself that, forget it forever, leaving no room in his workshop for anything but the old verities and truths of the heart, the universal truths ... love and honor and pity and pride and compassion and sacrifice.

—William Faulkner, Nobel Prize acceptance speech

A NOVEL IDEA

A novel can begin when you pick up the newspaper—and sometimes does. You read about Senator Ted Kennedy undergoing therapy for a brain tumor and he's quoted as saying that it's not time for eulogies; he's planning to stick around. And, no matter what side of the political fence you sit on, you start to wonder what it would be like to be diagnosed with a deadly cancer and still feel that you have so much work left to do in your life. And in that moment of bravery—or maybe that moment of delusion, as the writer in you needs to decide—you have an idea for a novel.

You delve into the poignancy of Senator Kennedy's situation. You may decide to change his name. You may make him a congressman or take him out of politics all together and make him a grocery store owner.

However you choose to alter the facts of the situation, at some point you have to ask yourself if this novel idea can really become a novel. Everyone dies, so we know the ending—so where's the conflict? What kind of structure would the novel have? Do you want to make it a 300-page postmodern rumination on a life well lived? And, if you do, how would you make it interesting to a reader?

Ideas for stories are everywhere. A conversation overheard in a bar, an experience in your own life, even the newspaper—all serve as great resources for ideas, but these ideas may not make great novels, or novels at all.

Novels are built, not discovered. Your inspiration is just the beginning. Once your interest is peaked, the building process begins. How you build your story depends on who you are.

If you're a mystery writer who came across Senator Kennedy's quote, or if you know a person struggling with cancer, you may take a route similar to that which Tom Cavanagh did in his comic mystery, *Head Games*. Cavanagh, in an effort to understand his father's cancer, created a hero, former Orlando Police Detective Mike Garrity, who has a tumor in his head. That tumor's name is Bob, and, unfortunately, Bob is the most significant relationship in Garrity's life.

Now while this may sound flippant, it's really not. Cavanagh used the great love he has for his father and his intimate knowledge of the situation to create a work that is indeed funny—and at the same time gentle and wise—and is still a bona fide murder mystery. It's truly a novel idea.

Of course, Cavanagh could have written a memoir about his father, or a family saga based on the possibility of losing him. Or, like Alexs Pate in *Losing Absalom*, he could have used a father's brain cancer as a way to speak not only about loss but the choices we make in our lives and the issues of race. But, as most writers do, Cavanagh dealt with his interest in a way that reflected his own history and disposition—he used the tools of his own life to build a story.

In his past life, Cavanagh was a writer for Disney television. He still lives in Orlando. So when he sat down to write the plot for *Head Games,* he drew upon his days working in children's television and had his detective search for a lost member of a boy band (who bore a striking resemblance to a member of The New Kids on the Block, a boy band that the author worked with). He also set the novel in Orlando. Those intimate details gave his idea the energy it needed to become a novel: They gave it life.

The word *novel* is both a challenge and a promise—it means "new or unusual, the first of its kind." So, it's your job to take your novel idea and pay it off in a way that is new, unusual—and truly your own.

As you flesh out your story, ask yourself, "How can I make this different? What's the twist? Given the parameters of the situation, what's the unpredictable thing that no one is thinking of here?"

Always remember that writing is an art form, just as painting is. The purpose of art is to make people rediscover what they think they know and to assist them in incorporating this newfound or rediscovered knowledge in their own lives.

Consider the work of Andy Warhol. He painted large canvases of Campbell's soup cans in vivid colors. He put them on the wall as if to say, "Look at these, these are art." And so we had to look at them closely, more closely than we did when we opened a can of Cream of Tomato for lunch. And through the process of that examination we may not think it's truly art, but we have a chance to think about our relationship to the image, the image's relationship to our lives, and what the image means to us. We may even ask ourselves, *When is a can of soup more than a can of soup?*

That's what art does—it enriches our lives and our understanding of our experience.

And that's what a writer brings to writing—she takes an everyday event or object, like being ill or buying Campbell's soup, and makes it so vivid that we understand our own world in a slightly different way. She make us think outside of the box of our own making.

Everything you write, even if you define it as a paperback romance, is art. Art is crucial to society because it asks us to imagine—and when we imagine, all things are possible. Virologist Jonas Salk imagined a world without polio, and made it so.

So when you have a novel idea, no matter what the source, you need to test it, to verify the fact that it can become something bigger than just a notion—you need to know if it can inspire you to build a world, which can inspire the world.

THE NOVEL LITMUS TEST

To see if your story idea can turn into a real novel, you have to decide if it has "legs." Can you run with it? Can you somehow take the idea that sparks your interest, find meaning in it, and create a world from it that is real and meaningful to others? Can you turn it into something that sparks your reader's imagination as much as your own?

To answer these questions, approach your idea as a journalist approaches a story. Begin by asking about the who, what, where, when, why, and how of what you think your story might be. The more precisely you answer these questions, the deeper the understanding you'll have of your novel's potential.

Keep in mind that if you do decide to write the book, you may find that as you work, the circumstances of it could change, or the characters, or any number of elements—that's very common. As the Emergency Broadcast System used to say when it interrupted your favorite television show, "This is a test. This is only a test."

The Litmus Test allows you to see if you have interest, and if the story is deep enough, to actually begin writing. It is by no means an outline of your work, although it can become one.

As you go, write your ideas down in a notebook. You'll want to keep your responses for reference in case you decide to go ahead with the project.

Step one: Answer these questions to the best of your ability. There are no wrong answers, but there are answers that inspire you to write on … and that's what you're looking for.

1. **What about the idea draws you in?** What's the most important element of it to you?

2. **Who could the players be?** Not just the people who inspired you to follow your idea but the supporting characters. What type of people would be involved in the situation? Who are the friends? Who are the acquaintances? Who are the enemies? Try to create a quick biography of each in which you explore their relationships to each other and to the protagonist. Try to engage all your senses. What do they sound like when they speak? Don't forget to add physical descriptions, aspirations, and even cologne choice, if you "know" it.

3. **Where does the story take place?** When? Keep in mind that the details of the incident that sparked you may not be where you choose to set your novel. Whatever you do, make the setting as concrete as possible. Every reader needs a sense of being grounded in a time and place. Nobody likes the feeling of not knowing where they are.

4. **What are the possibilities for conflict?** Don't just settle for what actually happened. Now that you have a chance to imagine this idea in a more fleshed out manner, ask yourself what could happen given who the characters you've created are, in addition to where they are in this world that you've made.

Step Two: Write. This is the difficult part. Once you've decided the particulars of the story you want to tell, just start writing it. Begin with what you think is the first chapter. Then write the next. Or, just write a couple of chapters out of sequence. When you reach fifty pages, try to write an outline. If you can't, keep writing until you can't write anymore, and then try again.

You're not looking for publishable pages, you're just looking to unlock the possibility of the story and give yourself an understanding of the depth of the project. These pages will be more about what's possible given your idea, and not necessarily part of your final text—although that's possible, too.

Whenever you feel blocked, put the pages away and come back to them the next day. If you continue to feel blocked, or if you have written fifty pages and have run out of ideas for the 270 more you need, put the project away for a while—a week, a month, a year, whatever.

Whatever you do, don't throw any of this away. While you may not be able to write this particular project right now, the fact that you were inspired in the first place may mean that there's some part of this story that you need to write. When you're ready to do that, it'll be waiting for you.

THE FINAL CONSIDERATION: A SHORT, AND YET NOVEL, IDEA

The sneaky thing about writing is that every story needs to be just as long as it takes to be told. You can't make a story longer if it doesn't need to be. It will just run out of steam. And so will you.

Sometimes you can sense how big a story is as soon as you hear the idea. Your mind is filled with all sorts of characters and conflicts. You can think of multiple resolutions and scores of themes that could be played out. Your mind races at the possibilities.

But, sometimes, you get fooled. You think you have a big redemptive story on your hands and then you begin to vet it, you run it through the Litmus Test, and it comes up short—quite literally. You may just have a short story on your hands.

For example, the idea that sparked you only has three characters: let's say a husband, a wife, and her former employer—a blind man who is recently widowed. The wife has maintained a friendship with the man for a great many years, but they haven't seen each other. Still, she invites him to spend the weekend because he's lonely.

You've tried to add other characters, but they don't fit. They make the story feel flabby.

And even though you try, you can only think of one setting, and that's a suburban living room. And you've tried to imagine the action of the story taking place over a year or a lifetime, but you discover that the time frame is short and actually seems to stem from these three people having to spend this one weekend together. And all you know is that it's going to be a very strained weekend because the husband is a cocky, insecure drunk who is insolent and prejudiced towards the visitor because of his blindness.

You could abandon the project, or put it under your bed for later. But if you're Raymond Carver, you write "Cathedral," one of the most memorable stories of contemporary literature. The beauty of Carver's story is in the intimate, and sometimes churlish, details that are provided by the husband and the touching redemption of the man at the story's close.

Sometimes, what you think is a failed novel attempt is actually a short story. So how do you tell the difference? How do you know how much space you need for what you want to say?

You begin writing.

The length of any tale is judged by the complexity of what the story is about—and the complexity is something you discover by writing it—and as you write it. While running it through the Litmus Test is a good indicator, you still can be fooled. You can actually begin writing a short story, but sometimes, through the act of writing, you discover that what you're trying to say is much more complicated. And, of course, the reverse is also true.

As a general rule, short stories usually focus on only one incident. There is often a single setting, a very small number of characters, a short time frame, and one primary plotline. Although you'll often see two plots twining together, only one can be dominant.

If you're trying to say something small, you'll need to keep it simple, or your reader will be confused.

Some stories are so short that they're called flash fiction. They're quick, engaging, and they usually expose a single truth about a condition, situation, or person. The entire arc of a flash story can fit in 50 to 300 words and is more akin to haiku than a novel.

When you write, think of every story as if it were a movie production. You have certain scenes you need to tell the story, crucial images, and a cast of characters. Unfortunately, you have a budget, too. So when you write, spend your words like money, use what you need and nothing more. Nothing should be wasted, but nothing should be spared, either.

Novels have a complicated structure because they usually try to say complicated things. Since they have more depth, they need a large framework. Most novels contain all the classic elements of dramatic structure, including:

- exposition (the introduction of setting, situation, and main characters)
- conflict (a problem)
- rising action (the problem heats up)
- the decisive moment (the problem is so heated that something has to be done)
- climax (the moment everything changes)
- resolution
- moral (sometimes thrown in)

Because a short story is, by definition, short—it doesn't play by these rules. Exposition is usually forgotten: The writer flings you right in the middle of action, and only backtracks a little. While short stories do have a climax, that's the only element that you can usually count on. Endings often *suggest* a resolution rather than give one, and the closing moral is usually implied, if there is one at all.

If you have a question about the length of a story, write it and see where it goes. You may find that the limited space of a short story plays to the strength of what you're trying to say, or you could discover that your vision is too unwieldy to be trapped in 3,000 to 9,000 words.

Or you may find that what you want to say *can* fit into a small space, but when you're finished it doesn't feel quite done. That's not uncommon. It often seems like we're just telling parts of the same story because we are. Since writers work within an emotional landscape that's based on their experiences, it's uniquely their own and always unfolding.

Richard Ford is a good example of that. A master of the sorrow of modern man; he moves from short story to novella to novel, but the heart of his work is still, always, the state of man today: his betrayals, his moral dilemmas, and his mortality. As Ford ages, his stories become wiser, as time has made him wiser.

If a work doesn't feel quite finished and yet functions as a short story, publish it and later cannibalize it to create your novel or novella. When the longer works are published, you can cannibalize them to create short stories that help you rediscover your themes in a deeper way. Just as a point of reference, the Science Fiction and Fantasy Writers of

America define the novella as having a word count between 17,500 and 40,000. Most novels hover around 60,000 to 90,000 words, although they can be much longer.

Exercise

Your Vision as a Writer

You can change the names and the circumstances, but you're always working within the boundaries of your own heart. The ideas that spark you will all have common threads. Short or long is really just a momentary decision. You'll always have another chance to rediscover what you're trying to say, and what you're trying to say will change with age and your own experience, but it will still be part of your landscape. The only time you're ever finished with a story is when you take your last breath.

Take a look at the books you enjoy reading and compare them to your own writing. Then ask yourself, what are the themes and traits that define the work you like? What defines your own work? Make a list of both. For example, Isabel Allende is known for lush historic Latin American novels steeped in romance, magic realism, sorrow, and hope. She once said, "I have stopped asking myself why; now I trust that in every book I am exploring my own soul, my past, myself. Certain things interest me deeply: strong women, mothers, love, violence, death, loss, grief, friendship, loyalty, justice, and redemption. Those seem to be constant themes in my writing and in my life."

What are the things that are part of your life that you explore? What interests you deeply? Once you know, you'll better understand where each story will take you.

CREATING YOUR
PROTAGONIST

Form is easily learned, but vision is the challenge. All ideas for novels come from you; you just have to be able to recognize that. The day you are born, your stories begin to take shape. How you shape them—your vision of your place in the world—is what distinguishes you from other writers. In a sense, we create reality but not as a god would—we do not have the finesse, the elegance, or the nuance of a creator—we are clumsy gods. So we write from our own personal experience, bruised and tarnished as it is, not as journalists would, but as witnesses to the travesties of our own human hearts.

The process of fiction begins with a moment that takes root under your skin and grows until you have to write about it. You may not even be that conscious of it. Stories often wake you up in the night and tug at you until you get out of bed and make some odd notes that you won't exactly remember the details of when morning comes, but you'll have a sense of what you were trying to say. And so you'll sit down and write. When you're finished, someone will ask, "Isn't that the story of your Uncle Joe?" And it will be. And won't be.

Stories are tricky that way.

Fiction is the process of forgetting. Through time your memory softens, becomes malleable, and suddenly you find yourself telling a story that is what happened to you, and not what happened to you—both at the same time. The more you allow the real truth of what happened to fade, the more the universal truth of what happened surfaces.

If you tried to write the story of Uncle Joe, you'd get tangled in truth and loyalty. But if you find yourself writing about a man who, like your Uncle Joe, always wanted to go to Rio de Janeiro but, unlike your Uncle Joe, died of a stroke as soon as his foot touched the tarmac (Joe really only bought the ticket and never took the flight), then you're on the right track. If you're writing about the heat and sorrow of a moment that you know, and a loss that you understand, then your work is freed by it and yet still tethered to the compass of your heart.

That's the way it is with stories. They take you on journeys. You don't have a map or an itinerary, but you keep pounding away in the dark until you finally figure what story you need to tell and then you refine it until it shines brightly for all to see.

PUTTING FLESH ON THOSE BONES

Your brain wants a story to tell because you are alive and dying, both at the same time, and it must be entertained, must be obsessed by something other than your own personal tragedy. And that's where you begin—with the obsessive distraction that living demands.

Dangerous wisdom—lessons learned from mistakes, mishaps, and wanton disregard—is the seed of all stories.

Both short stories and novels are such long projects without definable outcomes that you need to have an obsessive commitment to stick around and tell the tale properly. But while commitment is where your job begins, you can't assume that others will share your obsession. People have to care about your protagonist, and it's your job to make them care.

"Protagonist," "main character," and "hero" are words that are often used interchangeably, but there's a difference between them. While all protagonists are main characters, not all protagonists are heroes. The word "hero" refers to someone who has the courage needed to face danger and overcome it. So a protagonist can be a hero, and is most certainly the main character, but a hero is not always the protagonist.

In John Irving's *A Prayer for Owen Meany,* the story is told by John— a character who is most certainly *not* a hero, but he is the protagonist. The story he tells is about how his life was changed forever by his heroic friend, Owen Meany.

The protagonist is the first to take the stage and is clearly the main character because the story revolves around him, and he's the one who undergoes change. Sometimes, a story will focus on a character who appears to be the protagonist but then is killed off. This is called a false protagonist.

The protagonist is yours for the making. Make him equal parts haplessness and charm, but don't make him an unredeemable monster. If he kills people, you need to give him traits that endear him to the reader, such as a code of honor and strong values, just as Mario Puzo did with *The Godfather.* Or make him a vampire who longs to be in God's graces, as Anne Rice did with Lestat. You can even make him a serial killer, like Jeff Lindsay's Dexter character, if your friendly neighborhood serial killer is a police department blood-spatter expert who just happens to murder other murderers on his days off.

If he's charming and knows he's a monster, the reader loves it because it reminds them that even the flawed can be forgiven. Writing, indeed, is an optimistic art.

Once you decide whom your protagonist is, what his flaws are, and why he should be loved, you can begin. Your most important job is to make him both interesting and human.

In Jonathan Lethem's homage to the hard-boiled crime novel, *Motherless Brooklyn*, protagonist Lionel Essrog is a detective suffering from Tourette's syndrome. The novel introduces this charming tortured man in the very first sentence.

> Context is everything. Dress me up and see. I'm a carnival barker, an auctioneer, a downtown performance artist, a speaker in tongues, a senator drunk on filibuster.

The opening, "Context is everything. Dress me up and see," establishes the sense of helplessness of the protagonist. He's like a Ken doll. Dress him up to provide the context for his uncontrollable ranting. We immediately feel sympathy for him, relate to him, and care about his plight. It's a fascinating premise. Lethem has us right from the start because Lionel is both interesting and human. And even though we may not know what it feels like to have Tourette's, who hasn't felt helpless?

You can never assume your story is intrinsically interesting. You have to make us care about the protagonist. Instead of using first person, Lethem could have just begun in third person and told us that Lionel Essrog is a detective suffering from Tourette's syndrome. He lives in Brooklyn. And we would all say, "Oh. Okay. So, what else have you got?"

But to put us in the room with Lionel, on his side, inside of his head, makes this story matter to us. Lionel is speaking to us about his helplessness, and it's interesting because unlike our own personal helplessness—lack of money, love, or status—you just don't work at fixing the problem of Tourette's, you can only work around it. How one does that is compelling to a reader.

How do you decide how to make your protagonist human? Everything you need to know is buried within the story you want to tell. But again, don't take your characters directly from real life or your work may be limited and have little dimension. You can change the names all you want, but something in the back of your mind will always pull you back on the course of truth—and the facts are never as interesting as the possibilities they suggest.

One thing I learned from being a reporter is that fiction is a better version of the truth: It's what should have happened.

Start with what you know. Use it as a springboard and dive deep into the dark waters of what you don't know. And don't forget to take your heart with you.

Keep in mind that even if you think you know who your protagonist is, she will change on you. When you think she's a safe driver, she runs five lights. When you think that she believes in happy endings, she leaves a loved one at the altar.

Protagonists are often fickle, so it's important for you to create a framework for your hero that's flexible, and you need to be flexible, too. Take the journey that presents itself on the page, the one you're not sure of. Trust the story to lead you.

Here are a few more tips for building your protagonist:

- **Create a fully drawn person, with both good and bad points.** Make notes such as, "Eats hot sauce and voted Independent," but draw the line at writing small sketches of everyone. While all these mechanical things may help keep some writers focused, they also tend to exert too much influence on the writing. If you've written an essay about your protagonist's childhood dog, it's only natural to try to fit it into the story—even if it doesn't fit at all. You have it and if it's good writing you're going to want to use it. Plus, who has the time to flesh out every character? Some of them, like some people you know, just play a minor role and then leave as they came—a mystery.

- **Name your character as soon as you can.** Newspapers, phone books, and Internet-based name generators such as thinkbaby names.com are good places to start. Just make sure that whatever name you choose is appropriate to the age of the character and the time and place in which the book is set. You don't want a grandmother in the early 1900s being named "Mandi;" your reader will question the spelling and the use of that name during that time period. Also, try not to name your female characters with male names and vice versa. Pick a name that has energy for you, but also one that won't confuse your reader.

• **As soon as you have a general idea of who your protagonist is, begin to craft the supporting characters needed to help with the quest—friends, bosses, loves.** Think of them as real people. What would they look like? How old would they be? What's their job history? Who's in their family? Who do they love? What do they eat?

Exercise

Building Your Own Hero

E.M. Forster once said, "I have only got down on to paper, really, three types of people: the person I think I am, the people who irritate me, and the people I'd like to be."

Since it's easier to create characters from people we know, open your photo albums or take that old shoebox down from the closet, and spread out your pictures. Choose fifteen to twenty and photocopy them in black and white. When you're done, cut the faces, hands, and feet in the photos into small squares. Throw the rest away.

Keep in mind that you're not looking to cut an exact square of Uncle Joe's head; what you're trying to do is to cut the square so that you get a part of his face. You want to make these squares evocative, and not true representations of these people because you're culling bits of them and not their entire selves.

Yes, it seems a trifle sacrilegious to chop up poor defenseless Uncle Joe, but metaphorically that's what you're going to do with him when you turn him into a fictional character, anyway. You might as well get used to it.

Once you've finished, tape these snippets onto 3x5 cards. Shuffle the deck and chose a card and then another until one sparks you. When you've settled on one, look at it very closely:

---

this is your protagonist. Don't think about who it is in the picture, but think about who it could be. What are the possibilities? Imagine him grocery shopping, celebrating a birthday, driving through traffic. What color are his eyes? What's his favorite shirt? Open your notebook and write it all down.

Remember that actions are often the best way to describe any character, protagonist or not. Don't tell us that someone is befuddled. Show him driving aimlessly around his city, stopping at café after café trying to figure out what he wants for lunch and then deciding that lunch isn't at all what he's after. Be specific with your descriptions. Make extensive notes.

INTRODUCING THE PROTAGONIST

In the short story "In Cuba I was a German Shepherd," Ana Menendez sets up a leisurely introduction of her protagonist. The man is sitting in a park under a tree with three other men. He's brought a box of dominos with him. In the very first paragraph she says of the quartet, "Sometimes the way the wind moved through the leaves reminded them of home."

She's setting the tone of homesickness and displacement that these Cuban immigrants feel. She then gives us the name of her main character, Maximo, and writes, "And because he was a small man his grandiose name had inspired much amusement all his life." She ends with:

> Judging the men to be in good spirits, he cleared his throat and began to tell the joke he had prepared for the day.
> "So Bill Clinton dies in office and they freeze his body."

Not only do we understand the time in which the story is set, during Clinton's presidency, we understand exactly who Maximo is—he's a joker. He's the elderly gentleman we walk past sitting in the park every day. He's the one who, given the irony of being an unassuming man with a very grand name, uses humor as a way to comment on life. The pace of this introduction, and the pace of the story, is fitting to the nature of the protagonist, who is lonely and too far away from home.

On the other hand, in the novel *The Kitchen God's Wife,* Amy Tan throws you in the middle of the moment because her character is that whirlwind kind of person.

> Whenever my mother talks to me, she begins the conversation as if we were already in the middle of an argument.
>
> "Pearl-ah, have to go, no choice," my mother said when I phoned last week. After several minutes I learned the reason for her call: Auntie Helen was inviting the whole family to my cousin Bao-bao's engagement party.
>
> "The whole family means the Kwongs and the Louies. The Kwongs are Auntie Helen, Uncle Henry, Mary, Frank, and Bao-bao. And these days, "the Louies" really refers only to my mother and me since my father is dead and my brother ...."

This character, in first person, is doing exactly what she says her mother does—she's beginning her conversation with you as if you're in the middle of an argument. You've met this person before. She's telling you all about these people who you have no idea about; they're not even described to you so you can't picture them—they're just names. By using this technique, the reader instantly relates to the "type" that Tan is presenting and the story begins to take shape.

When you develop characters, you have many tools to work with, but the most important thing you can do is find their heart and your own. All stories are written with the bold heart of childlike wonderment and abandon. The technical side of the work, transferring your vision onto the page, is mechanical. You wield all your available tools to create the right mix of dialogue, action, and description.

Exercise

...•••• ✳ ••••...

Introducing Your Own Hero

...•••••••••...

Rewrite *The Kitchen God's Wife* text in a more traditional manner using the classical approach presented in "In Cuba I was a German Shepherd." Note the difference in energy between what you've written and what Tan has.

Take your newly created hero and write an introduction for him in the style of Tan and then of Menendez. Which suits your purposes better?

15

TECHNIQUES FOR CRAFTING YOUR ENTIRE CAST

Characters do two things: They either evolve or reveal themselves. When characters evolve, they're not the same people they were when you started the story; something profound has changed them—usually the plot. The protagonist of your story often evolves, although other characters can too. It's only natural. Whenever you deal with life-changing events, which are usually the linchpin of all storytelling, people's lives are going to change.

Characters who reveal themselves usually do so through dialogue and action. You as a reader know them just as you get to know a real person because all you have to go on is what you can piece together from what they do or say. The author shapes what you know and when you get to know it, which can create tension and compel you to keep reading because you want to discover who this person really is.

In *The Book of Ruth,* Jane Hamilton uses first person to tell the story of Ruth Grey, a woman who seems to be a slow-witted victim. At least, that's how it seems until the end of the book. And, because it's clear that you've been duped, the end of the book is quite shocking.

Hamilton expertly builds the reveal by starting out making Ruth likable. That's crucial in a first-person reveal of this nature because people must always be able to imagine a bit of themselves, their humanity, in the protagonist. If you're going to make your protagonist evil, you really need to make him likable at first so that your reader identifies with him and is reluctant to see anything amiss until it's too late. Then, of course, they're going to feel surprised, maybe even tricked—but that's the function of a revealed narrator.

A revealed character can provoke strong feelings in readers when the character is not who they thought she was. Authors use the method to allow the reader to make a discovery about the protagonist that will shed new light on the narration. With an unreliable narrator like Hamilton's, at some point in the story you understand that the narrator is lying to you and that changes everything you thought you knew about the "facts" of the story.

Of course, you don't need to just use the same form of character development with all your characters. In *Mystic River,* Dennis Lehane both reveals and changes characters. The story is about three childhood friends whose lives were changed forever when a strange car pulled into their neighborhood. Two men, pretending to be policeman, tried to convince the trio to get into the car. One of the boys got in and the other two stayed behind. The boy who went with the strangers was presumed raped, then released. Twenty-five years later, the daughter of one of the friends is murdered and the three come together again.

The protagonist of the story is homicide detective Sean Devine, one of the boys who didn't get into the car. When the story begins, his pregnant wife has left him and his life is a mess. By the time the story ends and the murder is solved, this conflict is resolved and his life, and outlook, has changed. He's evolved.

Jimmy Marcus, the other boy who didn't get into the car, is revealed to be a violent man and an ex-con. When his daughter is murdered, he wants to kill the man who did it. From the first moment we're introduced to him when he's eleven years old, he's crazy and reckless. Time didn't change him. The event of the kidnapping exacerbated his condition, but his behavior was still what you'd expect from Jimmy, the tough kid who grew up on the wrong side of town. The more we read, the more is revealed about Jimmy until we can't help but think that he's a dangerous man and yet, we're sympathetic to his loss.

The boy who did get into the car, Dave Boyle, has grown into a troubled man, but at the beginning of the book, we're not quite sure *how* troubled. Nobody is. Something obviously happened to him when he was kidnapped, but no one knows what exactly. As the story progresses, though, we begin to see what damage had been done to Dave, and why, and how his kidnapping not only shaped his life but the lives of others.

Unlike Hamilton's Ruth, this reveal makes the reader both horrified for and sympathetic towards Dave. In the end, when "justice" is served, we feel deeply about the outcome because by using the reveal method, we've slowly come to an understanding of Dave as one would understand a friend.

SHAPING DIALOGUE

While it's important to know the facts of a character—color of hair, age, job, and marital status—he won't come to life until you have him speak.

How a person speaks, not just what he says, is an important part of building characters who seem like real people. Do you want your characters to speak proper English or use slang? Should they curse? And, if so, how vulgar should they be? Do you want them to have a regional dialect, like Cajun, or speak in another language?

While the answers come from the characters themselves—who you think they are in the world—there are some practical considerations, too. Vulgar language turns some readers away. If you use a dialect, or have your character speak in another language, you could also lose readers. Slang, like "wicked good," is particular to certain regions and often has to be explained to readers who live outside of the area. If someone speaks in broken English, you need to figure out a way to portray that so the character doesn't seem too comic or cartoonlike.

Whatever you do, you need to present the character in a way that won't lose too many readers. If they need to curse, you have three options:

1. Let them curse to excess so that it becomes comic and therefore neutralizes the impact.

2. Just refer to a person's swearing, as Jean Shepherd did in *A Christmas Story* when Ralphie Parker tells the audience, "My father worked in profanity the way other artists worked in paint or clay. It was an art form, his true calling."

3. Just save up and use it sparingly.

As far as dialect goes, in most cases, it's always best to use *any* variation of American English, such as regional dialects, with a light hand. Using foreign languages falls under the same rule. Anytime you stray away from what the reader knows, it calls for some invention to help him understand what you're getting at. Since one can't assume that your reader knows even the most basic of any other language or dialect, you have to help them deduce meaning.

Ruth L. Ozeki set her book *My Year of Meats* in Japan. The novel is about Jane Takagi-Little, a Japanese-American documentary filmmaker who is so desperate for a job that she signs on to coordinate an odd television series that's designed to bring America's heartland, and America's meat, into the homes of millions of Japanese viewers. Naturally, there's going to have to be some Japanese in a book that's set in the country and involves working with native speakers. Ozeki chose to write some of the sections in first person, so she peppers her dialogue with Japanese, while maintaining the meaning in English. Here's an excerpt from the prologue, where Janet, or *Takagi* as they call her, is trying to help the Japanese crew shoot the final scene of the series.

> The cameraman, eye pressed to the finder, groans in exasperation.
>
> *"Takagi, tell her not to move!"* he says.
>
> "I'm sorry, Mrs. Flowers, but I have to ask you once again not to move your head ...?"
>
> "Muri desu you," the cameraman tells Oda. "It's impossible. We can't go in any closer than this. Her face is all shiny and blotched. She looks ugly."
>
> *"Takagi!"*
>
> *"Hai!"*
>
> *"Ask her if she has any makeup she can use to cover up her unattractive skin!"*
>
> "Uh ... Mrs. Flowers? Mr. Oda is asking if you happen to have any foundation? We are having a bit of a problem with the camera, and there's this one little area .... It's just for the close-up."
>
> "Should I go and get it?" Suzie asks, her jaw is still frozen.
>
> *"She has makeup. Do you want her to go and get it?"*
>
> *"Baka ... Don't be stupid. I don't want her to move. Ask her where it is, and you get it!"*

It's interesting to note that when one writes foreign words, they are usually in italics. Here, the writer uses italics to suggest that some words, while English, should be in Japanese, as in this passage: *"Takagi, tell her not to move!"*

As long as you provide a consistent, comfortable, logical, and accessible framework for your reader, you can give your characters any kind of language "tic" they need.

Making It Real

Being too polite with characters is a problem. Most of us have a moment when we want to make our protagonist too nice, too lovable, too perfect, or just too much. It's an understandable reflex. We live with our characters day and night, so we want to make them likable—who wants to hang out with boorish idiots? But the only thing we really need to do is make them real. Jimmy Cagney once said that acting is simple: "Learn your lines ... plant your feet ... look the other actor in the eye and tell the truth." The same is true for writers: Be grounded and don't blink.

Believable dialogue is crucial to building your characters, and your novel in general. But be careful not to confuse the idea of believable with "real." In real life people stumble, make all sorts of misstatements, and often don't get to the point. This is why dialogue is written much like poetry—every word needs to be resonant and necessary to build the plot or the character.

Dialogue always works on two levels, the text and the subtext. The text is straightforward, as in, "Is there gas in the car?" The answer to this would be either "yes" or "no." But the subtext of the question is what is meant by the question itself—as in why is it being asked? You would never write dialogue in which a character would ask if there was gas in a car, just as a matter of housekeeping. Dialogue does convey information but it must be *important* information. Who cares about gas? You don't—unless there's a reason that you should.

Let's say that you're writing a scene between a man and a woman in the throes of an argument. The man says, "You don't have the courage to rob that bank." And the woman says, "Is there gas in the car?" The sentence now takes on a whole different level of meaning—and that's the subtext. Writing dialogue is all about economy: You want to have characters speak the way they should, and only as much as they need to.

Mystic River begins with the flashback of Dave getting into the kidnapper's car more than twenty-five years earlier. After Dave is taken, Sean and Jimmy both feel uneasy about what happened but can't articulate it until they reach home. Mr. Devine, Sean's father, confronts the two on the sidewalk, notices that Dave isn't with them, and demands to know what happened. Sean explains that they were fighting and the cops came and took Dave home.

"What are you talking about? Sean, what the cops
look like?"

"Huh?"

"Were they wearing uniforms?"

"No. No, they ..."

"Then how did you know they were cops?

"I didn't. They ..."

"They what?"

"He had a badge," Jimmy said. "On his belt."

"What kind of badge?"

"Gold?"

"Okay. But what did it say on it?"

"Say?"

"The words. Were there words you could read?"

"No. I don't know."

As you can see, there's a lot of subtext going on in this short passage. The father begins by saying, "What are you talking about?" If you look at this question textually, it's really unnecessary—the boys are talking about what happened to Dave. So the question isn't asked for information's sake, it's asked to establish that the father thinks that something is wrong.

This passage doesn't have much in the way of attribution, or what's known as dialogue tag, as in "he said." Sean is addressed at the start and then there is an exchange between father and son. Then Jimmy speaks and Lehane makes sure that his dialogue is attributed to him. We then assume that the rest of the conversation is between Jimmy and Sean's father, even though we're not told that. We don't need to be because the structure is already set in place.

It's all about economy; there's not one wasted word in this exchange. Attribution would slow the pace, so it's not used. The writer spends his words wisely; even when someone repeats what's being said, as in when Jimmy says, "Say?" it builds tension and helps establish the confusion over what's just happened. When the exchange "I didn't. They ..." "They what?" happens, you can just feel the father's anxiety because of the writer's choice to repeat the word "they."

The two boys' speech patterns also help build the tension. If you look carefully, you can figure out what each boy is feeling at this moment because the writer makes grammar work for him. When Sean speaks to his father, he begins to trail off after every sentence. The writer indicates this with "…". You get the feeling that Sean realizes that something is amiss and is wondering about it and is ashamed of his role.

Lehane also uses grammatical incorrectly structure to develop the scene. "Sean, what the cops look like?" is not a proper sentence. It should read "what *did* the cops look like?" but this wouldn't serve the author as well. By taking out the "did," Lehane quickens the momentum of the exchange and makes it seem as if a real person said it.

Of course, he could have just told us the information in a summary. He could have written, "When the boys came home, Sean's father had a feeling that Dave was in trouble." But, as you can see, the scene in summary loses the richness of the moment. It is now just information. The subtext that defined the characters and their relationships is lost.

There are times, however, when a summary is exactly what you need. So how do you tell?

There's just one rule—go with what gives energy to the moment that you're working on. Each style choice creates a different outcome, so write and rewrite passages until they function in the way you want them to.

Well-drawn dialogue makes a reader pay attention to the interaction of characters, so when drama is required, as in the exchange from *Mystic River,* consider this technique. You'll also want to keep in mind that the sound of words can create rhythm, a music of sorts, and add to the momentum—like Lehane did with his repetitive use of the word "they." When you want to amp up the tension, focus on the sound of words.

Description, or the straight reportage of facts, makes readers step back a moment to try to imagine it in their heads. It slows them down, and can often break the rhythm of a passage, but is sometimes necessary to convey a great deal of information in a small space. Whatever you do, try to avoid description in a dialogue tag. Phrases like, "he sadly said" instead of "he said" stop the reader and break up the dialogue in a non-productive way. If what the character says is sad, and his body language or gestures communicate that he's sad, then you don't need to say that. If you've laid enough groundwork, you can trust your reader to understand.

Silence Matters, Too

Whatever you do, don't underestimate the power of silence. What is unsaid is often more important than what is said.

Playwright Harold Pinter was known for his use of odd unforgettable moments of quiet that the theatergoer, and reader, infuse with their own terror, outrage, and black humor. Plays like "The Caretaker" and "The Homecoming" were illuminated by what's known as the Pinter Pause, and the word "Pinter-esque" was coined to explain his succinct and ferocious style that allowed the emotion of moment, rather than words, to say what was too horrible to be said.

In this scene from *Betrayal,* you'll see the [...] and the word *pause,* which are stage directions that indicate Pinter's desire for silence. In this section, Jerry apologizes to Robert for having an affair with Robert's wife, Emma. Jerry thinks that Emma had just told her husband two days ago, but in fact, she'd told him four *years* ago and Robert never said a word even though, as Robert says, the two men have "seen each other ... a great deal ... over the last four years," having "had lunch," but they "Never played squash though."

Jerry is ironically outraged that Robert didn't feel close enough to him to confront him. "I was your best friend," he says.

Robert agrees—"Well, yes, sure."

Jerry says, "Why didn't you tell me?" *pause [...]* "That you knew. You bastard."

"Oh, don't call me a bastard, Jerry."

Which provokes Jerry even more and he goes on about the "seven years" that he's lived with Robert's wife "in the afternoons." Robert knows this, and then, after a pause says, "I hope she looked after you all right."

And the scene ends with a friendliness between the men, because even though Jerry betrayed Robert, they still like each other.

In a 1964 interview, Pinter said, "Actually, I write the pause because people are going to stop talking at this point."

The silence just makes this exchange more creepy.

So, if you find that something overwhelming happens in your plot and your characters have stopped talking, trust that. Your reader will fill in the blanks because they know that sometimes words tend to be inadequate. There are certain things that you can't name or describe because that would cheapen them and make them maudlin. You just have to trust that sometimes there's dignity in silence and allow your reader to draw his own conclusion, which will subsequently strengthen the narrative bond.

BUILDING CHARACTER THROUGH SETTING

Setting is the canvas on which you craft your tale. Where something happens always dictates how it happens, why it happens, and to whom it happens. And where a person lives defines who they are. A widow on the Upper East Side of New York City will act substantially different from a widow who lives in the home of Winnebago Industries, Forest City, Iowa, with its population of 4,500 and recently built YMCA. Setting matters a great deal. And how one lives in the place is a great indication of character.

Chang-rae Lee's *A Gesture Life* is set in a small town that the narrator Doc Hata tells us is, "fifty minutes north of the city ... a picturesque town that I will call Bedley Run." Hata is not a doctor, but an elderly man who once owned the medical supply store in town and ran what he calls "an informal clinic" geared to making sense out of the prognoses doctors were fond of giving and not explaining.

Even though it quickly becomes clear that Hata is not a reliable narrator, as he seems to be in the early stages of dementia, he is a keen observer of his world and his place in it. The novel begins:

> People know me here. It wasn't always so. But living thirty odd years in the same place begins to show on a man. In the course of such time, without even realizing it, one takes on the characteristics of the locality, the color and stamp of the prevailing dress and gait and even speech—those gentle bells of the sidewalk passerby, their *How are yous* and *Good days* and *Hellos.*

As Hata recognizes that he has become the place he lives in, your characters also are the embodiment of the particular time and place in which you place them. So, don't make arbitrary choices. Don't decide that you want to set the story in a midsized American city and then think that either side of Kansas City will do—it just won't. Both areas are lovely, but the part of Kansas City that's in Missouri is much more urbane and urban than that part of Kansas City that's actually in Kansas—and that makes a huge difference when building a character.

When choosing a setting for your character, try to find a place that you're familiar with. You'll need to know things like when people get up in the morning (in farm communities that can be anywhere from 3 to 4 A.M.). Do most drive to work or commute? What's the education level? What's the median income and housing price? What gives the people pride about where they live? What are they ashamed of?

Much of this information can be found on the Internet; even the smallest of towns seem to have their own official Web sites. In addition there are many oral history sites, and bloggers live everywhere. Of course, it's best to have firsthand knowledge of a place and its people. So, if you don't feel familiar with a setting that you want to use, travel there or find someone who lives there and ask about it.

All places are unique, even the smallest of towns, and it's your job to figure out why. It's just not something that you can fake.

And don't forget to find a map. Yes, even if you chose your own hometown, it's often amazing how the mind can play tricks on you. You may have lived in Sarasota, Florida, all your life and think you know the streets as well as you know the lines on your own face, but the first time you get a letter from a reader who tells you that Fruitville Road does not intersect with University Avenue, and they're right, you are going to be embarrassed.

Familiarity breeds mistakes. A map costs about $5—trust me, it's a good investment. You'd be surprised how many people find the time to correct your mistakes and how much time it takes to write them back and eat crow.

Imaginary Settings

Imaginary places are a little more difficult for readers to relate to, since you made them up in your own mind, but at least you get the street names right. Still, it takes a lot of explaining to use an imaginary setting. Everybody knows something about Miami or Detroit, so you can get on with your story more quickly. But if you create a city called Downyberg, you have to be prepared to build it brick by brick for your reader—just as Lee did in *A Gesture Life*.

Of course, you sometimes can use a shortcut. Robert Olen Butler's book *Hell* is set in a place that most people have some idea about. His twist on the location is that all the streets are named "Peachtree."

If you do think you want to go the imaginary route, pick a place that you think your city, village, or town is most like and use it as a model. This approach is easier on you. In addition, if you're writing about an imaginary town that's like New Bedford, and you live in the real New Bedford, you can easily draw on your own experience, and the lives of the people you know, to create your world. People may recognize that you did this, and shun you, but luckily they can't sue you for it.

If you're going to create a town, be careful what you name it. Sherwood Anderson used his hometown of Clyde, Ohio, as the model for his story collection *Winesburg, Ohio* and based his fictional characters on people he knew in the area. Unfortunately there *is* a Winesburg, Ohio, and Anderson's book made people from both towns rather upset.

One last thing about setting—use it every chance you get and use every element of it that you can. Employ all the senses. What does the place smell like, sound like, or feel like? Instead of words, it's sometimes much stronger to let the physical world carry the emotion. Remember that nature continues despite wars and personal tragedy, but the wind is never colder than on the day your character's daughter dies.

Exercise

Your Hero on the Move

Take the protagonist you created earlier and write a scene in which he's talking to a loved one about taking a vacation. This conversation can take place wherever seems natural— a café, a church basement—any place in keeping with your character's life. Make sure that he's firmly grounded in the place and that you use all your senses to draw the scene.

After you're finished, change the location of the scene to the Paris Metro and make your protagonist a Moroccan living in the city post-WWII. If you know nothing about the discrimination of Moroccans in Paris at that time, look it up before you rewrite the scene.

BACKSTORY

Creating backstory is like being at a cocktail party and trying to figure out how much information you need to give someone so that they can connect with you, understand who you are, and get a good idea of why you say and do what you say and do. And you have to be quick about it. You can't begin at childhood and ramble all the way up to the moment you walked through your host's door. What you're really looking for are tiny, yet germane, packets of information that will give people all they really need to know—for the moment. When the need arrives, you can always offer a little bit more.

Backstory is a very important way for writers to flesh out characters. While we learn a great deal from what characters say and do, everything can't be forward motion in a story. We'd have no sense of history or context. Backstory adds depth and perspective to a character. It also slows the reader down a moment, so they can digest who this person really is.

In Ha Jin's *Waiting,* he begins his novel with the smallest amount of backstory, and yet this is the pivotal bit of information that a reader needs to be prepared to listen to his tale.

> Every summer Lin Kong returned to Goose Village to divorce his wife, Shuyu. Together they had appeared at the courthouse in Wujia Town many times, but she had always changed her mind at the last moment when the judge asked if she would accept a divorce. Year after year, they went to Wujia Town and came back with the same marriage license issued to them by the county's registry office twenty years before.

As you see, the crucial thing with backstory is brevity. We don't need to know why Shuyu won't divorce her husband—at least we don't need to know this very minute. But to set the book in motion, we very much need to know that this is the case. The entire book rests on this fact.

Of course, you can devote an entire chapter to a character's history (I certainly have), but you have to be careful not to confuse the reader when you do this. It's really a big risk. Most people read in bed, and they're tired. Confusion happens easily.

It's much better if you think of the use of backstory as an explanation for an action. In *Waiting,* it explains why Lin Kong is, indeed, waiting.

Exercise

Backstory Experiment

Using your protagonist, write a scene about that person's first kiss. Now, write a scene in which your protagonist meets the recipient of that kiss, many years later, because they're involved in a traffic accident together.

When you write the second scene, choose parts of the first kiss narrative and intertwine them as backstory elements. When you settle on one version of the car accident, rewrite it. Try other elements in the kiss narrative that you didn't use the first time to see if they are stronger or weaker than the ones you chose. Don't forget to use all the senses—not just the tactical elements of the kiss but the taste of it, etc.

CRAFTING YOUR STORY

Once you've decided on the basics of your story, it's time to figure out how you're going to tell it. What are the tools you as a writer have at your disposal, and how will you use them?

VOICE AND STYLE

The difference between voice and style (or tone) is often confusing for most writers. The basic definitions are simple. Voice is usually defined by word choice and the way a writer speaks and thinks on the page, which is made manifest by the way the characters speak and think and the writer's narrative approach.

Style, on the other hand, is about the tools the writer always chooses, such as sentence length, punctuation, and sometimes topic matter.

Voice (which is sometimes called tone) can change from project to project. But a writer's style usually doesn't.

Now here's where the confusion comes in: A writer's style always influences the voice of a project. And so, in cases where a person writes a series of work with the same voice and style, it's sometimes difficult to distinguish what one's style is versus what the voice of the book is.

That said, it's always easy to tell the style of one writer over another. No matter what book you're reading, you couldn't confuse the style of Ernest Hemingway, who is known for his spare evocative prose, with that of Thomas Pynchon, who is often elegantly loquacious. Whatever choices they make about the voice or tone in their individual works may vary, but it still is very easy to tell them apart. Similarly, you'd never confuse Candace Bushnell with either man. Her choice of topic and scope is just too dissimilar.

Voice, on the other hand, does vary from project to project. Lewis Nordan, a darkly comic Southern writer, has a very distinctive style. He blends the fantastic with the everyday and writes about Sugar Mecklin, a small boy growing up in a mythic town named Arrow Catcher. He's also extremely adept at creating the perfect voice for each tale he tells.

Here's the opening paragraph from "How Bob Steele Broke My Father's Heart" from *Music of the Swamp*:

> Naughty demons accompanied my father wherever he went. All misery did not seem to be of his own making. In his home, the telephone often rang with no one on the line. Hoses broke on the Maytag. Pipes froze in spring. Pets came down with diseases that they had been inoculated against. Wrestling and "The Love Boat" appeared on television at unscheduled times. Lightning struck our house and sent a fireball across the floor. He was the only man in Mississippi to buy a bottle of Tylenol that actually had a cyanide capsule in it.

As you can see, this list begins with things that are fairly common, like hoses breaking on the Maytag. Then Nordan takes it to another level by having wrestling and "The Love Boat" appear at unscheduled times, which seems odd and unbelievable. Then he moves on to the lightening and cyanide capsule incidents in which no one gets hurt but which makes his father seem quite lucky while still being quite cursed. At the end of this paragraph, Nordan makes the father seem quite hapless, and still cursed, by accepting collect charges for an obscene phone call.

This opening paragraph sounds like a child would have written it, a child who didn't quite understand that a broken Maytag, which is a normal thing, and finding a cyanide capsule, which is a wildly unlikely thing, were not both the products of "naughty demons." There's a simple acceptance of the facts that engages one as a child would. On the other hand, in *The Sharpshooter Blues*, Nordan employs a difference voice: a more knowing and worldly narrator for this opening salvo.

> The island where Mr. Raney had his fishcamp was a strip of high ground far out in a strange bayou, the vast, unbounded backwaters of many lakes and rivers; from underground, somewhere, salt water, brackish at least, mineral salts, filled up the swamp and broadened it far across the Delta. The water seemed limitless, everywhere, even to a boy who grew

> up on the island; it was a black mirror, colored by the tannic
> acid that seeped into it from the knees of cypress trees.

As you can see, the voices are different, but both are the work of Lewis Nordan; his style is marked by the geography of Mississippi and his simple, yet often poetic diction.

Your Style, Your Choice

Look at what you've written already, your body of work. Can you distinguish what your style is?

How do you use words? How are you planning to use them? Are you playful, respectful, or bold? How do you use character development, diction, dialogue, syntax, or punctuation? What are the topics you care about?

A writer's style is like a fingerprint, and every writer should try to cultivate a unique approach to the page—the best often do. In great writing, style and voice combine to turn a simple tale into a memorable read.

Annie Proulx's *The Shipping News* provides a wonderful example of how both style and voice can breathe new life into an old story. A man being left by his wife is a tale that's been told millions of times, but Proulx brought to it her own experience of living in Newfoundland and knowing the people there, and discovered her protagonist, Quoyle, a third-rate newspaperman. Quoyle, which means "a coil of rope," is announced on the first page of the book by way of a laundry list of characteristics:

> Hive-spangled, gut roaring with gas and cramp, he survived
> childhood; at the state university, hand clapped over his chin,
> he camouflaged torment with smiles and silence. Stumbled
> through his twenties and into his thirties learning to separate
> his feelings from his life, counting on nothing. He ate prodi-
> giously, liked a ham knuckle, buttered spuds.

The boldness of the voice sets this work apart. It's so no-nonsense, much like Newfoundland itself, that you're engaged immediately. Proulx lays out the core of this man in a paragraph and, in the next, his place in the world and what this book will be about.

> His jobs: distributor of vending machine candy, all-night clerk
> in a convenience store, a third-rate newspaperman. At thirty-
> six, bereft, brimming with grief and thwarted love, Quoyle

steered away to Newfoundland, the rock that had generated
his ancestors, a place he had never thought to go.

Proulx piles images upon images, like one sandbags a door. You're trapped inside this man's life now. You're here for the duration.

Michael Ondaatje's *The English Patient* uses voice and style to set a completely different tone. His first paragraph unwinds gracefully, and it's filled with evocative language that brings this prelude full circle and invites the reader into a mystery.

> She stands up in the garden where she has been working and looks into the distance. She has sensed a shift in the weather. There is another gust of wind, a buckle of noise in the air, and the tall cypress sway. She turns and moves towards the house, climbing over the low wall, feeling the first drops of rain on her bare arms. She crosses the loggia and quickly enters the house.

Once she enters the house, she goes directly into a room, which Ondaatje writes "is another garden—this one made up of trees and bowers painted over its walls and ceiling." And there, on the bed, lies the English patient, "his body exposed to the breeze, and he turns his head slowly towards her as she enters."

The difference between the two pieces is remarkable. Proulx's pace is nearly frantic at first. It's all expository; she wants you to be very clear about what's at stake and who this poor man who is named after a coil of rope is. She even heads several chapters with real definitions from *The Ashley Book of Knots* as a way to explain what kind of knot (love knot, strangle knot) this particular Quoyle is getting himself tied into.

Ondaatje takes a mysterious approach, as he often does. It's his style. And so he begins by crafting an elegant image of an unnamed woman in a garden who is forced to move indoors into "another garden," as he says, a room painted with a garden mural, because of a change in the weather. Of course, this is a metaphor for the book. Set in the last throes of WWII, which can be seen as a "change in the weather" from everyday life, *The English Patient* is a story of a young nurse whose last patient, an unknown dying Englishman, is someone in whom she feels that she has seen something that she "wanted to learn, grow into, and hide in."

Each author's style gives birth to a particular tone, or voice, that serves his or her work well. Both approaches lure you in, just in different ways. As you can imagine, *The Shipping News* is quite comedic, while *The English Patient* is lyrical and dark.

Exercise

Test-Drive Style

In an effort to find your own style and the appropriate voice for the story you wish to tell, you need to try on the words of others. Walk around in them as you would new shoes. See where they rub and where they are comfortable; pay close attention to the fit. Every writer learns the craft from emulating others until she begins to hear her own voice.

Write the opening of a love story in the style and voices of the enclosed pieces from Proulx and Ondaatje, and then in what you think may be your own style and tone. Keep in mind that a love story can be between two friends, a man and his dog, or a mother and child. It could even be a story of a man and his car. As long as there is a strong feeling of attachment to guide you, along with a chance for an unhappy ending, it's irrelevant who (or what) loves whom. As in the above samples, write only two paragraphs, but make them as wild or reverent as your story demands.

POINT OF VIEW

After you've found your protagonist and you think you have an idea about how your own style works and what type of voice you'd like to use, decide how you want to structure your story. It's your job make things seem fresh. How you tell your story matters.

What point of view (POV) you use is usually one of the early choices you'll make. There are only three basic choices, so it's not that difficult a decision, but it is crucial. Each point of view brings a different feel, texture, and meaning to your story.

First Person

When writing in first person, you'll use pronouns like *I*, *me*, *my*, *mine*, *we*, and *our*. This is an extremely intimate way to have your protagonist relate to the reader, but it's also very limited. The protagonist only knows his own thoughts, what people tell him, and what happens in front of him. And, in the case of an unreliable narrator, he may or may not be truthful when he speaks. In addition, he must be present in every scene. F. Scott Fitzgerald employed first person in *The Great Gatsby*.

> In my younger and more vulnerable years my father gave me some advice that I've been turning over in my mind ever since.
> "Whenever you feel like criticizing anyone," he told me, "just remember that all the people in this world haven't had the advantages that you've had."
> He didn't say any more but we've always been unusually communicative in a reserved way and I understood that he meant a great deal more than that.

The great benefit of first person is that you really come to know the protagonist, and in a book like *Gatsby*, that intimacy is what gives the story its impact.

Second Person

When writing in second person, you use pronouns like *you*, *your*, and *yours*. When you use it sparingly, readers become active participants. When you use it as your main POV, they become the protagonist.

Stewart O'Nan's *A Prayer for the Dying*, a gothic novel set after the Civil War, employs this technique to make you its protagonist: a war-ravaged sheriff who also serves as his hometown's pastor and undertaker during an epidemic.

> Today they send for you, or Old Man Meyer sends his littlest Bitsi. She comes running, kicking up dust, getting her stockings dirty. "Sheriff Hansen! Sheriff Hansen!"
> You're standing on the stairs outside, ignoring the big bay hitched outside of Fenton's dipping at the water trough. That's

one thing you'll admit is strange about you: you don't like to be around horses anymore. It's understandable, having had to eat them during the siege, to burrow into their warm, dead guts for cover, but you don't talk about that, or only to Marta, who'd never let it slip.

Second person can be a very intense POV.

Third Person

When writing in third person, one uses pronouns like *he, she, it, they, them*, etc. Third is the most flexible POV, because you can share anyone's thoughts, foreshadow events to come—whatever you want. Ann Patchett's *Bel Canto* is about a terrorist takeover at an embassy party. It begins in third person:

> When the lights went off the accompanist kissed her. Maybe he had been running towards her just before it was completely dark, maybe he was lifting his hands. There must have been some movement, a gesture, because every person in the living room would later remember a kiss. They did not see a kiss, that would have been impossible. The darkness that came on them was startling and complete. Not only was everyone there certain that there was a kiss, they claimed they could identify the type of kiss: it was strong and passionate, and it took her by surprise.

TENSE

After you've decided on a POV, tense is the next thing you'll need to think about. Past? Present? Future? All of the above? And once you do choose, what are the implications?

Luckily, you don't have to choose only one tense. Many novels combine them. In *Bleak House,* Charles Dickens tells half in first-person past tense and the other half in third-person present tense. The key to mixing tenses is to create a logic system for it. If a book is set in both the past and present, and you move between both past and present in alternating chapters, then you can use past and present tense in the respective chapters; your reader will understand the logic system of that. If you try to move between past and present in a single paragraph, you're going to drive your reader crazy.

It's important to know what each tense brings to your story. Present tense provides a sense of urgency to a narrative: a sense that things are happening right now and that nobody knows how anything will turn out. It sets forth a mystery. It's very suspenseful. However, you don't see many genre novels that use present tense.

Past tense is the most comforting, and the most widely used. It tells the reader that everything is okay; we made it through the problem and it's now in the past. Even if your story is tragic, the use of past tense will still reassure.

Exercise

Trying On POV and Tense

Once you think you have a basic, yet flexible, understanding of your protagonist, what story you want to tell, and how you want to tell it, you're ready to begin. To have a clear understanding of how POV and tense affect your story, write the first two pages of chapter one in first person. Then rewrite them in second person. Then in third. And then, just for fun, break a few rules and try a combination of POVs. Do the same with tenses.

When you're finished, look at what each narrative mode and tense taught you about your protagonist, and then choose the one you want to take you on your journey.

GRAMMAR

Now that you know where you're going with your story, who is coming with you, and you have your course mapped with your POV and tense suggesting which roads will be taken and which will not, you have to figure out what car you're going to drive. Because what you drive—from a 1971 VW Beetle, to a Hummer, to a brand new Caddy—will shape the journey, too. And that's where grammar comes in. How you use grammar provides rhythm, texture, and depth to your adventure.

And yes, you do have choices as to how you use grammar.

Unlike what your third-grade teacher told you, grammar is a tool just like any other tool, and you *do* have a choice as to how you use it—or don't use it. It's just a road map that keeps the reader from getting lost and indicates the direct route to the meaning of any work. However, sometimes you want to toss your map out the window and take the scenic route or maybe a new unchartered route—and that's when you get to break the rules. Of course, you have to know the rules to break them, but if you do, you can add a level of texture to your story, which can have a large payoff.

In *Blindness*, Portuguese author José Saramago's tale of the unraveling of society and the triumph of humanity, the rules of grammar are retracted midway in an effort to break down the wall between text and reader. The book is about an outbreak of a virus that causes blindness. At first, Saramago employs standard punctuation, but as more and more people go blind, the structures of grammar break down—just as the society breaks down. At the height of the outbreak, the work is written with limited punctuation and dialogue that has neither quotation marks nor attribution.

This may seem challenging for a reader, but Saramago has given his characters specific styles of speech and tics, so you really do know who's speaking when. The style contributes to the narrative's building tension and to the reader's involvement. You really begin to understand what it is to be blind.

Grammar is dynamic. It evolves. It can be re-created based on the need to tell more and more complex stories. In *A Million Little Pieces*, James Frey is writing about a breakdown, so he breaks down the conventions of grammar. Although there was a great deal of controversy over this book because it was discovered to not really be a memoir, it still is a very moving text.

We needed a new grammar to tell our stories. Television, video games—they changed the way we comprehend; therefore they changed the way we read. Our attention spans are shorter and we are much more visual, so many writers use white space to set the tone of their work. We now need a sense of rhythm, and so sentence fragments are now acceptable. We need to have the story surround us, and so in *Blindness*, the rules of grammar are re-created to fold us into the story because today's reader has to be inside the world of the story—not just taken by it, but tactically connected to it. When you shake up punctuation you can create that connection.

The possibilities are endless and the density that these texts create is amazing. Some metafiction books, or books that use fiction to comment on the relationship of fiction to reality, like Mark Danielewski's *House of Leaves* and Junot Diaz's *The Brief Wondrous Life of Oscar Wao*, re-create and reshape footnotes to tell their stories while commenting on them. They also play with the conventions of white space, attribution, and POV—to be honest, they mix it up on all levels. And, at the same time, they also follow the rules.

For example, in the Pulitzer Prize-winning *Wao*, chapter two begins like this:

> It's never the changes we want that change everything.
>
> *This is how it all starts: with your mother calling you into the bathroom. You will remember what you were doing at that precise moment for the rest of your life: You were reading* Watership Down *and the rabbits and their does were making their dash for their boat and you didn't want to stop reading, the book has to go back to your brother tomorrow, but then she called you again, louder, her I'm-not-fucking-around voice, and you mumbled irritably, Sí, señora.*

When you look at this passage closely, it's quite dense. The first sentence is fairly simple in structure, and yet also very evocative. The writer is declaring this condition to be true.

The second sentence is a new paragraph that is entirely in italics, which suggests internal thought, and it's in the second person. However, note that the book title, *Watership Down,* is not in italics. This is because the use of Roman here sets the title off from the text that is in italics. So what can we gather from this use of grammar?

By using italics, we can assume that Diaz is telling us that the character is thinking this. The use of second person can lead us to believe that these thoughts are urgent and need to be shared, as he wants to put you in his shoes. Finally, the colons alert you that what "changed" is something of import.

At least, that's a standard reading. Diaz seems to be re-creating grammar completely; or maybe our assumptions, which are based on standard usage, are incorrect. Or not. It's a puzzle. You have to keep reading to find out.

One book that breaks nearly every rule is *Infinite Jest* by David Foster Wallace. First of all, most publishers feel that books shouldn't be too much over four hundred pages. *Jest* is a whopping 1,104 pages long, with nearly one hundred of those dedicated to endnotes. It relies largely on footnotes, which you really have to read because they do move the plot along, and way too many characters but, if you are up to the challenge, it pulls you in and you read it all.

Of course, not all readers want to be *that* challenged. And if they do, you have to know what you're doing, to keep a plot moving in such a tangle. Picasso was a master in the classical style of painting before he began to reduce the world into the suggestion of form and movement with single stroke, or color. It's a good idea to start out with a more conventional structure and then, if you wish, slowly break down conventions.

"Screwing things up is a virtue," the painter Robert Rauschenberg once said. "Being correct is never the point. I have an almost fanatically correct assistant, and by the time she re-spells my words and corrects my punctuation, I can't read what I wrote. Being right can stop all the momentum of a very interesting idea."

These days everybody seems to have his own stylebook based on an internal logic and worldview. For a more standard approach, there's the Strunk and White version of grammar. Most publishers work with a modified version of the *Chicago Manual of Style*. For emergencies, *Write Right!* by Jan Venolia and *The Everyday Writer* by Andrea A. Lunsford are easy to use reference books that can quickly clear up any confusion you might have.

Use grammar as the tool that it is. Be playful. Be thoughtful. And, most of all, be accurate to the needs of your work.

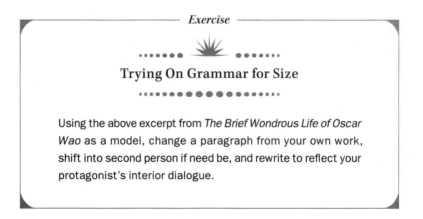

Exercise

Trying On Grammar for Size

Using the above excerpt from *The Brief Wondrous Life of Oscar Wao* as a model, change a paragraph from your own work, shift into second person if need be, and rewrite to reflect your protagonist's interior dialogue.

Does the new paragraph change your intent? Does it illuminate anything about your protagonist? Does it give insight that the reader may need? Does it help you make any new discoveries?

Consider the value of using grammar in a more edgy way in your own work. Based on your sample paragraph, would it help tell your story or just muddy it? If you think it may help, try a sample page. Be bold and break rules if you want to—just keep in mind that you have to be consistent. You need to create a logic system. If you decide to forgo all quotation marks around sentences, another thing that Diaz does in *Wao*, then you always should do that or always do that when a certain situation arises, such as in *Blindness* when the epidemic is at its height and everyone is blind. A logic system grounds readers in the world of the book and allows them to understand the reasons why you've broken with convention.

If you find that this exercise brings new energy to the work, write a chapter. If you think it bogs readers down, abandon it.

THE STRUCTURE
OF YOUR TALE

PLOT

Plot is the shape of the surprise. You need to craft it carefully, taking into consideration what you want to say and how you want to say it.

According to Aristotle, all plots need a beginning, a middle, and an end—that was the gold standard back in 300 B.C. and it's still true because people have been told stories a certain way ever since the birth of language.

But while all stories can be divided into three acts, the acts don't actually have to appear in the prescribed order. They just have to appear to or, at the very least, be suggested.

Here are standard acts in their standard order.

Act I: The Beginning

You lay the foundation for your story and set the stage by introducing your setting, the protagonist, and the conflict that's going to take the protagonist on a journey in which he may be changed or may change others. You need to tell us the "who," "what," "when," and "where" of the tale.

If you don't begin your story by introducing your protagonist, you still need to set the groundwork for his later introduction. The story is about him, after all. If it's a murder mystery and your detective is the protagonist but you don't want to introduce him in the first chapter, you could begin with the murder and the murderer, because this is the circumstance that the protagonist will enter into and be changed by.

This is the place where you announce to the readers what the story is about, what's at stake, and why they should care. It's crucial to get all these elements in so that you have their attention right from the beginning.

Tips for Beginnings

1. Streamline. Don't introduce too many settings and too many characters all at once. It confuses readers. Each chapter can be set in a new place, but try not to move locations more than twice within a chapter.

2. Get into the action as quickly as possible. You don't want to spend too much time in your set-up or you'll lose your reader.

3. Make your elements work double duty. In *The Last Girls,* Lee Smith uses setting to give us a glimpse of her character, Harriet. "... Mississippi begins in the lobby of the Peabody hotel. Waiting to check in at the ornate desk, she can well believe it. Vast and exotic as another country, the hushed lobby stretches away forever with its giant chandeliers, its marble floors, its palms, Oriental rugs and central fountain, its islands of big comfortable furniture where gorgeous blond heiresses lean forward toward each other telling secrets that Harriet will never know and could not imagine." How Harriet sees this world explains exactly who she is.

4. Avoid starting with an extended backstory. It can be done, but unless it has a lot of action, it's tricky to hold the reader's interest. The device of backstory is used to explain the past. If you start with the past, people confuse it with the present. So make sure that we know your characters before you start making excuses for how they behave. We won't care about them, and won't be able to try to understand why they are who they are until we've bonded with them. Give us a scene, or some dialogue, or at least observe them from a distance before you use backstory to explain their actions.

Act II: The Middle

There are crises, complications, and obstacles that present themselves and then seem to be solved but are actually moving the plot towards an ultimate crisis, also known as the climax. The focus here is conflict: Your protagonist should undergo many struggles and emotional challenges. At the moment when hope is gone, he will suddenly be able to draw upon new strength, or a lesson that he learned from his loss, and will solve the final crisis.

Tips for Middles

1. Don't overdo. Too much conflict turns a reader off. You really want to set in motion just enough obstacles to make a struggle work. For example, if you have a blind protagonist who suddenly loses the use of his limbs and can no longer hear, you better have a good reason for it, because your reader will think the situation impossible and may walk away.

2. Don't introduce a new theme or a group of new characters. Keep in mind that this is the point in your novel where you should be using all the elements you've already introduced.

3. Be plausible. Throughout the entire middle section of a book, you should be asking yourself, "Given the elements that I've set in play, could this *really* happen?"

4. Don't shift genre in midstream. If you can't resolve the conflict or tie up another loose end, don't suddenly go science-fiction on your reader and have aliens appear or have the problem solved via *deus ex machina,* which translates into "God from the machine," a literary device in which God actually appears at the end of the story to provide resolution. It's a rather lame plot device that went out of fashion about the same time Homer coined the phrase. If you do find that you'd like to have an otherworldly ending, then start from the beginning and give the reader clues. If you don't, the reader will feel cheated.

5. Be clear. It's amazing how much readers love some ambiguity but hate too much of it. So while it's important not to tie up all the loose ends, you must still give your reader something. For example, if you set in play a murder mystery with a possible love interest—pay off the most compelling story of the two. In the case of genre fiction, like a mystery, it's important that you pay off what is expected in the genre—like who did it. In literary fiction, who did it can take a backseat to the romantic aspect.

6. Every element must lead to the ending. If you write a novel that includes a woman who is blind, you better have a good reason for that. If you don't pay off this choice by giving it meaning and making it important to the story, when the reader finishes

she'll wonder why—and the story will feel unfinished. Once you have the end set in place, if a point of action isn't working—either because it feels superfluous and doesn't contribute to the ending, or because it gives you writer's block and you just can't seem to write it—then you can feel free to get rid of it.

7. Don't forget to let your protagonist fail at some point, feel lost, and move out of their comfort zone.

Act III: The End

Also known as the denouement, this is where the climax and some of the loose ends of the story are resolved. This is also where we get to see the outcome of the protagonist's actions and how he is now changed.

Tips for Endings

1. The real ending of a story always comes *after* the climax or denouement. If you think of it as a hurricane, the denouement is the moment of calm after the winds have moved beyond you and you can finally see what's left of your life and landscape. That's true of endings, too.

2. Endings should always be plausible. Once your characters are "in play," just like cards in a poker game, they are moving toward a logical conclusion that will, hopefully, pay off, or the reader will feel as if you were just being gratuitous. The Russian playwright Anton Chekhov once told a young playwright, "If there is a gun hanging on the wall in the first act, it must fire in the last." The advice still holds.

3. A story begins and ends with your protagonist. You can break that convention, but you'll need to make sure that everything you offer the reader—the character, plot point, etc.—is designed to tell the story of the protagonist's journey. Even if you kill the protagonist off before the book is over, the end must reflect back to her somehow.

You Can Mix It Up

Some books begin with Act II, and backfill the information from Act I. Some even begin with Act III. How you structure your story depends on the story you're trying to tell. It's good practice to try a few variations and see how they affect your story.

One of the biggest problems in creating a plot is not losing the threads of it. If your protagonist becomes a father in chapter two, the baby and his relationship to it can't be forgotten. Everything has to pay off.

Mystery writers often have the worst of it. By nature, their plots twist and turn, confound and surprise; that's not easy to do unless you make some sort of outline. Some suggest taping 3×5 note cards to your walls, with each card having a plot point, in an effort to keep things straight. It's usually just as good to write this information in your notebook. All those cards can lock a writer into a course of action that, perhaps, his characters would not follow. Plus, it ruins the paint.

BUILDING PLOT

All plots grow out of characters, and yet there are certain elements and actions that a reader needs in order to be satisfied with your story. So while your characters drive how the story plays out, there are some universals that you'll need to include based on what type of story you want to write.

Since everyone understands the idea of revenge, we'll create a plot for a book that will deal with this most basic of human desires.

By definition, revenge is simply retaliation by a protagonist who is wronged or feels that he is wronged. This is usually a good person (and that makes it easier for the reader to relate to him) and the act of revenge usually happens outside of the law.

There are some basic rules with revenge stories:

- The more heinous the wrong (like murder or rape) the more heinous the response.

- The protagonist's revenge can't be greater than the initial wrong. Simply put, if somebody steals his parking space, you can't have him shoot the thief, because that changes everything. The old adage—an eye for an eye and a tooth for a tooth—comes into play here.

- The protagonist doesn't need to pay a price for his revenge, like jail time, but should learn a lesson about what he's capable of, or be changed somehow by the act. If you're confused about this, you can use any Clint Eastwood movie for reference.

Now plot your revenge story using the three-act model. Keep in mind that while this is just an exercise, not a book you'd actually write, you'll still want to create a new take on this classic tale. Try to make it your own.

1. Choose a character. It can be a character that you've been working on. Or, you can choose someone who already exists, real or imaginative, like Madame Bovary, George W. Bush, or your dry cleaner. Write a paragraph that establishes his normal life before the event. Do this to connect with readers and have them understand the protagonist in terms of their own lives.

2. Choose a lesson the character needs to learn. Make it one sentence. Some classic possibilities include:

- Never take the gift of life for granted.

- You can't trust everyone.

- Love is the greatest gift.

- Money can't buy happiness.

- Looks aren't everything.

3. Choose your antagonist. Again, you can choose someone who is real or imagined. Since a good revenge story often includes a betrayal of sorts, it should be someone close to the protagonist like a friend, spouse, parent, child, lover, or even an accountant.

4. Based on your characters, choose the reason for revenge. You can pick one of these or come up with your own:

- A betrayed trust, like a love affair.

- Embezzlement.

- Someone scared them, perhaps threatened them with a gun.

- Someone destroyed something they valued (like a painting or a car).

- They were scammed.

5. Now that you have your reason, and your characters, it's time to flesh out Act I. Write down the details of the offense. If the hero's girlfriend was murdered, write out the details. After you're finished, make a list of the reasons why this happened. Pick the one reason that angers you the most, the one that makes you want to take revenge, and use that.

Keep in mind that you probably want to wait until the end of Act I to disrupt the protagonist's life and have him vow to seek revenge. If you wait, your reader will be able to understand what the hero has lost, identify with him, and forgive him anything. Show that your hero has moral justification for vengeance. Again, if you have any questions about this, Clint is your man.

6. Flesh out Act II. Write notes about how you think the middle of your book should be. This is the place where you should plot out the revenge and act upon it. Keep in mind that matching a violent act with a violent act is not your only option. Sometimes one can inflict great psychological pain on a person—pain that would be tantamount to violence. Again, you want to be creative in your response.

If you're like most Americans, you've seen a lot of movies and television, which will taint how you go about this. As you work, keep asking yourself, "Is this the plot from any Clint Eastwood movie I've seen?" "No" should be the answer. While Clint understands the revenge story form better than most mainstream artists today, and does make for a great point of reference, you don't want to rip him off. He is, after all, the master of the art of revenge.

In Act II, you'll also need to decide how far the protagonist is willing to go to get vengeance—would he try to go to the police first? If so, this needs to be an unsatisfying experience because the whole point of a revenge book is to change the hero by making him take action. If the hero doesn't take action, it's not much of a book.

You should also have him fail at some point and try to create a series of surprise twists and turns. Make him improvise. Make it a real struggle—and an inner struggle, too.

This section should end with the act of revenge and whatever wild justice you feel is appropriate.

7. Flesh out Act III. After the act of revenge, your hero should be changed. This is the place where you show how much his life has been altered, how he's not the person he was at the start of Act I. You'll also have to consider how he feels about this and how he can learn the lesson that you feel he needs to. As a guide, keep in mind this quote from Buddha, "If a man speaks or acts with an evil thought, pain follows him. If a man speaks or acts with a pure thought, happiness follows him, like a shadow that never leaves him."

SCENES

Now that you have your plot in place, it's time to build your story. A plot is just a promise of things to come, an outline. Scenes are the building blocks of story. A reader moves from scene to scene, taking in information and passing judgment.

When I became a television reporter after a decade of being a print journalist, I had to learn an entirely different way to tell a story. In print, you have the freedom to mention anything. If a shooting took place in a church, you can describe the church in great detail if it's germane to your story.

In television, however, you have to write to the images that you were able to catch on tape. If you didn't get footage of a parade, you can't do a story about it. And, when you write a story, everything you write in it must have an image to accompany it. If you didn't get video of a fire in progress, you have to show the remains of the building.

The reason why you need photos is that the viewers need to feel as if they're at the crime scene. As if the fire is their own fire. Or the embezzlement is their own loss. That's why reporters always try to show photos of the victims. Like novelists, they are trying to establish a sense of humanity, the sense that the person who lost everything is just like you—a person with dogs and kids. Television is about community. Reporters are trying to tell you what is going on with those who shop at your stores, eat at your cafés, and drive down your streets. You have a right to know. They are a part of your life, after all.

A TV news story is a series of words and images packaged together in segments that convey a story that is important to the viewer.

A novel is a series of words and images packaged together in scenes that convey a story that is important to the reader.

As a writer, it's your job to impart in your readers a powerful emotional experience, just like a reporter can do. If you're a romance writer, your readers must feel as if they are falling in love. If you're writing a mystery, they must feel the outrage and fear that killing imparts. If you're writing science fiction, they must feel as if they live in a brave new world.

Each scene you write builds that emotion, like an image within a news story. Each scene must be important, must build the story that you're telling, and must be vivid. And each scene must also have an arc, which means that it must change the character, or reveal him in a new light, and move the action forward.

There really are no such things as throwaway scenes. However, some scenes are not as exciting as others—and that's the way it should be. There's a sense of rhythm to scenes. You want to use them to create enough action to keep the readers reading, but also to give the readers enough breathing room so that they have a moment to think about what they've read.

Here are some of the basic types of scenes:

1. **Establishing scenes.** The opening scene, or first scene, of any story is the most important. It sets the tone, lays out the stakes, and introduces the players. Besides the first chapter, there are other places for establishing scenes. Anytime the "reality" of your story substantially changes, you'll need an establishing scene (which technically, at this point, could be called a reestablishing scene) to show the reader how life has changed. For example, if a protagonist's wife dies in your book, you'll want to establish what his life is like without her. This scene will then give the readers a clear understanding of what your hero has lost.

2. **Forward action scenes.** These are those breakneck moments when things happen: The detective gets a break, or the little girl wins the spelling bee. These scenes advance the action of the plot. If you're writing a suspense novel or thriller, you'll want to have more of these than any other scene because these types of works are action-based. Keep in mind though, that if you have all forward action, you're going to give your readers intellectual whiplash. Every now and then you have to change up the pace and let them take a breath.

3. **Breather scenes.** Sometimes you need to give your readers a pause so that they can regroup and think about what you've already told them. Or, maybe, you want to give them a little time to anticipate your next move because stories are often like roller coasters; you build towards the death-defying corkscrew because it's so much more frightening if you know it's coming—eventually. Suspense is built when you allow the moment of anticipation to build.

Breather scenes are quiet, simple moments that you use to reestablish a character after he's gone through a major change or to introduce a new character or give backstory. They advance the texture of the plot while they move the story forward.

4. Big scenes. Juliet takes the poison because she can't be with Romeo; this is a big scene. Books will only have two, maybe three, scenes like this. They are the major action on which the book is based. The first big scene is the reason why you're telling this story and the second is the usually the life-changing event that affects your protagonist. Set your big scenes up so that the reader knows they're big. Slow down the narrative line, or storytelling, with a breather scene, and then render the important details of the moment with surgical skill. Set it up; build it up: pay it off.

Exercise

Crafting Your Own Scenes

Based on the plot lesson on pages 108–113, write a sample of each of the four basic types of scenes. They don't have to be in order, nor should they be the first four scenes in the book. They just have to meet the above criteria.

When you're finished, find a book that's similar to the one you've been working on in this exercise. Try to find an example of each of the scene types within it. Compare your scenes to the published ones. Pay special attention to how the writer builds each scene type and what methods she employs to create the arc and pay off the scenes.

TELLING THE DIFFICULT TALE

Every story has different demands, and they require different forms, with substantially different expectations. Form follows function, not only in architecture but also in writing. Here are some tools that can help enliven the standard plot format and may help you tell the story you're trying to tell.

Overall Considerations for Fiction

- Poetic language is the embodiment of passion: It overrides the brain and speaks directly to the heart.

- Plain language invites friendliness, comfort, and ease of understanding.

- Craft is the practice of subtlety.

- Don't focus too much on plot. Yes, you need to understand how stories are shaped, but the plot is just a series of events that aid you in your development of the character—after all, all stories revolve around a protagonist. Once you decide on the story you want to tell, the plot will develop organically. Books are never so much about what happened, but to whom it happened. So, it's more practical to begin writing your story by thinking about whom your protagonist is and what journey you think he should take. When you come up with an idea of what you're going for, take out your notebook and write it down. This is where your novel begins.

Magic Realism

In 1967, Gabriel Garcia Marquez broke literary ground with his novel *One Hundred Years of Solitude* and made popular a style known as magic realism. The style, first identified with the work of Cuban novelist Alejo Carpentier in the 1940s, elevates realism into a hyperrealistic state by borrowing heavily from the traditions of fable, folktale, and myth to create a story of social relevance.

Solitude, which is set in the midst of an endless civil war, begins with the protagonist, Buendía, standing before the firing squad. Before Marquez returns to the action of that moment, his protagonist tells the story of his town, Macondo, including the time when everyone was struck with insomnia, a man ascended to heaven while hanging laundry, and a woman who seemed to be followed by clouds of yellow butterflies:

> ... when Mauricio Babilonia began to pursue her like a ghost that only she could identify in the crowd, she understood that the butterflies had something to do with him. Mauricio Babilonia was always in the audience at the concerts, at the movies, at high mass, and she did not have to see him to know that he was there, because the butterflies were always there.

There's also a ghost who haunts Buendía's house searching for water with which to clean its wound. When Buendía's wife, Úrsula, sees him, she knows what to do:

> ... the next time she saw the dead man uncovering the pots on the stove she understood what he was looking for, and from then on she placed water jugs all about the house.

What's most interesting about this style is that the fantastic appears in everyday life; there are butterflies at the movies and ghosts in need of water. Everyday events are magical and yet still grounded in a framework of reality—and that's why the reader is willing to accept the fantastic worlds of magic realism. No matter how amazing the images are, they're still based on something that we can relate to. Everyone goes to the movies and everyone needs a drink of water.

"My most important problem was destroying the line of demarcation that separates what seems real from what seems fantastic," Marquez once said.

And you can see his point. It takes a gentle hand to create these fantastic scenes and not tip over into the realm of fantasy.

While this style is closely linked to Latin American authors, writers of all cultures have used it to illuminate political tales. Günter Grass's *The Tin Drum*, Salman Rushdie's *Midnight's Children*, and most of Isabel Allende's work are rooted in magic realism.

If you think you have a story that may be made stronger through the use of magic realism, here are a few guidelines:

1. **Root your story in the everyday.** Make the real life of the book as ordinary as possible so that readers will be able to relate when the world of the book takes a magical turn. If you don't do this, the reader won't have confidence in the truth of your story. For example, of the film made from Vikas Swarup's

Q&A, *Slumdog Millionaire,* Salman Rushdie told *The New York Times,* "I have problems with the storyline. I find the storyline unconvincing. It just couldn't happen. I'm not adverse to magic realism but there has to be a level of plausibility, and I felt there were three or four moments in the film where the storyline breached that rule." There were just too many ordinary details, like the distance from Delhi to Mumbai, that made this book seem implausible, even within the realm of the form.

2. **Whenever an extraordinary event happens, your characters will need to accept it as if nothing too out of the ordinary happened—it's just reality shifted slightly.** They must embrace the magic as somewhat commonplace so that your reader will as well. If they don't, you run the risk of crossing over to the realm of fantasy. In fantasy, what is fantastic, even in a fantastic world, is treated as such.

3. **Use the fable as your model.** Magic realism is used to make a point, more often a political point but not solely. Like a fable, there should be an implied moral to your story. In *Q&A,* Jamal teaches us all not to let tragedy define our lives. You need to embrace abundance and hope, and then you can win a million dollars and get the girl.

4. **Less is more.** Minimalist architect Ludwig Mies van der Rohe used this saying to explain his aesthetics, but it also applies here. You have to be careful not to overdo the fantastic in your work; let your images be profound, such as the woman who is followed by butterflies, and open them to many interpretations.

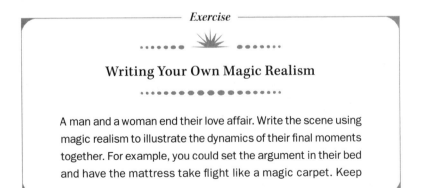

Exercise

Writing Your Own Magic Realism

A man and a woman end their love affair. Write the scene using magic realism to illustrate the dynamics of their final moments together. For example, you could set the argument in their bed and have the mattress take flight like a magic carpet. Keep in mind that whatever choice you make, it needs to speak to the emotion of the moment. If the mattress flies, it should be a menacing journey fueled by anger, sorrow, and rage. It is, after all, the end of their relationship.

Metafictive Structure

As mentioned earlier, the quest for a new structure has brought the modern writer to all sorts of variations on metafiction, a type of fiction that draws attention to the devices of fiction, the tricks we use to get readers hooked. It's a way for a writer to tell a story and at the same time always remind readers that they are reading a story. Metafiction doesn't want to break down that third wall, as they say in theater. It wants to scale it.

Despite its recent popularity, metafiction can be traced back to the ninth century with Cervantes' *Don Quixote.* It's a very useful device when you're trying to tell a story that will benefit from a close look at the relationship between fiction and reality. Metafictive works usually employ irony and self-reflection to make their points.

If you think your story might benefit from a metafictive structure, there are some basic structures you can use as models. Books about writers writing books include *Atonement* (Ian McEwan), *The Curious Incident of the Dog in the Night-Time* (Mark Haddon), and *The World According to Garp* (John Irving). On the other hand, books about readers reading are Italo Calvino's *If on a winter's night a traveler,* which actually has a character who is called "The Reader," and *House of Leaves* by Mark Z. Danielewski, a work whose structure allows the reader to create meaning. There are books that can be read in a nonlinear fashion, such as *Finnegans Wake* (James Joyce), and books in which the author names himself as a character just like Tim O'Brien, a Vietnam War veteran, did when he wrote his short story collection, *The Things They Carried*, about a character named "Tim O'Brien" and his experiences in Vietnam.

The biggest problem with all these devices is that they are, well, devices. Unless your story will benefit from reminding readers that they are reading—and many stories don't—then you need to structure your work so that readers tumble into the world of the book and are reluctant to pull themselves out.

Humor

Mark Twain once said, "Humor must not professedly teach, and it must not professedly preach, but it must do both if it would live forever." Most stories, even the most serious ones, use humor. It's a very versatile tool. It can humanize a character, deflate the darkness of a moment, allow a reader comfort (as in comic relief), and serve as a reminder that there still is joy in the world.

Humor scratches away at the veneer of polite society to reveal truth. That's why we need it, but that's also why it's so difficult to write. It's difficult to get under the skin of things: It's human nature to cling to the status quo. To write humor we must break down our own inhibitions and be willing to kill our own sacred cows before we can successfully dig deep enough to discover what makes something funny. And who wants to do that?

E.B. White, who cowrote the excessively unfunny *The Elements of Style*, once said, "Analyzing humor is like dissecting a frog. Few people are interested and the frog dies of it."

Writing humor is a "gut-art"—you just know in your gut if something works. If you're laughing, you can be assured that others will laugh, too. The more you understand your own sense of humor, and trust it, the better writer you will become and the more people you will make laugh.

Humor is about connection, and so you should always come to the page with an insider's knowledge of what makes crazy seem crazy. Write as if you're not above the insanity of human nature but wallowing in it, celebrating it, and chastising it.

Unfortunately, what is funny is *not* universal. Some people like the physical slapstick of The Three Stooges and some prefer the gentle humor of Wallace and Gromit—everybody is different. But, as we all know, there are basic needs, desires, actions, and experiences that all humans share—no matter who we are. In order to write a piece that most people will find funny, you need to build your story on that common ground. Your readers must connect on a basic level so that you can build their trust. If you create a world that is true to your own heart and experience, readers will understand it and trust it, even if it's a fantastic world. And most will laugh.

In the totally irreverent novel, *Lamb: The Gospel According to Biff, Christ's Childhood Pal*, Christopher Moore takes a very common household chore and begins to build his wild house of words on it.

Moore begins the prologue of this book with an angel cleaning his closet. We might not be able to imagine what being an angel is like, but cleaning is something everybody understands. In Moore's imagining, the closet is filled with all sorts of angelic things.

> Halos and moonbeams were sorted into piles according to brightness, satchels of wrath and scabbards of lightning hung on hooks waiting to be dusted.

Cleaning your closet is a humble act. Right away, Moore has us trusting the angel Raziel. Although Moore doesn't tell us this in the prologue, Raziel is reputed to be one of the Cherubim, the guardians of originality and the realm of pure ideas—and a bit of a writer himself. He's a perfect choice for the plot. Once Moore has created this somewhat familiar world, and has your trust, he gets to the intent of the chapter and why this particular angel is being sent "dirt-side," or to Earth. Apparently, there's a rumor of a new gospel. And who might the author be? "Levi who is called Biff," the archangel Stephan says.

At this point, you are either with Moore and his tale, or not. But he has taken every opportunity to help you identify with this outrageous world. He's created as much common ground as he can give the broad comic story that he's telling.

A blueprint for the payoff of this chapter is a good model for you to follow in your own work. Here's a quick outline of it:

1. He begins with the sentence, "The angel was cleaning out his closets when the call came." It's charming and surprising, which makes it funny. And, best of all, we can all relate to it. Once we are on board, Moore "pays off" the idea of an angel cleaning by delighting us with the heavenly mess that is Raziel's closet: "Halos and moonbeams were sorted into piles according to brightness ..."

2. Moore raises the stakes by introducing an archangel who uses corporate jargon—he refers to Earth as "dirt-side"—and brandishes orders.

3. Now that Moore has lulled us into believing that we understand this world, he ends with the wild imaging of Christ's childhood pal, "Levi who is called Biff."

Note that Moore built his humor on a strong foundation of common experience, like cleaning out a closet, and then bit by bit started to create this increasingly fantastic world in which Christ's best friend could actually be a boy named "Levi" who is called Biff.

The important part of all humor is the build. In order to be truly funny, you have to find the humanity of the moment, crawl inside of it, make it real, and make yourself laugh.

Exercise

Mining Humor in Everyday Life

Humorist Carl Hiaasen says that he doesn't make anything up, he just reads the morning paper and allows his outrage to take over. It's understandable. The odd, the offbeat, the well meaning, the misguided—all you have to do is illuminate their insanity with the skewed logic of the world they represent. Come at it with an angle that most never think about. Make it fresh, but real.

Select an article from the day's news, or use one of the following as a foundation and write a one- to three-page story based on it. Don't settle for stereotypical responses or ideas. For example, consider this recent news item: "An Iowa man called police this week to report the theft of a blow-up doll fashioned to resemble a porn star."

At first glance, this appears to be a story about a man who misses his sex toy so much that he'll do anything to get it back. However, what if the situation was sadly innocent? What if the man is in love with the blow-up doll? *Lars and the Real Girl* is a movie that explores this very idea. It begins as a farce and tells the tale of Lars, an introvert who becomes delusional and believes that his newly purchased, realistically engineered blow-up doll is not only real, but that she is the woman of his dreams. Encouraged by a psychologist, Lars' family and friends play along and meet the "fiancée."

There's a huge amount of comic potential here, but this isn't just played for laughs. Because the film makes Lars an endearing character, not a pervert at all, the comedy is gentle and allows for a more serious discovery about human nature. The unexpected makes it an interesting choice.

Here are some story ideas to get you started.

1. *CBS News Sunday Morning* reports that "Doggie Dancing" is all the rage with the canine crowd and covered an international event held at the Airport Ramada in Portland, Oregon. According to CBS, "Carolyn and her golden retriever, named Promise, were dancing, sort of, to the *Beer Barrel Polka*.

   Some story options include:

   - Taking us to the dance and telling the story of the "wallflower" dog whom nobody wants to dance with.

   - Telling the tale of a dog who forces his reasonable and embarrassed owner into taking him dancing.

2. According to *World Weekly News*, "Man Dates Gal on Internet for Six Months—Turns Out She's His Mother!" Apparently, a skirt-chasing playboy spent weeks sweet-talking a woman on the Internet before arranging a romantic rendezvous at a remote beach—only to discover that his new love was his own mother.

   Some story options include:

   - Telling this from the mother's POV. You could make her a widow thinking this was her last hope for happiness.

   - Telling this story from the father's POV. The man knows his wife is cheating on him and is amazed and confused when he sees his wife with their son. Not half as amazed as the mother is, but still—you get the point.

STARTING AT THE END: HOW TO OUTLINE

We can all benefit from a sense of organization. I like to think of a novel outline as the bones of a story. As a child, your bones grow to the place where they'll support who you are meant to be on this planet. If your genes determine that you are tall, you bones will form that foundation, and your flesh will grow accordingly. As you grow older, you need calcium, and bones provide it to the point where they become brittle and can easily break.

The same is true with outlines. You need to create the basic framework for your story to grow on, but not so much that it takes away the energy from the work.

So where do you begin? Arthur Miller once said, "If I see an ending, I can work backward." So start with the end.

BEFORE YOU START: KNOW YOUR ENDING

If you start with the end of the story, the ending won't be set in concrete; it can change. Starting with what you think is the end allows you to have a firm idea of where you are going when you begin a journey with 60,000 to 80,000 words in tow. And you'll need that. Once you decide on your ending, everything in the book will be shaped to arrive there. None of your characters should be superfluous, nor should your scenes. It's all about bones. You never get more than you need.

Of course, the most difficult part of writing any story, long or short, *is* ending it.

In order to write your ending, you have to ask yourself what action you want to set forth in the start, but be careful not to create a "purse string" ending—with all the elements brought together in a tidy bundle. At the end of your story, you don't want to give the reader the sense that all there is to know is already known. You really just want to give them a whisper and a dream and send them on their way.

Once your ending is in place, you can weave your tale. Tony Earley always says, "A story is about a thing and another thing." So it's your job to plan your story so that you give your reader the satisfaction of getting closure from one "thing," the most obvious thing, but keep the mystery of the other "thing" intact.

A good example of this can be found in Sherman Alexie's "What You Pawn I Shall Redeem," a short story about a homeless Spokane Indian's circular attempts to raise $1,000 to redeem his grandmother's Pow Wow regalia from a pawnshop. It was stolen fifty years before, and the shop owner would like to give it back, but he paid $1,000 for it himself. So he gives the homeless man $5 as seed money and twenty-four hours to raise the rest of the cash.

In the first paragraph, Alexie gives the reader notice and sets up the ending of his story:

> One day you have a home and the next you don't, but I'm not going to tell you my particular reasons for being homeless, because it's my secret story, and Indians have to work hard to keep secrets from hungry white folks.

The idea of a "secret story" is the key to the ending. While the protagonist does manage to earn money, he drinks, gambles, or gives it away. After twenty-four hours, the money has not been raised, but the pawnbroker gives him the regalia anyway. This is the last paragraph of the story:

> Outside, I wrapped myself in my grandmother's regalia and breathed her in. I stepped off the sidewalk and into the intersection. Pedestrians stopped. Cars stopped. The city stopped. They all watched me dance with my grandmother. I was my grandmother, dancing.

Because the regalia is given back, the story does seem to tie itself up (that would be the first "thing"), but this really isn't about getting a stolen dress back. It's about the struggle to regain one's spirit—and that could be seen as the "secret" story (or the other thing) wrapped in this tall tale.

The ending that satisfies the reader, or ties things up, is never the real ending of the story. We discover that the grandmother's regalia is returned, and yet the story continues on for a moment to put the act into context. Alexie left readers with a whisper and a dream and sent them on their way.

Exercise

Another Use for Outlines

Outlines are not only important to your writing life, they can be the key for economic survival. When your agent goes to sell your second novel (or third or fourth), if you haven't finished it yet, he can sell it using an outline and fifty pages. So it's your job to create a document that will sell your book both to you (because writing a novel is a long process) and your potential editor.

Your outline should be a chapter-by-chapter summary of action, a general guideline of where you see the book going and developing. However, it may not represent the book you actually publish, although the overall tone and story should be the same. It's more of a notation of where you think you're going.

One caution: If you do sell off of your outline, your finished project should not be substantially different. For example, if you created an outline for a comedic work, sold it, and then turned in a tragedy, that would be a problem. Your editor may have all the dramas on his list that he needs for the year and your contract could be considered void.

OUTLINE GUIDE

There is no set amount of pages in an outline because it all depends on how large a story you're going to tell. The story of *Harry Potter and the Order of the Phoenix* had thirty-eight chapters that spanned 870 pages. Its table of contents provides an interesting look at the bones of an outline. It begins:

> One: Dudley Demented
>
> Two: A Peck of Owls
>
> Three: The Advance Guard

If you were J.K. Rowling, and this was your outline, all you'd have to do is write a short summary paragraph after the title of each chapter. In the first chapter, you would tell us why Dudley is demented and make sure that there are bits in your description that set the action of the book in play. Then move on to the next chapter.

To build the bones of your own outline, begin by writing a short description of what happens in the last chapter, and then move to the first chapter. After that's done, divide the rest of Act 1 into as many chapters as it takes to properly introduce your protagonist and the conflict—the "who," "what," "when," and "where" of the tale.

Move on to Act 2 and, again, create as many chapters as it takes to explain the crisis, complications, and obstacles that present themselves on the protagonist's way to the climax. Make note of the emotional challenges that he faces.

Once you've written the climax, it's time to create as many chapters as you'll need to lead to the final chapter.

Try not to get too fancy with the writing. If your agent is going to pitch your outline, he's going to take fifty pages of the draft with him, so you don't need to show any style in the outline. This is all about bones.

Exercise

A Model Outline

Take a well-known novel or story that someone else has published and create an outline for it. The story you choose should be similar in style or plot to your own work. After you're finished, do one for your own fiction. Compare the two. Look at how the acts work within the published work, paying special attention to how quickly the climax is reached, what the ending is, what the dénouement is, and how the protagonist is either changed or revealed. Examine your outline and see if you want to make revisions based on what you may perceive to be the efficiency of the published work's form.

RESEARCH

When you've done your research, it shows. In *The Curious Incident of the Dog in the Night-Time*, Mark Haddon writes a (dog) murder mystery in first person from the perspective of Christopher Boone, a fifteen-year-old Sherlock Holmes fan with Asperger's Syndrome who is also a math savant. Christopher has a photographic memory and is extremely observant. He also has a pathological inability to tell lies. In a sense, he's the perfect narrator.

> My memory is like a film. ... And when people ask me to remember something I can simply press Rewind and Fast Forward and Pause like on a video recorder .... If someone says to me, "Christopher, tell me what your mother was like," I can rewind to lots of different scenes and say what she was like in those scenes.

But because of the Asperger's, he doesn't understand who his mother was—just *how* she was, the mechanics of her. And he still ends up solving the mystery.

About his research, Haddon says, "Many years ago I worked with people with a variety of disabilities (all of them more seriously disabled than Christopher), so I feel comfortable writing about the subject and have what you might call an interested layperson's knowledge of autism and Asperger's. Beyond that I reasoned (rightly, I think, in retrospect) that the novel would work best if I simply tried to make Christopher seem like a believable human being, rather than trying to make him medically 'correct.' In short, if I treated him like any other character and didn't make him a special case."

It's interesting to note that the title of the novel is a quotation of a remark made by Sherlock Holmes in Sir Arthur Conan Doyle's 1894 short story "Silver Blaze." When Haddon decided to make his savant a

Holmes fan, he did his research and came up with a title that is exactly what Christopher would have called his own murder mystery.

When you weave specific details through your story that are realistic and based on fact, you make it more believable. It makes it breathe.

Research is something that all novels need. If you say that in Santa Fe, Guadalupe Street intersects with Paseo De Peralta, it should intersect. People know these things, and if they find that you've made a mistake, you break that delicate trust that a reader extends to a writer. Always check those kinds of facts.

There are many ways to do research. What tools you use depends on the nature of your project and how deeply you want to go. One caution, though. Research can be great fun. You can get grants and fly all over the world to find out about things, and because of that, many writers have gotten so enthused about the research of a book that the novel itself never seems to get written. You really want to be careful that you don't get carried away.

TIPS FOR INTERNET RESEARCH

The Internet is a great source of information, but also a great source of misinformation. Be careful that you are using reliable sites and always try to get a corroborating source. For example, Wikipedia.com relies on the general public to supply information and then has a series of volunteers to verify. While there are staff people who do oversee this process, the people who verify facts are a mixed bag—some are wonderful, some are not. This a good place to begin, but there are much better sources.

For general information, Bartleby.com is a comprehensive site featuring all the best reference books around, including *Gray's Anatomy, Bartlett's Familiar Quotations, World Factbook*, and the sixth edition of the *Columbia Encyclopedia*. Merriam-Webster.com features language-related reference books including a medical dictionary and a Spanish-American dictionary.

If you need a word translated, you can get some general help at babelfish.yahoo.com. The site will give you a rough translation of French, German, Greek, Chinese, Portuguese, Spanish, and other languages. Keep in mind that this translation process is still quirky. If you really want an accurate translation, it's best to find a language teacher or professional translator in your area.

Most research facilities including the Smithsonian (smithsonian. org) and the United States Holocaust Memorial Museum (ushmm.org) have an online presence that allows you to search for information and can put you in contact with librarians who can help you if necessary. Some charge a fee, some don't.

The Statue of Liberty Ellis Island Foundation (ellisisland.org) features a free search engine that allows you to search the Port of New York records to trace immigrants' journeys into this country. But keep in mind that oral histories are risky to use as facts. Even if well-respected institutions like Ellis Island have collected them, they are still one person's remembering of an event and not usually fact-checked. Oral histories make a great foundation for a story, but the actual facts surrounding the situation must be verified through other sources.

If you can't get what you need online, there are several granting institutions, including the NEA, NEH, and Fulbright Programs, which help writers get the funds to travel and collect information in person. (See chapter 10.) For more information, check the listings at *Writers Digest, Poets & Writers,* and *The Writer's Chronicle.*

REFLECTIONS ON HISTORICAL RESEARCH FROM NOVELIST SUSAN VREELAND

Susan Vreeland's books, including *Luncheon of the Boating Party, Girl in Hyacinth Blue*, and *The Passion of Artemisia,* focus on famous painters and their art. All are painstakingly researched. Below, *in her own words*, she offers some advice for those wanting to write historical fiction and wondering what the considerations of such a daunting task really are.

Author's License

There is no universal answer to the issue of just how accurate a fiction writer must be. In fact, great literary masters come down at opposite poles of this question. In a letter to his aunt in Dublin, written from England, James Joyce asks, "Is it possible for an ordinary person to climb over the area railings of #7 Eccles Street, either from the path or the steps, lower himself down from the lowest part of the railings till his feet are within two feet or three of the ground and drop unhurt? I saw it done myself but by a man of rather athletic build. I require this information in detail in order to determine the wording of a paragraph." Astonishing accuracy.

Yet, in *A Room of One's Own*, Virginia Woolf notes that women's history cannot be studied since the books are written by, for, and about men. Instead women's history "will have to be read into the scene of its own exclusion. It has to be invented—both discovered and made up." Ah, made up, she says. Therein lies the novelist's permission.

To Joyce, scenic truth was important; to Woolf, a larger truth was paramount.

Nevertheless, there are some guidelines.

I see two types of historical fiction that form a continuum. At one end is the novel devoted to a specific historical event or historical person who plays the major role, and at the other is the more personal, domestic, narrowly focused story that happens to be set far enough in the past to require research. To some writers and critics, how historically accurate an author is required to be depends on where the work is positioned on the continuum.

I would add that the importance of a particular historical moment must contribute to the writer's decision. Stories that require a significant departure from known human history, or that distort truth gratuitously are to be avoided. In such cases, one ought to rethink one's purpose. At the very least, one must be willing to risk criticism. It isn't appropriate to change a historical figure's known character or opinions, or to have the outcome of a well-known historical moment different from fact.

In deciding how much license to take, one might consider that a historical novel is not a biography, a compendium of facts. Instead, it invites us into the privacies of a person's soul, which requires some well-founded invention. Its value is in its revelation of what it felt like to be a particular person at a particular place and time, which can often be delivered by a character's interaction with his or her intimates. However, archival and published history don't always record personal relationships, so characters must be invented to allow the subject to reveal the interior realm through intimate interaction.

For example, my novel, *The Passion of Artemisia,* traces the inner development of Artemisia Gentileschi as an unconventional woman and a seventeenth-century painter. The title character had no recorded women friends, and her mother died when she was twelve. My research revealed that she was "probably" raised in a convent from the age of twelve to fifteen. This allowed me to invent two nuns that provided Artemisia with an outlet for her feelings and thoughts.

Raped by her painting teacher and physically tortured during his trial, eighteen-year-old Artemisia goes to Sister Graciela for comfort. Having read the actual court transcript, I could create this scene that blends historic fact, the events of the trial, with invention, the interaction with the nun, to display Artemisia's feelings:

> "Today they had two midwives examine me, you know where, with a notary watching. ... They wanted to show me lying that way."
>
> "*Dio ti salvi.*" She held me and I laid my head on her lap. "It's just another way to break any woman who accuses a man. They are without conscience."
>
> "They're beasts, all of them," I wailed into her habit.
>
> "They may be, but they cannot destroy you." She cradled me, stroking the back of my head, letting me cry.
>
> "My own papa let them."
>
> "*Cara mia,*" she crooned. "Fathers aren't always fatherly. They may try, but many fail. They're only mortal. ... [Our Heavenly Father] does not betray us. ..."
>
> "He abandoned me."

I did not dilute the horror of the trial, nor did I change its outcome.

In other cases, a fact may conflict with what an author wants a character to do. When the fact is insignificant, one might need to hold one's ground and resist the tyranny of fact for the greater good of the narrative, *if* doing so does not *measurably* alter history. Insignificant departures from fact should not give the writer anguish. Emily Carr, the painter and central character in my novel *The Forest Lover*, wrote in her journal, "There is something bigger than fact: the underlying spirit, all it stands for." Following her advice, I reduced her native friend's unbelievable twenty-one documented infant deaths to a more believable nine, which still conveyed the shocking effect of white-induced diseases on the native population. In *Luncheon of the Boating Party*, I moved Renoir's broken arm forward by five months. These adjustments did not change the integrity of history, and served the narrative purpose better.

In the last analysis, the seeming lie of art, that is to say fictional art, can show more of the truth, a larger truth than many a collection of more easily verifiable facts.

Pitfalls

Clio, the muse of history, is a fickle mistress, teasing the novelist with her rich storehouse of enticing material, yet expecting a fair obedience to discovered truth. She tricks us with false paths, guards her secrets, yet showers us with delectable, irrelevant detail.

The discovery of some detail so appealing that one is tempted to deflect the narrative direction in order to include it is a danger. One must resist. Fiction is about character, not research. Every detail that enters the story should have an influence on the characters.

Failure to write in accord with that guiding principle could result in research dumps—long accounts of historical events, processes, or technical information not delivered through action, scene, dialogue. Literature has moved far away from Herman Melville's lengthy account of whaling, for example.

Overuse of interior monologue to inform the reader of the results of the author's research is also a practice to be avoided.

Another danger exists when an author falls in love with an historical figure so much that the person's shortcomings are overlooked. I've had to remind myself that while we are right to stand in awe at the great art of the world, the creators thereof are not gods and goddesses.

A Final Note on Purpose

The case for writing or reading historical fiction lies in its stimulation of the imagination. Through fiction that sets us down in another time period, we are offered a window to other lives, as well as sensibilities, attitudes, and values other than our own. We escape somewhat from ourselves. Each time we enter imaginatively into the life of another, it's a small step upwards in the elevation of the human race because it expands our hearts.

Consider the alternative: When there is no imagination of others' lives, there is no human connection. Where there is no human connection, there is no compassion. Without compassion, then community, commitment, loving kindness, human understanding, peace—all shrivel. Individuals become isolated, the isolated turn cruel, and the tragic hovers in the form of domestic and civil violence, terrorism, and genocide. Historical fiction is an antidote to that.

REVISION TECHNIQUES: A TUNE-UP TOOLKIT

The process of writing is really the process of revising. You prove your authority as a storyteller sentence by sentence; and so every sentence you write should be considered carefully—maybe not at the time that you write it but certainly afterwards. Great care is always given to the building of fiction because every word matters.

Before you begin any revision, make sure that you always keep a copy of the manuscript. In fact, you need to keep all your drafts. Title them with the date and a slug word from the title like: "WHALE 7-18-02." At the end of every month, select "Save As" and create a new working draft for the next month. Store all your drafts in a folder on your desktop. You never know when they might come in handy.

Put your entire manuscript in one file because you can use the search function when you go to revise. For example, you can search for a character's name and see exactly what he said or did in the scene immediately before or after the scene you're revising. Or you can search for a key word like "Volkswagen" that you need to edit around. One-file editing saves a great deal of time.

THE PROCESS

The overall process of revision takes place in four stages.

Stage One: Craft as You Build

Edit as you build your narrative. At the beginning of each day, before you start writing, print out and revise what you wrote the day before. When you've completed an entire a chapter, print out and revise it before moving on to the next.

Always make hard copies of your work and edit from them because you need to understand how your words look on the page. It's also easier on the eyes.

Besides looking for typos and grammar problems, at this stage of revision you need to ask yourself some questions:

1. **Is the narrative effective?** Think of your narrative like a TV news story—you should move from point to point or image to image. Also, don't talk about anything you don't show or don't need to talk about.

2. **Did you use every element that you introduced?** For example, if your protagonist is afraid of snakes, is that germane to the story? Are you planning to pay it off later in the work?

3. **Did you use hackneyed phrases or predictable outcomes?** If so, ask yourself how you can make it fresh.

4. **Did you engage the senses?** Can the readers feel as if they can hear, smell, and see elements of your scenes?

5. **How's the rhythm of the text working?** Are you varying the length of sentences when you need to?

6. **Is the work believable?** Are there points readers will question or doubt?

7. **How does this story's path differ from similar stories?** What will make readers want to read your book instead?

Stage Two: Structural Revision

Once your manuscript is finished, you'll need to edit the draft of it. You'll still be asking yourself all the same questions, but you'll also need to take a very close look at the entire structure of the work. The only way to do this properly is to read the entire book aloud—every single word.

No kidding.

If you want to get a handle on a story, long or short, it really helps to hear it. How you read is important, though. You don't want to read it as is if you're giving a public reading because sometimes you put emphasis in places where it isn't written on the page. You just want to read the entire text, as written, slowly, without missing a word, and in as neutral a tone as possible.

While the prospect of reading an entire book aloud seems daunting, it's really the only way to figure out what you've actually written. The computer screen gives you a limited look, just a page or two at a time. Even when you print it out, unless you read it aloud, you can't get a sense of what's really on the page because the eye often skips over words and your brain fills in the blanks. That's how we read—our minds make assumptions as to what is being communicated. If you've deleted a word or made a wrong word choice by accident, you can often miss that by not taking the time to force yourself to read each and every word.

Keep in mind that you don't have to read the entire book in one sitting. If you try, you'll find that you speed up, gloss over words, and miss a great deal. It's best to print out each chapter and then lay them out side-by-side on your office floor, two or three rows deep.

When you're done, pick up the first chapter and begin to read aloud. Once you edit that chapter, print out the corrected copy and put it back in the pile where it belongs. As soon as you find yourself rushing over text, put it down and start fresh in the morning.

When you lay the entire manuscript out like this, you can see the progression of each narrative element. You can read chapter 1 and the final chapter and actually place them on a table in front of you, side by side, and try to figure out if the end of the book has met the promise of its start. If not, walk through the pages and see where you may have taken a wrong turn.

You can also double-check timelines very easily. Sometimes, it's a good idea to create graphs at this stage, so you know that everybody is exactly where they should be in various chapters. Time lines are often confused—sometimes you have a person at the grocery store and two chapters later you write that he hasn't gone yet—so you really have to be on the lookout for that.

It's also a good time to look closely at some punctuation issues. When you force yourself to read every word, it's easy to do this. If you write on a computer, your work is spell-checked—somewhat. Never trust that. Often the writing program will make assumptions about what word you want to use and "autocorrect" you in a rather annoying fashion. So look very closely at the spelling of words as you read.

Although computers help us work faster, they also change how we think when we write. Sometimes we write in a breathless frenzy, so there can often be an abundance of unnecessary commas in the work. Missing words are another common computer issue because we just can't type as quickly as our minds think, but computers make us feel as if we can. Tense shifting is also common.

Stage Three: A Second Opinion

Once you've read the entire manuscript aloud and corrected all the issues that you've discovered, you should workshop it or send it out to a reader. At this point, you're too close to the project. You need a fresh pair of eyes to help you refine.

Many people will tell you not to use somebody who is close to you, like a spouse or partner. But if you're comfortable letting people close to you read your work, do it. Just keep in mind that they do love you and want you to be happy, so they may, at times, be more delicate than you need a reader to be.

When using loved ones as readers, take special care not to be sensitive if they say they don't "get it." In fact, you need to maintain that policy with all your readers, even the ones you pay or the ones (like your editor) who pay you. If someone doesn't get something, find out where they became lost; that's important for you to know. If your reader doesn't get something, that doesn't mean that it's bad. They may not "get" the work because they're not your market, the person you're ultimately writing for, but it could also be because you missed something. And if you missed something, you want to know that because you can go back and fix it. That's what editing is all about.

You have to try to accept criticism with an open mind.

Some writers workshop their books with other writers. The largest group I know has five writers working together on a weekly basis. They met in graduate school; one member is actually their former teacher, and they've been together for over a decade. They all enjoy each other's company and often try to time their books so they can go on tour together. It's a very club-like approach.

There are many ways to get a "reader" for your work. If you don't feel comfortable working with people you know, the back of any writer's magazine has dozens of ads from editors who will either just edit or coach you through the process to publication.

If you are going to hire someone to edit your work, ask your writing friends if they know anybody. It's nice to get a personal recommendation. If they don't, just start contacting the ads that strike your fancy. It's always best to get references and to call those references. Don't be shy.

When you're looking for an editor, you should explain what your project is, how long it is, and what kind of turnaround time you are looking for. If you write genre work, you'll want to ask if they have done work within the genre because the standards and conventions are very specific.

If you do find somebody, you'll want to sign a simple contract based on a per-page reading fee. Per hour can really add up. Per page is a clear way to pay. The reader should give you a line edit (which means correcting your mistakes line by line), and then give you several pages of notes for you to think about. These notes are designed to help you improve your work, but you need to keep in mind that they are one reader's opinion and may not be reflective of the direction in which you wish to go.

There's really no right way to go about this stage of editing your manuscript. Ask a friend, pay an editor, join a group—whatever works for your situation is what you should go with. With short stories, you can post them in online workshops, like Zoetrope.com, but some people do hire editors for short works, too.

No matter what option you choose, always remember that, aside from basic grammatical issues, editing is really one person's opinion. You always have to decide what you will pay attention to and what you will discard. The more you publish, the more you gain confidence and an understanding of your work, the marketplace, and where you fit in. You understand what you are trying to do. You begin to develop a sense of your work as being unique to you.

Stage Four: Your Manuscript in the World

Once you feel the work is as good as it can be, it's time to send it out. If you don't have a book contract, you'll be sending it to an agent. If you do have a contract, you'll be sending it to your editor for "notes." This is a very polite way of saying now it's time for your publisher to step in and tell you how they see the book, not just its merit as a work, but its place in the marketplace.

And so the editing process begins again. After the notes comes the first edit. And then the second pass, or second edit. And then comes the final pass, or final edit, which is usually the advanced reader's copy (ARC).

Each step of the way, you'll be asked to refine and redefine your work until it's as perfect as it can be. By the time you get to the ARC stage, you know the work so well you can recite it in your sleep—this is not good. The ARC edit is the most important edit of all.

Any final corrections you have must be done at this time. Your manuscript is already typeset so you can't make large edits because it will throw the page count off. If you do discover a problem that must be corrected and the printing process has begun, you'll have to pay to make corrections and that will be very expensive. So, at this point, you really will be looking to make minor corrections that are crucial to the integrity of the work. It's too late for anything else.

Since you are so very tired of your work by this point, read the ARC backwards, starting at the last page and the last sentence. Read every word aloud. It's painstaking work, but it has to be done. Nothing is more upsetting than seeing a typo in your book and nothing is more embarrassing than having a reader e-mail you about some problem with a manuscript you thought was perfect.

Of course, a manuscript is never perfect. It goes through too many hands and too many edits. Typos can even happen at the ARC stage when the corrections are transferred to the printer, and there's nothing you can do about that.

FIXING THE ISSUES

You'll usually get about two to four weeks to complete an edit. It's a lot of work done in a short time, so you have to be very careful not to get confused. It's a good idea to check off the edits that you wish to do as you complete them. It gives you a sense of accomplishment and keeps you from getting overwhelmed.

Most editing issues fall into a few basic categories with several easy fixes available.

> **1. No one cares about the main character.** People have to like your protagonist, even if he or she is an awful person. Keep in mind that nobody is 100 percent evil—even the devil has a sympathetic backstory as an angel fallen from grace. So, even if you're working with a dark character, try to find that bit of humanity. Complexity brings depth. Depth brings readers.

2. Too wordy. Get to the point. That's not to say that your sentences have to be short and choppy; it's just that all of them should work to create a framework for your plot. To train yourself to see flabby writing, try to eliminate one sentence in every paragraph and one page in every chapter. The arbitrary nature of this challenge will help you question the nature of your choices and force you to make decisions about what you do and don't need.

3. No one can figure out who the main character is. This is just a matter of restructuring. If no one can figure out who your main character is, you need to pull out all the chapters that he doesn't appear in and look at what remains. Make sure your basic plot line is clear. If you have too many intricate story lines running at the same time, you're going to need to do a little pruning, but it's not as daunting as it seems. Go back to your outline and revise it to match your manuscript. The chapter summaries will help you review plot points in a compact format, and that makes it a lot easier to see how the changes you're contemplating might affect the entire work.

4. Too slow of a start. Delete the first three chapters and see how it reads. As you know, it's always interesting to walk into the middle of a conversation and have to piece things together—it engages you. Dropping in mid-story does the same. File those chapters and re-insert the needed basic information throughout the rest of the work. If you find that you need entire passages reinserted, all you have to do is search for the key word, copy, and save.

5. Lack of suspense. If A + B = C in a direct lineal fashion, it's boring. You always need to build in a twist or two and make the reader, and also your characters, work harder to get answers they need. If you need to rework suspense, create a list of changes you plan to make and then outline the implications of each, such as "what if I add a romantic subplot?" It's always best to have an idea of where you're going with a structural change before you begin writing because it makes it less confusing and saves a lot of time.

6. **The writing is clumsy.** At the level of the sentence, this could mean that your sentences have no flow. You may write with all short sentences, which feels choppy, or go on forever in a series of very complex sentences, which is tiring to read. Long runs of text in which the sentences are the same length and the same structure is also clumsy. You should really think of your story as a symphony. It needs movement. Short sentences speed up the reader and cause a sense of urgency. Long sentences slow them down and make them dig deeper into the text. You need both. Also, try to avoid consecutive sentences opening with the same word, such as "She ran. She was afraid. She didn't mean to shoot him."

7. **Too many tics.** Everybody has them. There are words or phrases that slip in whenever we stop paying attention (like "that rocks"), or actions that we overuse such as having a character run their fingers through their hair. If your manuscript is in one file, you can simply search for key words like "runs fingers hair" and rewrite it. It's also good practice to make a list of your usual stylistic flaws and search for problems before you get into the final edit stage. Word processing programs sometimes overlook vague adjectives, adverbs, and passive sentences.

8. **Writing is flat.** The root of this comment often lies in the writer's failure to paint a distinctive and vivid world in which the action of the book can take place. Look at your scenes carefully.

   - Do we know where exactly the characters are? Not just America, but Iowa in the loft of a barn built in the 1800s. It really makes a difference. The readers need to be grounded in time and place. Being as vivid as possible will help them do that.

   - Always employ all your senses when you write; don't forget to tell the readers what your character hears and smells around him.

   - Be careful of what details you use, when you say that a character stands up, says something, and then sits down again, you have to have a good reason for all that standing and sitting. All action must support the scene.

9. **Boring dialogue.** Good fictive dialogue is direct. You have to get to the point far quicker than you would over lunch at the deli, and yet it has to sound natural. When you go to rewrite, you just need to ask yourself, *What would this moment actually be like? What's the texture of it? What must be said? What is the relationship between the people speaking?* An exchange between two lovers would be far different in tone and word choice than an exchange between two rivals.

While what is said between people is powerful, what is unsaid often speaks louder. Silence can be very evocative, as long as body language and internal thoughts reinforce it. In general, you don't need to use a long speech to get your point across. Instead of having a character say that he's angry, you can make that clear by tone, posture, and action. Slamming a door is the universal sign that someone is not pleased. And even though it's trite, it has much more impact on the page than the sentence, "I'm angry."

10. **Authorial confusion.** You don't always have to know why you are writing a story when you start, and it doesn't matter *when* you discover what your book is really about, as long as you do discover it. If you don't know the meaning of your work, and you're not refining the subtexts and making conscious decisions about what to do with them, the odds are good that your readers won't know what you're trying to say and will just get confused.

11. **Extraneous elements.** In fiction, everything you write must push the plot along. Things that don't contribute to the plot confuse readers because they try to make the extraneous make sense, as if they're putting together a puzzle. If the pieces don't fit, you lose them.

  - If you think you have too many characters, list the characters and their roles, and then get rid of those that are redundant.

  - If you think you have pointless actions or descriptions, ask yourself what you really need to move your plot along and then ruthlessly edit out all the rest—it's just noise.

12. **Your story is slight.** We're often in such a hurry to finish a work that we forget that readers like to take their time in a story. They enjoy the embroidery of it, the way it unfurls. If your beta reader says that your story is too slight, you may need to add a subplot. In life, many things happen at once. Fiction should be no different.

13. **Too many point-of-view shifts.** This can often be a judgment call, but if you hear it from more than one person, you probably want to look into doing something about it. Make sure you understand how POV works and be consistent with it.

14. **Lacking resolution.** Thematic elements that are introduced and then dropped with no resolution, or even progression, can drive readers insane. Plotting is difficult because all the subplots must pay off. If you're accused of not resolving themes or plot elements, make an outline so you can see where you wandered off.

A PLASTIC BUDDHA: THOUGHTS ON LANGUAGE WITH AIMEE BENDER

Aimee Bender is the author of *The Girl in the Flammable Skirt, An Invisible Sign of My Own*, and *Willful Creatures*. Her twisted contemporary fairy tales raise the stakes for all storytellers. The way she plays with language and point of view is breathtaking. Here is an excerpt from *The Girl in the Flammable Skirt*.

"THE REMEMBERER"

My lover is experiencing reverse evolution. I tell no one. I don't know how it happened, only that one day he was my lover and the next he was some kind of ape. It's been a month and now he's a sea turtle.

I keep him on the counter, in a glass baking pan filled with salt water.

N.M. Kelby: To me, language is a plastic Buddha from a five-and-dime store: It evokes, it triggers, but, without proper mindfulness, it's just another thing to dust. How do you, as a writer, crawl inside of it? Shake it around? Spin the cylinder and feel its kick?

Aimee Bender: I think of language as coming from two places—the mindful place (land of revision, for me) and the soupy place (land of first draft).

I think I get most into language when I'm not thinking verbally. In "Sonny's Blues," James Baldwin has this great line about music and jazz, about how the musician is imposing order on the void by playing. So, if I put that onto writing, I feel like we are dipping into that void, and a writer shapes the void with words, but first it is soupy, pre-verbal, immediate.

I find this part of the process relieving because when I have to think about words, I freeze up. I forget they are my friends. I feel like there are right ones and wrong ones, when, in fact, it is such a mess trying to express anything, and getting close to expressing something is such a triumph that clearly there are no right words and wrong words!

How do I get inside the soupy place? I try to distract myself as much as possible. I work on many things at once. I write fast. I space out and stare at the wall.

Mindfulness, editing, meditating—it's all part of the same process. It's all about the refinement of the world into some mysterious understanding that can be language-optional and often is.

NMK: The edge—that seems to be your territory as a writer. Darkness. Elegant outrage. What's a nice gal like you doing writing such nasty stuff?

AB: There's something aggressive about writing to me, and women can be aggressive, of course, but sometimes I do associate that quality more with men.

A certain kind of mindfulness is key, which is when you are just IN the story. Letting the story happen, without a writer imposing herself. I can tell, with other writers, or with students, when they're inside the scene, because the quality of the detail is better vs. a kind of "fancy-foot" writing, which isn't mindful, but performative.

NMK: What do we owe readers? I'm not trying to suggest that we think of pleasing an audience. But, perhaps, we should think of the place that our work—its joy, its terror, and its darkness—holds in the heart of our reader.

AB: My first thought is that we owe the reader some honesty, but that's a little easy, too, because honesty is complicated. I was just reading an interview with director Andre Gregory, talking about truth, and how it's not just truth we want, but many truths in a line, making a kind of "truth necklace."

I think we owe readers a window—meaning we need to get out of our own heads enough to show something past ourselves, something larger. But we also owe readers a voice, meaning we cannot pretend we are not there making the story as if we were making the glass of that window and the window frame. We have to be there.

It's a hard balance—both being there, and also getting out of the way.

My wonderful grad school teacher, the writer Judith Grossman, used to put it this way: In writing, if you break a rule, you accrue a debt with the reader, which is fine, as long as you know that. If you're reading *Ulysses* it's because you know you're going to get so much from all the invention, that it has value, in and of itself, and in the larger context, too.

NMK: When writers leave this world, what remains? Books go in and out of print. Lovers die. Children forget. Photographs fade. But I wonder if our work still remains as some trace element in the cultures—like the zinc of the world. And for some, like Mark Twain, the fluorescent green zinc oxide. What do you think?

AB: I like that the word "matter" and "matter," both noun and verb, are the same word. So maybe we just leave behind matter.

HOW TO CREATE A
BESTSELLER

According to *Forbes Magazine*, from June 1, 2007, to June 1, 2008, the top ten authors in America pulled in a combined $563 million. That's serious money. It's no wonder that a significant amount of writers at some point in their careers actively attempt to create a bestseller.

For example, John Updike's twenty-third novel, *The Widows of Eastwick,* was a return to the characters of *The Witches of Eastwick* for that very reason. "It occurred to me," he said, "that maybe the first book was a success of a sort. It had a movie, and I thought we might be able to sell a few more copies. ... I also thought a return to comedy would be a relief to my limited public."

Note that he says "limited" public. While many readers in America may know who John Updike is—if not for his short stories or the *Witches of Eastwick*, than for his famed Rabbit books, two of which (*Rabbit Is Rich* and *Rabbit at Rest*) he won Pulitzer Prizes for—he has certainly not sold as many books as Stephen King or even Danielle Steel.

Well-known writers, or famous books, are not always bestsellers. In fact, it's quite amazing how many distinguished books, such as Pulitzer Prize winners, sell only five thousand to ten thousand copies in hardcover.

Desire and talent don't always make you a best-selling author. On some level, the publishing house has the most control in your success because it has the ability to position your book in the marketplace so that it will sell. Its marketing and publicity staffs can't do this for every book the house publishes—there are just too many—so they have to make a choice and it all comes down to sales potential. If they think your book will sell, either because you've had bestsellers before or you've written something they feel will appeal to millions of readers, they will promote it in such a way that the public will feel compelled to buy it. You will be in every big-box store, at the front of every bookstore, and on every television and radio show in America that can make your sales numbers rise. There may even be trailers on the Internet and billboards promoting your book.

On the other hand, if you've written a beautiful book that because of a limited audience is perceived to sell *moderately* well, then all you'll get is the undying love of your editor (because books like this also add to the bottom line), a decent advance, and a modest promotional budget.

Yes, it does seem unfair, but you have to understand that this is a business decision. Blockbusters make up for all the beautiful books that didn't sell very well and are crucial to the current business model of publishing. One book that sells 3.5 million copies can quickly make up for a hundred that sold five thousand or fewer. Until the model changes, editors, in conjunction with marketing and PR people, will try to package certain books with a wide commercial appeal to become blockbusters. And while that's not the kind of thing they usually teach you when you get your MFA, it certainly illustrates that the business of writing and the act of writing have little to do with each other.

While you write, it's all about art. When you're finished, it's business. Because after that last edit is made you'll find that you've created a product, and that product will be printed in a factory and then sold and shipped by the caseload all over America. And it will be your job to help sell it.

While "selling" is a very un-artful word, the writer-as-salesperson has been a fact of life since Ovid read his *Metamorphoses* to packed crowds at the local coliseum. Charles Dickens and Mark Twain are famous examples of fine salesmen; their skill as writers, along with great oratory gifts, made them bestsellers in their lifetimes and secured their places in literary history.

Of course, things are more complicated these days. You just can't be a great writer and expect to be a bestseller by your efforts alone. Being a bestseller is a rather tricky thing because there are so many books out there vying for the public's attention, and if your publisher isn't paying for a big budget media campaign, the only thing you can really do is to write the best book you can and build your fan base in a way that suits your personality and temperament.

WHAT ARE THE QUALITIES OF A BESTSELLER?

It's easy to spot what books the publishers think will be this season's "must-haves." The quality of a book sometimes has nothing to do with sales of it; it's about marketability.

Sally Kim, executive editor of HarperCollins, says, "I always aim to acquire the kind of fiction I love to read myself: literary in quality, but with some commercial hook or angle to help make the story really accessible. The kind of book I find myself packing when I'm going on vacation.

"It's funny, some of my bigger successes were books for which I didn't have a lot of competition—I just saw something in them that others didn't. The same works the other way, where a project will go for a huge advance—and I was one of the first to turn it down! This is all to say there's a formula of sorts (we run numbers and try to predict what's going to happen by looking at comparative books), but the joy of this—particularly with fiction—is that it's so subjective, and you just never know."

Best-selling books are often packaged as bestsellers from the first moment they're pitched to a publisher or go to auction. They are usually bought for a very large price. The price then determines how much the publishing house is going to put into the book to make the money back. It also determines the print run. The larger the advance, the larger the initial print run.

Some books, however, are bought for a relatively modest price and then earmarked as bestsellers once everyone at the publishing house reads them. Algonquin Books' Executive Editor Chuck Adams loved *Water for Elephants* but wasn't sure how the public would respond. But when Director of Marketing Craig Popelars read the manuscript, he knew exactly. "I can give this to my mother, I can give this to my father, I can give this to my wife, I can give this to my old college roommate. This book is universal."

That's the key to a blockbuster. It somehow speaks to the widest audience possible. And so Algonquin put their energy behind the book and it took off.

While this isn't an exact science, if you look at various catalogues from the publishing houses, you can see what books they think will do well. A mid-list writer, someone who sells moderately, or a new writer who is just building their career will have an announced print run of about fifteen thousand to twenty thousand copies. That's what's called a ghost number. The actual number of books in the first run will depend on the orders from bookstores. If the sales department only gets an order for seventy-five hundred books, the publisher will print about eight thousand and try to keep an eye on stock just in case the book takes off.

The ghost number of most "bestsellers" begins at about sixty thousand to eighty thousand copies. Some, like the Harry Potter series, will have a print run in the millions. Because so much is being gambled, great emphasis is placed on the first month of sales. If the book hits the *New York Times* best-seller list within thirty days, there's a pretty good chance it will stay there for a little bit—as many readers still buy off the list. If the publisher paid a high five- to six-figure advance for it, they are going to try everything they can to get the book on the list and keep it there.

HOW THE MACHINE WORKS

When a book first appears in the marketplace, there's a lot of emphasis on media. You'll see it in magazines, newspapers, ads, and, if the topic is trendy or the author is media savvy, you'll also see it on talk shows. The publisher wants to get people talking about it right away.

Sometimes this works. If the book has some sort of appeal, it sells. Sometimes, however, it doesn't. Even though a publisher pays to package a book to be a bestseller, that still may not be enough. If people don't hear about the book right away, the momentum is lost and the campaign begins to become unfocused and less effective. Dr. Phil McGraw of Oprah fame was so worried this might happen to him that he hired an outside publicist to ensure that his first book had the most exposure that it could have in the marketplace—and he has a daily television show.

It's really difficult to put a book into the world these days. Publishers can sweeten the odds of landing a book on the *New York Times* list, but they can't really make a bestseller, no matter how hard they try. In the end, the public decides if the book is of interest. If it isn't, no amount of expensive advertising can make it a hit.

Unfortunately, a blockbuster-driven system makes it difficult for most writers to find a robust audience early in their careers. Because all this money is spent on pre-determined bestsellers, all those *other* books—the well-written delightful books that were deemed by the publisher to have a smaller audience—have limited promotional monies available to them. They often get lost in the marketplace, and that's not a good thing because the current business model allows booksellers to return unsold stock after 90 days.

This could be changing, though. Recently, HarperStudio, an imprint of HarperCollins Publishers, and the retail chain Borders reached an agreement for ending returns. In exchange for a discount ranging from 58–63 percent, Borders will buy HarperStudio books on a non-returnable basis. What impact this will have on the writer is yet to be determined. While the return policy did allow bookstores the ability to take a chance on new writers, it also gave them the luxury of not having to sell their books because it wouldn't hurt their bottom line if they were returned. So, this could be a good thing.

On the other hand, some speculate that it could make matters more difficult because some booksellers will take on only bestselling authors. I'm not entirely convinced: Booksellers are an independent folk—that's what drew them to the business—so common sense says that they'll be more likely to promote titles that they love, and now have a vested interested in. Of course, we'll see. It's difficult to tell how this will impact the system, and this is why writers should never worry about sales. You have enough to do writing.

CREATING YOUR OWN MARKET

Some authors do attempt to take matters into their own hands by bulk buying books to raise their own numbers and either giving them away or returning them at a later date.

In 2003, Al Franken suggested that Ann Coulter owed her best-seller status to bulk buys. Coulter was not pleased. She and Franken began a rather public spat that helped raise her visibility and increased book sales. But bulk purchasing is not something that can fool most of the public. *The New York Times* places a dagger next to books that "some bookstores report receiving bulk orders" for. This practice began in 1995 after authors Michael Treacy and Fred Wiersema spent $250,000 to buy ten thousand copies of their book, *The Discipline of Market Leaders*, and also arranged for the bulk purchase of thousands more.

So, if you can't buy your way onto the best-seller list, and it's extremely difficult to write your way on by just writing a beautiful book, the logical question then becomes: How do I fashion a book that will, without a doubt, capture the public's imagination and make me rich and famous?

Unfortunately, there's no formula for writing a bestseller, or for picking one. Editors are just as clueless when it comes to the process as writers are. Every season is littered with books that were hyped and have now been shredded. Still, there is one basic guideline for acquisitions that is pretty consistent throughout the industry: Go with your gut.

WHAT YOU CAN CONTROL

Since no one can predict a bestseller and there really isn't a formula to write one, then write your own voice and stop worrying. Your audience will find you. Carl Hiaasen didn't make the list until *Strip Tease* was made into a movie, and it took five years to sell two thousand copies of *Walden* by Henry David Thoreau. Building an audience takes time.

Christopher Moore once wrote to me, "I had stellar reviews and won awards for fifteen years before I got on the list. *The Today Show* did not put me on the list. *CBS Sunday Morning* didn't put me on the list. Being a Booksense 76 pick for six straight books didn't put me on the list. Touring didn't put me on the list. What put me on the list was a cumulative build-up of audience, and a mailing list, combined with an enormous print run and a great cover (and paid placement in the front of Borders and Barnes and Noble). What all that effort in the past did was add numbers to the first week of sales."

In the past, there've been books that didn't fit the model, or the trajectory, of a bestseller, such as *The Red Tent* by Anita Diamant, that are still selling ten years later. In a brilliant stroke of marketing genius, Diamant wrote all the wives of rabbis in America and offered them a book. The word of mouth carried *The Red Tent* to the best-seller list and beyond.

Unfortunately, times are different now. The big chains ate up a lot of the smaller booksellers and are now themselves facing difficult times. Big-box chains like Costco and Internet booksellers like Amazon are able to discount books, and that cuts into sales.

Studies show that many customers, often frustrated by inexperienced staff, no longer see bookstores as an inviting social destination, a place to meet friends for coffee and a chat. They just want go to buy a book with the least amount of hassle possible, so Costco and Amazon are good options for them.

The economic downside of this is significant. Booksellers, large and small, are ordering only the books they feel can sell, books by household-name authors, and they often are unwilling to reorder once their initial order is sold. Some won't even take orders from customers anymore. They all need the cash flow for the next big book and don't want to get stuck with stock. Most unsold books get returned within ninety days.

While it's more difficult to become *The Red Tent,* it is not impossible. Once your book is written, you need to identify and build your audience. That's what Diamant did, but she just did it in a rather bold and expensive fashion. There are many ways to gain visibility. You can be like Dan Brown and *The Da Vinci Code* and drive around the country with books in your trunk and talk to booksellers. Or you can get a force of bloggers to talk about your work.

Every day there are new opportunities that you can take advantage of; just be careful that the promotion of the work doesn't replace writing. You are not a marketer, even if you find that you enjoy it and are good at it. Don't ever lose sight of the fact that you're a writer. Marketing is just a vehicle for you to meet your audience, your readers. While money is a wonderful thing to have, increased sales shouldn't be the goal of your marketing plans. It's not realistic to think that those five thousand bookmarks you ordered are going to bring in five thousand more book sales.

Marketing for writers should be about building an audience by connecting with people. The more you interact with your readers, the greater understanding you have of them, and the more you grow yourself. All this unrelenting hawking of one's book seems to degrade both the writer and the work—and it certainly dehumanizes the readers by equating them with a possible unit sold.

UNDERSTANDING THE COMMERCIAL ENVIRONMENT

If you want to follow the publishing industry, there are several sources that will help you do that. *Publishers Weekly* is the industry's trade magazine. Publishers Lunch, a feature of Publishers Marketplace, is a daily news and sales update sent directly to your e-mail inbox. You can register at publishersmarketplace.com/lunch/free. GalleyCat (mediabistro.com/galleycat/) is Ron Hogan's inside look at the publishing industry. It's lively and current and housed at mediabistro.com, which is also worth looking at. For an overall look at the arts, including publishing, the ArtsJournal (artsjournal.com) is a really interesting compendium of news gathered from all over the world. In addition, Google.com allows you to see how your brand and product, also known as your name and work, is being disseminated across the Web.

There's a huge amount of information available about the business side of writing, information that often seems to directly affect you. But as nice as it is to be aware of what's going on in the industry, don't spend a large amount of time following it because, as an outsider, you can jump to conclusions that you really shouldn't reach. Whatever you read on these sites, things like "YA readership is down 28 percent," shouldn't affect your desire to write, even if you write young adult books. You always need to put this information into perspective. For example, in 2004, the National Endowment for the Arts (NEA) released a survey titled "Reading at Risk: A Survey of Literary Reading in America," which reported that the number of people reading, especially young people, dropped greatly, with a whopping 28 percent occurring in the youngest age groups. At the time, then NEA Chairman Dana Gioia was quoted as saying, "This report documents a national crisis."

Naturally, the report's conclusions sent many writers into a tailspin, but it's important to understand that these figures were taken from the Survey of Public Participation in the Arts, which was conducted by the Census Bureau in 2002 at the NEA's request. The sample was a group of about seventeen thousand adults who were simply asked if "during the previous twelve months they had read any novels, short stories, poetry, or plays in their leisure time, that were not required for work or school."

While that is a valid approach to gathering numbers, one census question asked about one specific year hardly seems worth getting upset about, especially in light of the mammoth sales of the Harry Potter series and other books that were geared toward young readers.

NAVIGATING TOUGH TIMES

It's no secret that 2008 was one of the worst years for the economy in American history. The stock market was near collapse, houses were being foreclosed on, gas prices were rising every day, and there were massive layoffs from one coast to the other. Even the bestsellers didn't sell many books as other bestsellers have in the past—they just sold more than everyone else, which really wasn't saying a lot.

The economy was in trouble and writers and publishers took a beating in the marketplace. In that kind of environment, there's really not a single thing that you can do to sell books, no matter how great your marketing plan is. No contest, personal appearance, or fun giveaway can sell books to people who feel they barely have enough money to pay for a tank of gas.

But people were still buying books when they could. *The Story of Edgar Sawtelle* managed to have 300,000 copies in print right before Oprah chose it for her book club. People really liked that book. It connected with them and so they bought it. Good books always find an audience, even in a weak marketplace.

Don't lose hope. There will always be readers. The gloom and doom of one year will, eventually, give way to an upswing. It always does. All you need to do is stay focused on the fact that your sales numbers bear little reflection on your worth as a writer, even though they do control a certain amount of your economic life.

While making yourself into a bestseller is a near-impossible task, you do have some control over your sales numbers. If low sales are hurting your ability to continue writing because your publisher doesn't see a market for your book, then you need to be flexible in your approach to your work. If several publishers reject your new book, then you might want to try something different. Change your style or genre. Or, take some classes to help you explore and grow.

Never let numbers dampen your creative spirit. Never give up. John Grisham didn't, but he could have.

For three years, Grisham woke up at dawn to write *A Time to Kill* before going to work. When the book was finally published, it had a run of five thousand copies, most of which he bought himself. That didn't discourage Grisham, but it did make him think that he was taking the wrong approach, so he followed a set of *Writer's Digest* guidelines for creating suspense novels. The result was *The Firm,* a story about a Harvard law graduate who is recruited by a firm that's a cover for the mob. It was the bestseller that he'd hoped for, but despite his effort, *The Firm* was not an instant success.

After the poor sales of *Time to Kill,* it was difficult to find a publisher to buy it. What Grisham didn't know was that his manuscript was being circulated around Hollywood. When Paramount offered him $600,000 for the film rights, *The Firm* became a hot commodity and eventually stayed on the *New York Times* list for forty-seven weeks.

All good writers really do find an audience. And, if they keep working at it, keep trying to make it universal, they sometimes they find a very large audience indeed.

YOUR WORK IN THE WORLD

There are two important reasons to send your work out: The more you are published, the larger your audience becomes, and the more you send your work out, the more you learn about it.

If you're working on a novel, you can send parts of it out while you're working on its completion. Many magazines will print chapters from longer works, if the chapter itself can stand on its own. It's nice to have that sort of promotion for your novel before it comes out because it gets people interested in the longer work, too.

Don't be worried about rejection. People will like your work or not—it's that simple. You don't need a thick skin to send it out; all you need are some stamps and envelopes. This is a business after all, a transaction between yourself and the editor. If you've taken the time to research your market and have sent a well-written query or cover letter with a clean manuscript, this should be a mundane experience, just one of the things on your to-do list this week. Editors will accept or reject your manuscript based on two criteria: taste and need.

Rejection letters are nothing to fear. Most editors, unless they are egotistical morons, will not insult you. They won't say awful things about your work or skill level because they're busy and don't have that much time. They will either write something specific on the standard rejection note (which helps you understand how your work is seen by this one person), or just send the note as is.

You have two basic options when you send out for publication: You can send to a publication directly or to a contest.

SUBMITTING YOUR WORK TO CONTESTS

Contests are fun, especially when you're first starting out, because if you don't win, you can place, and that's sometimes as rewarding as winning. Sometimes a story can lose a contest, but the judges (who are often editors) like the story so much they publish it in their journal or anthology at a later date.

Stories sent to contests get special attention, but there are some things you should keep in mind when you send. First, check who the announced judge is and read his or her work. Often people like work that's similar in tone or style to their own: not always, but often. So if you have a story with a lot of violence in it and the judge seems to forgo violence in his work, you might not have the best chance of winning. There's still a shot, though. So, if you feel like sending, go for it. It will just cost you the reading fee and postage.

Second, follow the submission guidelines. This sounds simple, but you'd be amazed how many writers don't do this. For example, if it says the manuscripts must be anonymous, then please don't put your name on it because it will get thrown out. And if the contest is designed for English speakers, do not submit a story that has not been translated; no one will read it. And never, ever, include a résumé if it's not asked for. No one is interested in what you've done as a writer, they just want to know if they like this particular story or not.

Third, make it easy for the judges. There are some unwritten rules that create professional entries; most of them revolve around making the submission easier to read. They must be followed for all contests, unless otherwise stated. Luckily, they're easy to do.

- Submission pages need to be numbered.

- No staples, because the judge will just flip through your pages and staples slow them down. Paperclips only.

- Use standard typefaces only. Times New Roman is always a good readable choice. A font size of 12 point is usually called for.

- Double space all entries.

- Print on one side only.

- Use clean white paper; it's easier on the eyes and looks more professional.

- Unless stated otherwise, send a self-addressed, stamped post-card (or SASP) so that you know your manuscript arrived. Don't send anything that requires a signature, so no "Return

Receipt Requested," UPS, or FedEx. Most contests just want submissions sent via regular mail.

- Don't forget the check. It costs a good deal of money to run these contests and, depending on how much you make as a writer, you can take the fees off your taxes. Don't send the check in another envelope or your entry might get thrown away.

SUBMITTING YOUR WORK TO PUBLICATIONS

While contests are fun, they are difficult to win because they usually provide a cash prize, which means you're competing against a large number of applicants. If you really want to be a professional writer, you need to send your work out to the publications themselves. It's always a good idea to send to paying markets first. Yes, they are swamped with submissions, but you need to see if your work is market ready and editors can provide valuable feedback.

Of course, you'll need to follow the submission guidelines as closely as you did for contests. If they're looking for stories about New Orleans, don't send them anything else. Don't get discouraged if you don't hear from people right away, even if you e-mailed your submission. The submission process always takes a very long time.

For example, McSweeney's has just a few editors and so in their guidelines they admit that things move slowly. "On the other hand," they write, "every single submission gets read. Please be patient and understanding, for we want very badly to discover and nurture new and developing writers, and are doing our best."

Response time for McSweeney's can be anywhere between a few weeks and five months. That may seem like a lot of time, but this is pretty typical of most publications and publishing houses. A book proposal to a small press may take anywhere from three months to a year, if not longer.

On the plus side, the longer it takes to get a response, the more likely that it's being given proper consideration. I know some people recommend that you do a follow-up note if you haven't heard anything after the posted response time. Most editors hate that.

Still, if they say it takes three months, send a follow-up after six if you haven't heard anything. Sometimes submissions, and rejection letters, get lost. Since it *is* your work, you do have a right to know what's happening with it. A quick note that gives your name, the project's name, and simply says, "Just wondering about the status of my manuscript" is often all you need.

Don't forget to say "thanks." Being an editor can be a thankless job. It's good to thank people for their time and energy. Always send a thank-you after the final decision is made. It's nice to make a personal contact.

There are so many publications these days, it's often difficult to keep up with the marketplace. Luckily, there are plenty of Web sites that make the submission process easier. They keep up with staff changes and publication openings and closings so that you don't have to. WritersMarket.com and Duotrope's Digest (duotrope.com) both offer a submissions tracker and a search engine that allows you to look for markets according to pay scale and other criteria, within the short fiction, poetry, novel, and collections markets. WritersMarket. com, sponsored by Writer's Digest, is a more complete site featuring how-to articles and a social networking site for writers.

Submitting has never been so simple, so send away.

It's always good policy to have ten or more queries out at once. Not ten copies of the same work, most publishers still are not interested in reading simultaneous submissions, but a combination of résumé building queries, such as fellowship competitions, along with publication queries. A good spread would be two writing colony applications, a story collection, a couple of stories you've been reworking, a writer-in-residence query, a couple of festival queries, and an award or grant submission.

The more you have out, the less rejection hurts. And, if some sad editor does find the time to lay your work to waste, take it in stride. He could have been having a bad day or going through a very stressful time.

It's better for the spirit if you don't take things personally, but if the rejection is quite horrible, some writers have found they feel better if they post them on the Internet. While this seems like a good idea, the downside is that the writing community is very small and if you try to publicly embarrass someone, it will probably get back to them—and their friends.

You have to always keep in mind that writing is a solitary act, but publishing is all about relationships. Most editors won't choose to work with writers who are difficult or vindictive. You really want to avoid getting that kind of reputation.

So, try to play nice. Try not to take things personally. And keep sending things out. Writing is about the act of communication, and so you have to find an audience to communicate with. Never be afraid of being rejected. "Yes" is an answer, but "no" is, too. A writer always learns more from "no" (even though "yes" is more fun).

And if you believe that misery loves company, there are some great sites where you can read other people's venting. Literaryrejectionson display.blogspot.com is cheeky and published anonymously by someone who says that they are "a published, award-winning author of fiction and creative nonfiction—but whatever. In the eyes of many, I am still a literary reject."

One final note: While writing is a business, it's very difficult to make much money at it. So sometimes you'll find that an editor may send you a subscription form with the rejection letter. It's tough to keep these publications alive, so it does make sense that editors are going to use this opportunity to try to solicit a subscription because you're obviously familiar with what they do and want to be a part of it. While it may be tacky to reject a person and ask for money at the same time, try not to be offended. The editor is just trying to survive.

On the other hand, so are you. There's a good deal of pressure to subscribe to everything and you really can't buy every literary magazine out there. So, in an effort to get a sense of the market, every year try to get a subscription to the old reliable sources, *The New Yorker* and *Harper's,* in addition to at least three new magazines. It will give you a sense of what is being sold and where you fit the best. Plus, it makes for good reading.

If it's difficult to find the time to read all those publications, put them in places where you're likely to do some reading, like the kitchen table. During breakfast, make it a point to read a story. Sometimes you'll be successful and sometimes not, but the magazine shouldn't leave the table until you've read it, so the incentive is there to read and recycle as soon as possible.

You'll probably come up with your own prompt, but whatever you do, do read what's being published. You should know your market, and the environment of your market, before you submit anything. You don't want people to think that you're unprofessional.

If you have questions about submitting to contests or literary magazines, there are dozens of Web sites to help you, including Preditors & Editors (anotherealm.com/prededitors), FirstWriter.com (first writer.com), and Writer Beware (sfwa.org/beware), which are all great resources that will keep you up to date on all the scams out there, including nightmare agents, bogus contests, and publishers that you should avoid at all costs.

Whatever you do, always remember that you only fail when you give up.

PART THREE

The Business

Writing ought either to be the manufacture of stories for which there is a market demand—a business as safe and commendable as making soap or breakfast foods—or it should be an art, which is always a search for something for which there is no market demand, something new and untried, where the values are intrinsic and have nothing to do with standardized values.

—Willa Cather

AGENTS AND THE CONTRACT PROCESS

When you hire an agent, you're choosing someone to represent you in the world. It's a business arrangement. You want to find a reasonable person who is well connected and will work hard for you because they like your work and you.

The agent's job is fairly straightforward: Primarily, they are there to sell your work. How well they do is really based on three things: connections, tenacity, and personality. When trying to decide which agent to go with, you really have to look closely at the dynamics of these elements.

Books can either be sold at auction or through private offerings. Unless you're selling your book at auction, agents usually pitch books to a group of editors that they have a relationship with, have met, or know something about. An auction is usually open to all publishers, and the writer and agent look over the bids to determine not only if the money is right, but what house would be the best fit.

If you don't go to auction, your agent will usually send your book with a cover letter to five editors, more or less. And if no one is interested, they will send it out to five more. The list of who they send to should be made available to you if you'd like to see it.

It helps to have an agent who has been around for a while and has a good reputation with editors. An agent who lives in New York City or Los Angeles is often well connected and spends a lot of time at events getting to know editors and publishers in those cities. They have personal relationships with them.

But that's not to say that agents who live in other places aren't good. I met an agent from the Midwest who had never even been to New York or L.A. Regional publishers were her forte, and many of her writers had been with her for ten years or more, so I assume that it was a situation that worked well for everyone.

Writing is a profession with many paths. Some writers want to work with multi-national conglomerates; some just want to publish in the literary presses. The New York publishing scene isn't for everyone. The market-driven frenzy can be very stressful. Editors can lose their jobs if they buy too many books that don't sell—and sometimes they will take it out on you, even though they're not supposed to.

If there are any serious issues, either with sales or editorial, the editor is supposed to go through your agent. Then your agent calls you. That's the protocol. However, in times of stress, protocol can get tossed out the window, and you have to be able to deal with it.

It's understandable, of course. Nothing is more disappointing than to end a three-month tour and learn that only a few books have been sold. It's your best hopes dashed, and so people get upset. And that's where your agent comes in. A good agent can talk to your editor as a colleague and listen to the concerns and see if there is any solution to the situation. If they have mutual respect for each other or an established relationship, it makes the difficult times go more smoothly.

FINDING AN AGENT

Keep in mind that you are not "lucky" to get an agent; it's not like winning the lottery. You chose an agent who seems to be the kind of person that you want to be a partner in your business.

All agents are different when it comes to submissions. If they request an initial e-mail query, then that's what you should send. If they say "query first," they don't want you to send your sample. If they ask for an exclusive read, make sure you don't send out another query until you hear back from them.

In the case of an exclusive read, make sure that a time frame is specified. Four to six weeks are standard, although some may ask for more. You really should never accept an open-ended commitment. You have a right to sell your book in a speedy manner.

The query letter is a business proposal. You can begin simply: "I'm seeking representation for a 60,000-word literary novel about Gertrude Stein's Vietnamese cook, Binh, titled *The Book of Salt*." Then you should tell a little more about the book. This section is often known as a "pitch."

The next paragraph should be why you chose to write this particular book and why you're qualified to write it. "I was born in Saigon and am a distant relative of Binh. I've won the Lambda Literary Award and the Pen/Oakland-Josephine Miles National Literary Award."

Make sure the letter includes your phone number, in addition to your e-mail and Web site addresses.

The letter is very simple, but there are some pitfalls that you should look out for. If you don't have any credentials, don't make any up. Also, it's best not to tell the agent that you gave the book to your father and he said he liked it, even if that's true. However, if Tom Robbins read your book and then sent you to the agent, you need to put that in the first paragraph.

If you want to know more about what not to write in your query, you can go to The Rejecter at rejecter.blogspot.com. The Rejecter—with the tag line "I don't hate you. I just hate your query letter."—is a very enlightening site written by an assistant at a literary agency who says that she rejects 95 percent of the queries that come across her desk. She tosses the other 5 percent into the "maybe" pile. Depressing as that sounds, the site is filled with helpful tips including how not to do a self-addressed stamped envelope (with metered postage) and how to manipulate your Amazon.com numbers.

Because selling books is all about making you a commodity in the marketplace, having your own Web site helps a great deal. Before they contact you, both agents and publishers usually take a look at your site. They want to figure out if they can market you and how professional you are. It's very important to have your site represent the best of who you are and what you do.

Once your query is sent off, it will take about two to four weeks to hear from someone, maybe more. Check your spam folder every day—it's amazing how often good mail ends up there.

If an agent likes what you've sent and is interested and available, you'll speak on the phone or meet in person depending on where you live. The agent-writer relationship is about being a team. Editors will come and go, but your agent will be with you for most of your career.

To begin your search, you need to find a list of agents who are members of the Association of Authors' Representatives. Most listings give you a little snapshot of who the person is, but you'll want to visit his Web site and check out his client list and what he says about himself. There are many Web sites designed to help submit to an agent. They include:

1. WritersMarket.com, a comprehensive site from *Writer's Digest*. Subscription-based, it locates new markets for your work, finds expert insider advice, and tracks your manuscript submissions and publishing contracts. It also has a wonderful search feature that can comb an extensive agent database using specific criteria such as "agents interested in science fiction who attend writers conferences."

2. Litmatch.net, which lets you track your submissions, browse agents and agencies, and manage "titles." A "title" is the project you are seeking representation for. Once it's entered into the system, Litmatch performs a search that generates a list of agents who are looking for similar projects.

3. Writers.net/agents.html is a simpler tool that lets you browse for agents by location and topic, like "occult."

4. Writerbeware.com, a good place to go to see if there are complaints against an agency that you're looking at.

Keep in mind that agencies come in various sizes. Some are quite large, like International Creative Management and William Morris, and some are quite small. It's best to familiarize yourself with all the options available and think about what you might be looking for in an agency. Make a list of about five top agents that you think you'd like to work with and query them. Then five more. If you're at a loss for whom to contact, there are quite a few ways you can get some help.

1. **Ask other writers for recommendations.** Writer friends may know of agents they met at conferences who are looking for clients. They may also know if their own agents are be looking for new clients.

2. **Publishing news sites list firms that have hired new agents.** Query these new agents. The new kid on the block may not a have a great track record, or any record at all, but there are other considerations, such as whether the agency that she's with carries a lot of weight. A new agent at William Morris will certainly have a lot more doors open to her than a new agent who is setting up her own shop.

Also, look at a new agent's prior experience. A new agent who worked in the industry, as, say, an acquisitions editor, is often a good choice. She knows people and can pick up a phone to call an editor on your behalf. If an agent just came out of the Iowa Writer's Workshop, she may have great writing credentials and may be familiar to publishers because of her own work. That could work out, too. You really want to deal with people who are connected in some way to the publishing world. The more connected, the better.

3. **Check the acknowledgements page of an author's book who writes in a style similar to yours (most authors thank their agents there) and query *their* agent.** This is a long shot, but sometimes you get lucky.

4. **Get someone who knows you, like a partner or spouse, to read through the agent list and choose agents they think you should send to.** Since this person knows you, loves you, and works with you, he or she may have some interesting insight as to who would be a good partner.

WHAT TO BASE YOUR CHOICE ON

There are two basic types of agents. There is some crossover between the two, but for the most part, an agent is of one school or the other. It's your job to decide what you want in a business partner.

The first type just sells what you give them. It's a straight transaction. You can ask them for career advice, and they'll give it, but they won't offer it on their own. Their approach is strictly about the sale and making sure the publication goes smoothly. Whatever you give them to work with, they will sell.

The second type nurtures. They'll give you advice about what your next book should be or what you should wear for your author photo. This type of agent takes a holistic approach to you and your work. They plan your future with you according to your vision and their experience.

Both types of agents are good, actually. It really just depends on what you need. Once you decide whom you might like to talk with, here are some basic questions to ask:

- Why are you an agent?

- What do you like about your job?

- What did you do before this?

- How large is your agency?

- Do you have an assistant I can work with when you're away?

- What writers do you represent, and how long have they been with you? This is an important question because if the agent doesn't have any long-term clients, or it's quite clear that most leave after one book, than you may want to ask about that. It may be that she had to give up practice to care for her elderly mother, or it may mean that she has a horrific temper. It's good to call people listed as the agent's clients and get a reference.

- What percentage do you take? Is that divided between the foreign rights and film subagents? Currently the going rate for agents is 15 percent. If foreign or film rights are sold, those subagents get a part of that. Other agencies have a separate fee for subagents, usually about 5 percent.

- Do you have a legal staff or work with a lawyer? Since all these new electronic and Internet rights make contracts a tangle, it's good to work with an agency that has contracts vetted by a lawyer.

- Do you accept manuscripts via e-mail? This saves a lot of time and money.

- Ask questions about the agent's general game plan. Where will the agent send the book? To how many publishers?

- Are there any plans for selling secondary rights, such as film, foreign, audio, or electronic rights? Find out if they have sub-agents who will seek out these opportunities.

There really are no right or wrong answers to these questions. You need to decide what you want based on what you think will make life easier for you. For example, many perfectly good agents don't have access to lawyers. To me that's a deal breaker, but if you like the agent you're dealing with, that might not be a problem for you.

In the end, whom you chose for an agent depends on you and what type of partnership you want to enter into. You may be with this person for a good part of your professional life, so it's often nice to have something in common besides you and your work—baseball, opera, pool, cooking. Whatever you two share will help deepen the bond between you and make your professional life not only profitable, but also enjoyable.

THE SALES PROCESS

You really want an agent who will fight for you and go the distance. A good agent is one who will offer your work until it's sold—no matter how long that takes. If it needs editing to become salable, she'll give you direction on that (although how much varies with each agent).

You should be an active participant in the selling process. Whom your book is sold to is your choice; it doesn't always have to go to the highest bidder. When your book is offered for sale, your agent gathers a list of all possible buyers. You should have an opportunity to speak to your soon-to-be editor before the deal is done, if you want to.

It's always a good idea to take a moment and "meet" them, even if it's on the phone. Your editor will be your partner in the publishing of your work, your main ally and contact for any problems that arise; you need to make sure that you find someone you think you can work with.

Books can either be sold at auction or through private offerings. An auction is usually open to all publishers and the writer and agent look over the bids to determine not only of the money is right, but what house would be the best fit.

If you don't go to auction, your agent will usually send your book with a cover letter to five editors, more or less. And if no one is interested, they will send it out to five more. The list of who they send to should be made available to you if you'd like to see it.

Once an offer is made, the agent negotiates a contract. As important as the amount of the advance seems at the time, it's just one part of the package. For example, there may be a concern if the publisher offers an e-book royalty rate of 8 percent of list price as compared to 15 percent paid by other publishers. It's the agent's job to bring that figure more in line with industry standards.

Once these details are all worked out, the agent usually sends the information to you in the form of what's often called a "deal sheet," although all agencies have their own terminology. No matter what it's called, the sheet is usually a straightforward list of what the key points of the deal are, such as due date and payment schedule.

If you agree, the contract is drawn up by the publisher and sent to your agent who then can send it to legal (if they have counsel) to take the final look, which is often known as "vetting."

The reason why the contract is usually revisited after it's agreed upon is that some publishers have boilerplate language that may conflict with the terms that your agent has negotiated. Plus, most agencies insert language that makes clear your relationship to them. For example, they stipulate that all monies will be sent to the agency of record for distribution to you. All those details have to be cleared up before you sign.

It's really a good policy to find counsel of your own in addition to any legal services that your agency provides. Don't just hire any lawyer, but choose one who is familiar with book contracts. The publishing world has some very particular jargon in their agreements, so you really need to get someone who understands the language and its context and is able to protect your rights.

Having your own lawyer doesn't mean that you don't trust your agent: You're just being prudent. Every contract you enter into is geared to the requirements of the person who last handed it to you. For example, many reputable agents will ask you to sign an agreement, or include a line in your contract with the publisher, that commits you to their agency for your next book. If you don't want to make that sort of commitment, you need a third party to negotiate that item—it's really not something you want to do on your own.

THE OTHER DEALS: BOOK CLUBS, AUDIO, FOREIGN, AND MOVIE RIGHTS

After you sign your book contract, there are lots of opportunities to make more than just your advance. In fact, you can sometimes make back your advance before you publish if your publisher held onto foreign, audio, and book-club rights and has resold them before you go to print.

Each different deal has a set of expectations, and legal language, that your agent has to guide you through. Here's a basic guide to the deals, so you won't be surprised, or overly excited. Keep in mind that all deals will vary by author and book; they're based on what the perceived worth of the book is in the marketplace. And, as we all know, that's a judgment call.

Book Club and Book Selections

A few years ago, book clubs like Book-of-the-Month found themselves in a rapid decline. Membership is still down and the amount of money they can afford to pay for the right to offer your book is often very small. Don't expect a lot of sales from a book-club deal: it's really more about the exposure. Book clubs give you a chance to get your work in front of readers who wouldn't necessarily see it.

Some chains, like Target, will feature your book as a "Book Selection." While this is a great honor, it's also an issue because your publisher will often have to increase the print run by at least 10,000 (to accommodate the number needed so that you'll be placed in all the stores), and unfortunately, many of these books don't sell that well. This is even true of the bookstore chain selection. These books get placed in special places and have a better chance of being bought, but unless someone knows what the books are about, or the books are being hand-sold by an employee, as they would be in an indie bookstore, then the books still have a high probability of gathering dust and being shredded.

So, don't expect huge sales. It *can* happen, but if you haven't made a name for yourself, it's going to be a little tougher. Just expect the satisfaction of taking your family to Target and standing in front of the display and having your picture taken. Not to mention hand-selling and signing a few books while you're there.

Don't try to sign stock, though; if it's not a bookstore, the store's not usually equipped for that kind of thing (they won't have stickers to tell people the books are signed, for instance) and may make you buy the books because you defaced them.

However, if you know you're going to be featured in Target, Wal-Mart, or even the local grocery store, train station, or airport, call the store managers and see if they'll set up a signing. You never know. I was recently in the Baltimore airport, and the bookstore there had continuous signings going on.

Audio and Large Print Rights

Both audio and large-print rights are usually brought to you and your agent by the publisher. It's not something that an agent tries to seek out, but will certainly keep an eye on.

There are two kinds of audio rights that can be sold—unabridged and abridged. Abridged means that the audio book is designed for general consumer use and will be sold in stores. If your book has a print run of more than fifty thousand, these audio rights are a possibility—the audio rights publisher needs a certain market saturation level before creating abridged work becomes profitable.

Unabridged means that your audio book will primarily go into the libraries. They are bought on a perceived market and merit and your print run doesn't really make a difference. These audio books are mostly geared towards the blind or people with sight difficulties. They pay a very small amount of money.

Large-print rights are very similar deals to the unabridged audio market. It's more a courtesy for people who have vision problems. If you're a best-selling author, you'll get more, but the money isn't that great—usually not much more than $1,000.

Both large-print and unabridged deals are something that your editor usually is approached with and the deal is struck by the publisher. You and your agent have a right to veto the contract and, in some cases, make amendments, but most times they'll just be accepted as offered.

Foreign Rights

Not all books are sold to foreign countries. Books that are too American, for example, are usually a difficult sell. When a book is deemed universal, like *The Life of Pi,* you'll often see it translated into several languages. Books that are American in a quintessential way, such as the recent rewrites of *The Godfather,* are also good candidates.

Foreign rights can either be handled by a subagent at your agency or by your publisher. If your publisher does it, they usually deduct the amount you earned for foreign rights from the balance against your advance. For example, if they paid you a $50,000 advance and they sold translation rights for $5,000 to Germany, then the amount you need to earn before you can start receiving royalties is now only $45,000.

If your agent retained the rights to sell in-house, then that money would go directly to you.

The book industry is not big business in other countries. Princely sums are very rare. Still, while most foreign publishers don't pay that well and sometimes buy books years after their publication, they can be fun to deal with. The rest of the world loves their authors, and sometimes it takes a Hungarian publisher to remind you that this isn't about money, it's about the glorious alchemy of words. They will usually send you copies that you can put on your bookshelf. Sometimes, if they think your book will be a bestseller, they will even tour you. Nothing is more fun then flying out to Iceland for a weekend.

MOVIE DEALS

Don't ever blame your agent because you don't have a movie deal. Film options are a very tricky business and often don't benefit the writer. Here are some truths about that cursed blessing.

- A book and a film are two different artistic mediums. Your book cannot be transferred exactly to film. You have to recognize that the storytelling process is very different. Your story will merely serve as a guide.

- Your agent can only write in so much protection for you. Don't get upset when people don't ask or don't care what you think. Once you cash the check, your story is no longer yours alone.

- Because films are also an art form, they can spawn their own industry. The movie *Forrest Gump* inspired Bubba Gump restaurants. After the indie *Napoleon Dynamite* hit critical mass, there were licensed greeting cards and T-shirts. You have to be very careful to protect your rights as the creator of the characters. Even though your agent will enclose language that protects you and makes sure you get a percentage of the profit, you have to make sure that you're comfortable with this arrangement.

- You will be paid in several stages. First, you'll get money for the option—it's usually pretty small. Second, you'll get money as soon as the film becomes a real project, as in the money for the budget is raised and work begins. If the film is modest to low-grossing, this is probably the most you'll see; it's often capped at about $100,000 to $150,000.

- Once the film is distributed, you will (usually) get a small percentage of the box office and whatever sales are generated from DVDs, T-shirts, airline videos, etc.

- Tax laws have changed and so not as many projects are bought these days.

- Since a film is an entirely different art form based on your original vision, the people involved with the film are entitled to more money.

- If your book is deemed a blockbuster, it may be pitched to a studio. If not, most film agents will wait until George Clooney comes knocking on the door.

- Some publishing houses are connected to studios and may try to option your book when they publish it. Your agent will be very leery of this, and rightly so. This type of in-house deal may result in less money in your pocket. Of course, this all depends on your book and how bankable people think it is.

- Most projects are bought by actors and producers who came across the work on their own. That's right. Somebody was on vacation and bought your book in an airport. Or their assistant did. Or they were filming in your hometown and the bookseller hand sold it to them. They fell in love with it and are willing to spend years making it a film.

- Never speak to anyone who asks about buying about film rights. Always have your agent call them.

- An actor or producer's cousin, parents, or best friend should not approach you to buy a script on their behalf for a movie deal. If they do, run.

- If the actor or producer is not prominent or does not have a film-making track record, your agent probably won't call them back if they've contacted you directly. There are too many amateurs in the film game, and you don't want to have your project co-opted by some addle-brained idiot who is playing producer.

- However, if you think that having a deal is better than not having one, you can badger your agent until she sets the deal in motion. Just don't go crying to her after you sign and United Artists drops you an e-mail asking if the rights have been sold.

- At first, your work is optioned for a year or 18 months. Most writers get paid a small amount, say $5-$10,000 for the option. After the option ends, it can be renewed usually at a set percentage increase. For example, if you got $5,000 the first time, you'll probably get $7,500 for the renewal.

- Again—don't let just anybody buy film rights. If your book or story is optioned and shopped around by a producer or studio and there are no takers, it's highly unusual that it can be resold and re-shopped. Everybody's seen it. However, if an actor buys it because he wants to be in it, and takes it around and no one wants it, you may have a chance at re-sale. The project may still be viable, it's just that no one could imagine that actor in that particular role.

- Never talk to the person who optioned your film without your agent or a lawyer present. Many people use their fame to try to cut a better deal or get you to give up some of your percentage. If the producer says you agreed to something without your agent being present, you can get burned.

- If there's a strike, or an act of God, during your option period, your option gets extended to cover that time frame. So, if the actors go on strike, your one-year option can drag on for as long as the strike does.

- Don't fall for the "We'll make you a producer" line. Everyone on a film has to get paid, and they're not going to pay you twice unless you have produced before.

- Once you sell your story, you're like somebody's ex. It's nice if you get along, but it's better if you take the money and disappear.

- Don't complain, give advice, or offer opinions. No one cares. When your work is bought, it's just like selling a car. Whatever the new owner wants to do with it, he will.

- Selling a book with a recurring character is difficult. As soon as the movie is made, the producer owns your characters and, usually, has control over how they are represented in the future. This can mean that you won't be able to write about them again. If you want to, tell your agent going into the deal.

- If you have two or more books with the same character, you can't sell all of them and wait to see who can get the deal done. You can only sell one at a time.

- If a movie is made of your work, you can't sell another book for a prescribed amount of time. This is usually set forth in the contract.

- Never accept e-mails from opposing agents, managers, or the person who bought your script without CCing your own agent. Again, your representatives must always be kept in the loop.

- In most cases, if your agent doesn't want to be involved and you hire a literary lawyer (which is expensive but better than going on without real legal advice), you still will owe them their 15 percent. Most book contracts state that any sort of product that comes from the publication of the book entitles the agent to a percentage. So, do get your agent on board.

- Don't try to use writer's "legal aid" services. Yes, there are many fine writing organizations that will help writers through the film option process, but don't go that route. Well-meaning as this is, Hollywood lawyers have those people for lunch. These non-profits deal with basic boilerplate language, and no contract is ever a basic boilerplate. There are so many ways to take advantage of you, it will make your head spin—including having a clause written that gives the buyer an option for all your future work.

- If the film is made and it's bad, it can hurt book sales. Even if it's just mediocre, it can hurt book sales. If it's great, it can hurt book sales because everybody knows that a book is not the movie and if they like the movie, they don't need to buy the book. Still, since the public is unpredictable, it's best to have your book reissued just in case there's a sudden interest in your work. But, if your editor won't do this, there's really no recourse.

- While it's a good idea to reprint or reissue a book that's being made into a film, some editors will try to launch a book in conjunction with its film release, especially if it's a TV movie. This could be a very bad thing for you. If your agent can't change your editor's mind, there's not much you can do about this. Just let whatever happens roll off your back.

- The usual length of time from the moment you sign the contract to the time you're eating popcorn at Sundance is ... forever. There is no usual time. Keep in mind that a script is like a book, it takes a year or two to write. And then everybody has to rewrite it. And money has to be raised.

• If your book is a blockbuster, the process moves faster—about two to three years *if,* and that is a very big if, all goes smoothly.

• Nothing ever goes smoothly.

FIRING YOUR AGENT OR GETTING FIRED

It's never easy to end a relationship, and the agent/client relationship is no exception. If you and your agent decide to part ways for whatever reason, make sure you get legal representation. You'll need a lawyer to help sort out who will deal with your publisher about books already in print, how you will get your royalty statements, and if there is anything in your agency contract that prevents you from leaving. You'll also need to make provisions just in case your book is later discovered and made into a film or you decide to get another agent to represent unsold rights.

Even if an agent "fires" you, you need legal representation to sort out the details. You don't want to take a financial hit.

There are many reasons why people change agents. If you feel your agent has lost interest in representing you, or is too busy, or made some huge errors in your contract that has hurt your economic well-being, or just has a bad attitude and treats you in a disrespectful manner, you need to call her on the phone and talk about it. All relationships go through rough patches. Your agent should be on your side. No matter what happens between you two, both parties should always maintain civility and professionalism—not to mention a healthy dose of friendship. If you can't do this any longer, it's time to leave.

Whatever you do, try to legally sever one relationship before starting a new one. Most agents don't like to be in the middle and most won't speak to you while someone else is representing you. It's just not good form.

In addition, if another agent wants the details of why you left your agent, just tell him that the relationship didn't work anymore. Don't gossip because it only makes you look bad. Be gracious and move on as quickly as possible.

HOW DO YOU KNOW IF YOUR MANUSCRIPT ISN'T WORKING?

You've tried everywhere, and you can't find an agent. Or, maybe, your agent has sent your manuscript out over and over again and no one is interested. How do you know when your critics may be right? That's always a difficult question, but the root of the issue lies within you. You need to be honest with yourself because that will help you understand what to listen to, and what to ignore—and that's an art unto itself.

No one wants to hear, "The book isn't working," but it happens. The thing to do is not to panic. Take a minute, take a deep breath, and think about the situation. If this is your agent or editor telling you this, you really need to listen and find out why. Your agent and editor are your touchstones; they know your reader and know what you need to do to reach them.

On the other hand, if a friend, or a potential agent, tells you the book isn't working and why, you should listen, but you also need to wait and see. When people you deal with like potential agents who don't have a vested interest in the project, they can quickly dismiss something. A general rule of thumb for rejections is that if you send to five agents and five agents send you a form rejection, send out five more.

You really don't want to have more than five manuscripts out at a time because as soon as someone decides to represent you, you need to contact everyone who still has your work and tell them that you've already accepted an offer for representation.

If you receive ten form rejections, you may have sent to the wrong agents. Remember, this is a matter of taste, if an agent isn't interested in your style, she is going to pass—sometimes without explanation. Send out to ten more.

When you've sent your work out to twenty agents and have received twenty form rejections, you really should take a moment and consider sending it to a professional editor to get some feedback. You could send it to a friend to read or to a writing partner, but, frankly, you should have done that before you sent it to the agents. And, if you did do that, it may be time to get an unbiased opinion that you pay for.

Paying for advice is a good idea at this point. Just be sure to check out the references to see if editor is reliable. While it may seem like a lot of money to hire someone to read your work, look at it in terms of lunch. If it cost you $150, that's fifteen lunches out. You can always make a sandwich for lunch, but you can't always figure out what's wrong with your book, so it's money well spent.

If you send to five, ten, or twenty agents and get a few handwritten responses, you may be on the right track. You should seriously look at the agents' concerns and see if they mesh with your artistic ideals for the work. Keep in mind that if you're sending to agents, your work must be commercially viable. All the agents' responses will be geared toward what sells and what will sell. After weighing all the responses, you may just decide to give small and literary presses a try.

Always remember that the book is yours; your name goes on it. A book, or a story for that matter, is your mark on the culture. If you revise a work to please an agent, it must also please you. If you feel it's no longer your work, then it's time for you to reclaim it and move on.

POOR SALES AND
WHAT TO DO ABOUT IT

When a book doesn't sell, who *really* is to blame? The author? The publisher? Both? On the topic of failed books, an anonymous editor from a major publisher contributed his thoughts to galleycat.com:

> We have a policy called, Don't Ask Don't Tell. What does this mean? Well, it means that if a book fails in the marketplace, don't ask anyone and don't tell anyone. Nine times out of ten, the author is blamed for poor sales; even though the house more often than not does support the author in marketing the book.
>
> As an editor I can assure you that I have too many books to edit and there are too many books to promote. Why is it a safe bet to blame the author? Because we all want to keep our jobs, that's why. What I am telling you is very important because it will give you some insight into the mindset of publishers today. The bottom line is this: When sales are good we all pat ourselves on the back and take credit, but when sales are bad, we find fault with the author, when in fact many times the poor results are our own fault!
>
> At just about every publishing house I've worked at I've run into this problem of having too many books to publicize, as do most of my colleagues. Some you just have to send out into the ether blind, some you champion, others you do the bare minimum on because that's all the time you have. I've actually had my boss tell me to NOT do anything for a book because another book needed to take priority. I think poor sales could be blamed on the new corporate model of publish-

ing that thinks of books as widgets and tries to get away with less staff and more books.

So what can a writer do about it? Well, one course of action is to forget that book and focus on writing another. While that sounds simple, the reality is that since you're paid for each book based on sales of your last, it'll be difficult to sell the new work. Or, you'll sell it for a lot less money.

Some writers change their names and try to write under a pseudonym. This is also a difficult proposition. Agent Lisa Bankoff from International Creative Management advises:

> Fashion designers often employ different names in marketing different lines of clothing. For high-end goods, it's one name; for lower-priced goods, it's a variation or another name entirely. This makes sense. No one questions the logic in making a distinction and the same should be true for books. There are many different kinds of writing. For the literary novelist who wants to write a (formula) detective series, the series would be better served greeting the world with a pseudonym. It's cut from a different cloth. That said, I feel just as strongly that a literary novelist not use a new name in an attempt to counter faltering sales. This seems as unpalatable as a woman who loves to dance but gives it up because her partner won't move his feet. She should keep on dancing.

One of the biggest problems with changing your name is that you'll start all over again. With a new name, you lose your readership base. And, if you divulge that you actually are Anne Rice writing as A.N. Roquelaure, you'll defeat the purpose of using a pseudonym—at least at first. Once you're famous, it won't matter.

Instead of abandoning your last book or changing your name to write a new one, the best course of action is to take control of your career. Yes, write that next book, but also spend some time trying to build an audience for you and what you have to say. Your book may have had sales problems because no one knew it was out there. If that's the case, enlist bloggers and your mailing list to get the word out. Set up readings or workshops at bookstores and libraries. Never give up. If an editor liked it well enough to publish it, there must be an audience for it, and you, somewhere. You just have to find it.

SURVIVING YOUR PUBLIC LIFE

STARTING OUT: ARE YOU ACTING LIKE A HACK?

Unfortunately, the writing profession is filled with high-strung, overly confident practitioners who believe that they are the next Ernest Hemingway. They know they are brilliant; they're certainly better than you and they will tell you that at every turn. And yet, they never seem to write anything new, or anything good.

However, they do spend a great deal of time telling people that the publishing industry doesn't recognize their talent. They can't get published, but it's not their fault. Commercial publishing is for losers, they say. Sellouts.

Hey, wait a minute, you think. *I can't seem to get published, either.*

Now that's an uncomfortable moment, isn't it?

If you haven't been published, and you call yourself a writer, you're always going to wonder if you're delusional. What if you don't have talent? Or, maybe, what if you had talent when you were younger, everyone seemed to like your writing in high school, but now it feels as if you've lost it? So, what do you do?

First, always keep in mind that being a writer isn't about being talented. There are talented people who have had all the benchmarks of a rising career—they went to the Iowa Writer's Workshop, they were given a scholarship to Provincetown Fine Arts Works Center, and they were granted several awards for new writers—and yet, ten years out of college, they've never published a single book and they're trying desperately to hold on to a teaching position.

Writing isn't about talent; it's about hard work. Talent can help get ideas on the page, but hard work organizes them into art.

Still, it's easy to become discouraged. You dream of signing six-figure contracts and yet spend your days working without any guarantee of pay. So, after a while, the lack of a publication credit is going to make you wonder if you're not some sort of hack working on a pipe dream.

So, how can you tell if you're not? Here are a few tips:

Real writers know that there is a market for all good writing, and so they hone their craft. Hack writers know they'll be rich and famous if only they make the right connections.

Real writers revise and revise again. Hack writers say that the famed Jack Kerouac never revised and so they don't have to.

Real writers understand that editors who reject them have made that decision based on their own taste and the marketplace. They know that somebody else might fall in love with their work, they just have to keep trying. Hacks know the editor has no taste and is stupid—and isn't afraid to tell her that to her face, either. Or send her an e-mail to that effect, or twelve e-mails. More is better.

Real writers work, even if they don't feel like it. This is a job, after all. Hacks work when they feel inspired. Writing, after all, is a calling.

Real writers know they can always learn from their mistakes and grow. Hacks know that they are right and refuse change despite what everyone tells them.

Real writers write because they love to write. Hacks write because it's an easy way to get rich.

Real writers know that sometimes you write a weak book. Hacks know there's a cabal of publishers plotting against them.

Real writers know brilliance when they see it. Hacks know they are brilliant.

Real writers understand publishing is a cooperative, and flawed, industry. Hacks feel their talent makes them the exception to every rule.

Real writers know it's easy to get discouraged and sometimes do.

Real writers are leery of praise and know that a publishing contract is the only true sign that the work is good.

Real writers define success by being able to write and know that sometimes that big paycheck never comes.

Real writers follow their hearts.

Hacks bellow, curse, blame, gossip, and snipe. They do anything they can do to hide their broken hearts—except work.

SURVIVING YOUR FIRST BOOK

When you write, it's art. When you publish, it's a business, and business is a collaborative art.

Once you sell your book, you begin working with a staff of editors, copywriters, photographers, graphic artists, subagents for film, subagents for foreign rights, foreign editors, marketing people, publicists, accountants, direct sales people, and the sales force. You sometimes have to work with voice talent or even be the voice talent.

These people are all paid professionals working to make your book a success. A lot of these people have been in the industry all their lives—they're a great resource. But many writers will tell you about what a fuss they made over the cover they hated or the jacket copy they could not tolerate. "The squeaky wheel gets the oil," they often conclude.

Being oily is never something a professional aspires to—being thoughtful and respectful usually is the best route. These people are on your side, after all. You all need your book to do well.

Of course, in any business there'll be some people who'll make your life a trial if you let them. So don't let them. If you're having an issue with someone and you can't make it right, then call your agent and get some advice. After all, you are a team.

However, before you make that call, take a breath and try to put the incident in perspective. You need to choose your battles wisely because everyone in publishing is working under crushing deadlines and there's tons of pressure. Any complaint you may have can create an avalanche of overreactions and lots of grief for you. Here are some crazy-making areas that you may need to be understanding about:

> 1. **E-mail.** If someone never responds to your e-mail, just let it go. They've probably read it and forgot to respond or didn't have the time. Don't send e-mails to keep people "in the loop" about readings and such—it just clogs their boxes. Send e-mails when you have something interesting to say—like Brad Pitt bought a case of your books when you were in New Orleans. Everybody likes good news. If you *need* to reach someone by e-mail for something important and you've sent three and there's been no response, pick up the phone. You may have to leave a message, but calling will usually prompt some type of response.

2. **Mistakes.** If someone makes a mistake, like forgets to send an advanced copy to a contest, send an FYI to your publicist. You can CC your agent if you want, but that makes you look like you're really upset and want to make a big deal out of something. It's always best not to let these things get to you. You're one of thirty authors that they are dealing with. Mistakes will happen, and with great frequency. It's always best to call the publicist right around launch and get a sense of what went out and what didn't. Offer to help if you can.

3. **Frightening accommodations and impossible scheduling.** Every writer has a tour horror story about the lack of geographic training some publicists have had. If your publicist asks you if you can do a reading in Miami at 8 P.M. and then do a signing in Tallahassee the next day, it's time you offer to book the tour yourself. If you don't, you may go crazy. Since most business travelers have access to better discounts than corporations do, it's often easier for publishers and less expensive if you book yourself. It's a hassle, but you get to stay where you want and travel the way that best suits you.

4. **Awful bookstore experiences.** No one has any idea as to how your event will turn out. Everyone is hopeful, but you may get two people or two hundred. You may have a snotty event coordinator or the sweetest person you will ever meet. There's no reason to get upset about whatever happens; it just happens. If something awful happens, like the readings coordinator wants to take you out for a romantic dinner and won't take "no" for an answer, then report it in a neutral tone to your publicist—but don't e-mail something that's this serious. Call and talk it over. If you e-mail, your publicist may send that e-mail on, and who knows what problems that can cause. By talking it over on the phone, your publicist gets to know what happened so that it doesn't happen to the next person, and you'll probably feel better after talking it through. Remember, your publicist has seen it all before. He can be a great source of comfort in a stressful situation.

5. **No press for your event.** The local bookstore is in charge of the basic local press. They will contact the newspapers and

television stations about your event. Your publicist will also make an attempt to garner you some ink. However, if someone forgets, there's really nothing you can do about it once you're there. The best way to guard against these problems is to cultivate mailing lists that are based in areas you'll tour and to join social networking sites. Both of these tools give you a chance to tell people when you're in town and may, to a limited degree, circumvent any press issues you may have.

So, when should you call your agent for help?

- If you find yourself in any situation where you are clearly being disrespected, such as being cursed at or told to "shut up," then it's time to pick up a phone.

- If you find that there's any sort of deviation from the contract, then pick up a phone.

- If you were told that you would receive $5,000 to cover tour expenses and you did the tour only to find that you'll only be reimbursed for $2,5000, pick up the phone.

- If your editor tells you something that she says she doesn't want your agent to know, you need stop her before she goes any further. If she continues, you need to pick up a phone. You can't be put in the middle of anything, and your agent's job is to protect your best interest.

Most of the time, if something goes wrong, all you really need to do is send an e-mail clearly stating what happened, CC your agent if you think it's called for, and either suggest a remedy for the issue or request one. Nicely.

Needless to say, you should keep every e-mail that you send and receive—even if you think it's meaningless. You never know when confusion could arise. Most e-mail programs have a "sent" file, so it's not a difficult thing to do.

Deadlines

A deadline is that. If your publisher says May 17, they mean it. Most contracts have a thirty-day extension after the date written into them, but if you're going to be late, you need to tell your editor and your agent as soon as you realize it.

A publishing house is like an ocean liner—it's huge, moves slowly, and, sometimes, barely moves at all. It has no room for flexibility. If you miss your deadline, you throw everybody off track, and your book will not come out on time. Or, it might miss its publication slot entirely, and you may not get published.

GOOD THINGS TO DO ONCE YOU SIGN THAT FIRST CONTRACT

When Hemingway signed his first contract, he gave up his job as a journalist and moved to Paris to live as a writer. *A Moveable Feast*, his memoir about those years as an expatriate, provides important and lively insight into the creative process and the Lost Generation of the 1920s. It also serves as a chronicle of what not to do if you want to be a writer in contemporary publishing. Here's a list of things that may not be as glamorous as using the proceeds of your gambling winnings to eat oysters and drink champagne instead of paying your rent, but it will certainly help you navigate some of the craziness that often comes along with that advance check.

- **Get a post office box.** You're a public person now, and you want to act like one. Giving your home address to strangers is never a good idea.

- **Get an unlisted phone number, an untraceable line, and Caller ID.** Unfortunately, once you're published, many would-be writers, including your doctor, lawyer, and drycleaner, think you can help them publish their book. People will call you and ask you to ghostwrite, edit, send their book to your publishing house, etc. It will drive you crazy in a very short time. An unlisted phone number is a must, along with an untraceable line, one that won't show up on Caller ID. Caller ID itself is also very helpful because if someone has your real phone number, like the appointment person at your dentist's office, they may pass it along to a loved one who wants to be a writer. It happens all the time.

- **Never give your cell phone number to anyone.** Get a Black-Berry or another type of phone that allows you to pick up e-mail. If a volunteer coordinator wants your phone number so she can contact you during a book fair, tell her to e-mail you because you'll be notified immediately. You really don't want to give out your phone number to anyone who you don't know well.

- **Never accept a manuscript from anyone except a current student.** People will try to give you manuscripts that they want you to read or edit or help them publish. Don't accept them. There are not enough hours in the day for your own work; you can't get involved with someone else's. Plus, there have been a few cases where people have sued writers because they claimed that they gave the writers manuscripts to read and then the writers plagiarized them. So, it's best to tell people that you're busy—because you are.

- **Buy cases of books to give away.** You'll need books to send to contests, fellowships, residencies, and jobs. You'll also need them to give to people like your contractor who thinks that since you wrote a book, and he likes to read, you should give him one. It's amazing how many people will ask you for a book. They have no idea that you pay between 40 to 50 percent of the cover price for them, but you don't really want to say no to the person who's rewiring your house. It's also a good idea to give books to people who you like, just because you like them.

- **Talk to a tax accountant who knows something about the publishing business.** When you get paid for writing, you become an individual proprietor of a business. According to current tax laws, you should be filing a Schedule C. It should be that simple, but tax laws change at the speed of light. So, it's really best to deal with a tax professional who understands that this year, you're going to get a lump of money called an advance ... and next year is another story.

- **Thank-you notes go a long way.** Cards and envelopes with your name and P.O. Box address engraved on them can be bought for about a dollar a set from reputable places like American Stationery.

- **Business cards are important.** In other countries, everyday people have cards with their names and contact information on them. There's no reason why you shouldn't, too. Spend the $100 and get the cards printed professionally. There are many reasonable places that create a very professional looking product. Whatever you do, don't put your phone number on them. Name, P.O. Box, Web site, and e-mail. If you need to give out a phone number, you can always write it on the card at the time of the exchange.

- **Remember why you write.** The Web site of "The Writer's Almanac" (Minnesota.publicradio.org/radio/programs/writers_almanac) by Garrison Keillor is a daily reminder of why we write. Each morning, Keillor features a poem, and the birthdays and bios of famous writers. This short feature reminds you that even great writers had to work hard and faced a lot of rejection. It gives you hope, and that's a good way to start the day.

BURNOUT

You've sold a few books and never made the list. Or, maybe, your first book did well and the rest falter. So you feel like giving up or just finding a rock and hiding under it.

It happens to everyone.

Once the blush of being a new writer is over, you get the feeling that you're just one of masses. That's when things begin to get difficult. You may be mid-career with five or more books, or later career with a lifetime of work, but there could come a time when you suddenly feel that it's over.

There are countless stories, as we all know, of writers who just gave it one more shot and suddenly became famous. While those stories may encourage you through your darkest moments, they're hardly enough to get you through the day. And they really are not very realistic. So instead of giving up, which is really out of the question, you need to re-create yourself. You need to find that spark again.

Here are some tips from other writers on how to keep pushing through:

1. **Join or rejoin a writer's group.** As cranky as writers can be, we are, of course, all the same species. We go through the same problems. There's comfort in that. There's never a time in our writing lives when we can't benefit from the solace of people who've been there.

2. **Revive your creative energy with an exotic residency in a place you've always been interested in like Spain.** Or arrange with a local travel agency to offer a "writer's tour" through a part of the world that you know well and love.

3. **Take up photography to get a different perspective on the world.** Try anything new, anything that moves you outside of your comfort zone and sparks your imagination.

4. **Try nonfiction.** Many writers do make a mid-career jump into nonfiction as a way to boost their career. And it often works. As long as you can build an audience and write, life is good.

5. **Be the elder statesman.** Your experience and expertise is worth a lot. You are a writer and you have books to prove it. Maybe it's time you helped the next generation. Teach a class or offer a workshop. Sometimes when you see the process through their eyes, it sparks you to take risks you never would have thought of taking before.

6. **Fall in love with the word again.** Volunteer. You could be a reader at your local library—there's a shortage of volunteers for story hours and also readers for the blind. Many hospices and hospitals could also use a hand when it comes to reading. Your time as a volunteer will be well appreciated and it will certainly help you remember why you decided to devote your life to this madness we call a career.

7. **Try writing in a different genre.** If you've always liked science fiction, why not change your name and give it a shot? Or write a book for your grandchild. Many a career has been revived out of a grandparent's or second-time around parent's concern for a child.

8. **Go to industry-based conferences.** Yes, it is painful to listen to the details of everyone else's new book deal or upcoming made-for-TV movie, but at The Association of Writers & Writing Programs yearly convention, or The Edgar Awards, or any other gathering of writers celebrating the written word, you can recharge and revive your outlook. You can meet with old friends, maybe strike a deal with a new press, or even get an

idea for a book. Whenever there's that much creative energy in a room, it's difficult not to have your own spark rekindled.

9. **Don't be afraid to make a break with your past.** If you think you need to, it's sometimes good to find a new agent or publisher who has a different take on your work.

10. **If you feel you've written everything you wanted to write, go back to some of your earlier work and create a book around a minor character.** You'd be surprised what energy seeing a work from a different angle can give you.

11. **There are many later career grants and residencies that are designed to help you keep writing.** Apply to them all. Avoid sitting at your desk and feeling sorry for yourself.

12. **Don't stop writing.** Ever.

As we all know, the writer's life is very difficult if we let it overwhelm us. The key is not to let it overwhelm. Life is a grand adventure, if you let it be. You just have to let it. So let it.

28

THE $80 (MORE OR LESS) PROMOTIONAL CAMPAIGN AND OTHER CONSIDERATIONS

Sometimes it's overwhelming to be one of fifty thousand authors trying to promote your work. If you don't have a syndicated television show, a fan base, and a full-time publicist, even with the support of your harried publisher, it's going to be a little difficult for you to sell your book to the entire fifty states of America—but it's not impossible. The Internet has opened up a wide variety of opportunities for writers to get their books seen by the reading public.

A 2008 Zogby survey reported that 43 percent of book buyers of all ages turn to online vendors as their most frequent point of purchase. And 77 percent say they've bought at least one book online.

So if you're not well connected—and maybe even slightly disheveled and a tad on the unphotogenic side—you can still create media impact in the marketplace with about $200 to $500 (depending on what software you own) and access to a computer. An adventurous spirit also helps.

BUILD YOUR OWN WEBSITE: $80 TO $160

If you've never done this before, you're probably laughing right now, but this is actually quite simple. For example, Apple makes iWeb, a plug-and-play Web program that gives you professional results. You don't have to know code. You don't even need instructions. All you have to do is click and type; the program does the rest.

iWeb is included with new Macs, or it can be bought as part of the $80 iLife program. It has several attractive site formats that you can customize. Amazingly, it includes features such as podcasts, movies, and blogs. You can even broadcast your podcasts to the iTunes store with a click of your mouse.

When you build your site, be sure to include an e-mail sign-up for visitors so that you can build your mailing list. You want to create a very large list of people interested in your work because it's good practice to alert your readers when you have a new book coming out. If they don't know it's out there, they can't buy it.

Your mailing list is your built-in market. If you have five thousand names and you send out an advanced publication notice, you'll see your Amazon number climb within hours. Try to send out an e-mail "blast," a bulk mailing to everyone on your list, at least twice a year. Even if it's a holiday greeting, it gives you a chance to connect and also weed out old addresses that no longer work.

Do include an e-mail address on your site that the public can write to you at. Being accessible is good business practice, and if someone wants you to appear at a reading series, they can easily get in touch.

Also include downloadable photos, a résumé, and press releases. Many programs let you do this, and it allows journalists easy access to tools that they need to write about you.

Once you create your site, you need to register your domain name. With GoDaddy.com, and several other sites, you can register your own domain, such as www.yourname.com for as little as $10 a year. Once you register, you'll need to find someone to host your site. Again, Go-Daddy.com and several other companies offer low cost hosting. Total cost here averages about $70, but these places often run sales. You can also add more services that will help make your site more efficient and give it better visibility on the Web. Again, these upgrades vary from company to company.

Whatever you do, try to work with a provider that offers tech support with real people on the telephone. Even though these Web programs are easy, the actual technology is very complicated and if you have a problem you'll need to be able to speak to someone about it. FAQs and real-time chat lines are of no concrete help if your code is misfiring for some reason that you can't explain because, well, you really don't understand it. Only a tech person can talk you through.

Before your site is published, you'll want to sign up for a free service called Google Analytics. This is another easy-to-use program that will make a huge difference in your professional life. Analytics allows you to track where your Web site visitors are coming from (right down to the city) and what pages they visited.

It can also give you an idea of which media efforts are working. If you did a radio interview in Memphis on Saturday, the next day you can check the numbers and see if anyone from that city came to your site. Analytics gives you an idea of how effective you are and also what audience building needs to be done.

While not all readers are rabid Internet surfers, if you don't notice a few hits from a town that you've visited, and you didn't sell a lot of books at the event, you need to make a note of that. You may not want to come back with your next book. It's important that you use your time and promotional resources wisely.

One of the things you'll need to consider is if you want to sell things from your site, like signed books and T-shirts. If you do, PayPal and Google Checkout are programs you may want to explore.

The downside about doing this is that it is very time consuming and you really don't make that much money doing it. It's more of a PR gesture. Before you start, you'll need to create a business entity and register it with your state because you'll be expected to collect tax monies. While it's not expensive to do, the cost depends on where you live and there's lots of paperwork involved and many laws that govern you, so it helps to have a lawyer walk you through it.

From there, you'll need to order books. Some publishers don't allow you to resell the books you buy from them because they discount them at a lower rate than they do for booksellers. If that's the case, you'll need to set up a business account with your publisher and deal with a sales rep to place your orders.

You'll also have to investigate shipping options and boxes to ship your customers' orders in. All these costs add up and must be passed along to your readers.

Keep in mind that if you want to create T-shirts or hats with your book cover as a logo, you'll need written permission to do that from your publisher. Also, check your agent agreement. Some agents will receive their percentage of what you make from any kind of product that is directly related to your book.

Another thing you might want to check into is creating a trademark for products named in your book. If you have an idea for a restaurant named Bubba Gump's, and your book becomes a famous film, it's a great idea to make sure that it's trademarked because if anybody is going to exploit your work it should be you.

CREATING IMAGES FOR YOUR WEBSITE: $0 TO $300

Readers love photos of their favorite authors, so you may consider getting a digital camera. Most of them are very simple to use. The primary thing you need to keep in mind when buying one is the higher the megapixels, the better the photo. While most pictures that you post on your site will be very small files, when you need a headshot for your book cover, the megapixel number matters a lot.

Some digital cameras now have a video option that allows you to take short clips of video. The sound quality isn't very good with these, but they're not bad.

One inexpensive step up is an Internet-ready video camcorder, like the Flip camcorder. About the size of a BlackBerry, these videocams can record up to sixty minutes of video and are point-and-shoot only. After you've filled the memory, you download it, save the file, erase the memory, and start again.

While this type of video isn't the same quality as that provided by a video camera, the sound is very good and the image is quite clear. More importantly, all you have to do is plug the Flip into your computer and it downloads itself into several formats including VCR, e-mail, and Web-based. It's pretty amazing what you can do and the cost is about $70 or less.

So, the next time you make an appearance, you can set it up about three feet away from you and turn it on. The video will be static, but you don't have to use it all. Just a snippet of it will do. Or, you could edit it.

Many newer programs, like iMovie (which is included with iWeb in the iLife program), allow you to edit your video by just dragging the clips onto a grid. You can even add fancy effects just like the pros do, including fade-to-black and colorizations. In addition, these programs give you the ability to type in titles and include another sound source, like music. If you want to add other video to your own, there are sites like stockfootageforfree.com, which provide access to free stock video of a wide variety of things from animals to U.S. cities.

Once you're finished, you can post your video on networking sites and also your own Web site.

If this all seems like a lot of work, and neither you nor anyone you know is interested in doing it for you, you could, of course, hire a videographer or a photographer to work with you. There are many fine ones available in most large cities, but it gets really expensive. Not only do they charge a shooting fee, and also an editing fee when working with video, they also charge per use. That means you'll have to track every Web site, magazine, and newspaper that you send to, and then pay the photographer anywhere from $50 to $200 per use—or more.

So, it might not hurt to give these less expensive options a try. They're easy and fun and will help bring you a little closer to your reader.

BOOK TRAILERS: $0 TO $200
(OR MORE IF YOU HAVE THE PROS DO IT)

Book trailers are another way to promote your work both on your own site and across the Web. Much like movie trailers, they are short and designed to capture the reader's imagination. If you want to get a sense of what they are, check Amazon.com and YouTube. Many authors have them and some are quite entertaining.

While publishers have been creating book trailers for high-profile books, if you feel creative, you can always make one for yourself. It's easy to do using tools like iMovie and an Internet-ready video camera—and free.

But while the do-it-yourself option is fun and cheap, sites like Amazon.com currently accept only professional trailers. Costs for those can be quite high, so shop around. Or, just make your own trailers until the publisher decides to make you one. On most Web sites like YouTube, the personal touch often trumps the high tech.

BLOGS: $0

There are many well-read blogs that are looking to review books and speak to authors. Some are very stable and have a large readership. If you can v-blog, which means add a video to your entry, that's even better.

If you find a blog that you like, ask your publisher if the publicity department has already contacted the blogger. If not, drop the blogger an e-mail about your book and ask if he'd like to see an ARC. It's a good idea to attach a résumé, press release, and headshot with your note, just so the blogger has a sense of who you are.

One rather effective way to blog is to be a guest blogger on someone else's site. Some authors "tour" each other's sites, which means that a group of people get together when they launch books and write each other's blogs. This helps authors reach wider audiences and allows them to speak to their colleagues' readers.

To do an exchange, find a writer, or a group of writers who already blog together, and introduce yourself via e-mail. A simple approach often works well. You can write something like, "I'd like to give my blog another perspective, and I really like your work," or "If you'd ever like a guest blogger, I hope you'll think of me."

Be clear that if you become part of the exchange, you'll provide a link to their Web site on your site. If you like, you can suggest a topic for your post, or theirs.

Some sites, like Murderati.com, feature a large community of bloggers, and thereby have a large audience of readers. Journalistic sites, such as Salon.com, will take queries, so if you have an idea for a blog which has an interesting news or cultural slant, you may want to e-mail them, too.

A caution about blogging: Promotion is good, as long as you're not too blatant about it. Be discreet. The point of blogging is not to tell people that you have a book out, but to let them meet you and understand who you are. If you seem real to them, and interesting, they're going to want to know what your work is like.

Be careful about spending too much time at this. While it does help to get your name out there, all this chatting on the Web takes you away from your writing. You really want to limit your efforts to blogs that have a readership that you want to have. Just like a movie star promoting a new film, you want to make the most out of every appearance so that you can go back to work, the thing you love, as soon as possible.

NETWORKING SITES: $0

The more sites you're on, the better chance people will have to run across you and your work. But unless you hire an assistant, you're going to have to choose a couple of favorites and set up residence there. Facebook currently seems to have the most active literary world; there's a bevy of working writers, fan sites, and literary organizations that you can network with, but that can change in a moment.

When you become a member of an online community, you have two options—you can create a closed site where you just talk to writers you know and organizations that you are a member of or want to learn more about, or you can open your site to everyone who wants to be your "friend."

It's most useful to do a mix. Some sites, like GoodReads.com, are designed to bring readers to writers, and so the more people you allow to be your friends, the more information you can pass along to the reading public. Since Facebook encourages people to chat with each other, it may be a good idea to keep your number of friends down so that you can actually keep up with them. For instance, three thousand friends is a very large number to receive updates from on a daily basis.

All these tools are addictive—it's really fun to get an e-mail that says "Anne Rice in now your friend"—but they are just tools. They're there for you to help build an audience and to create a rich professional life for yourself. They are a means to an end and shouldn't be allowed to take too much time away from your work—because they can and will.

THE BOOK TOUR

Even if your book doesn't sell a single copy that first month, don't cancel your tour. It's crucial that you go out there and meet readers. Some publishers are currently not inclined to tour authors, but tours are still a fact of life for writers, even if the only stop is the local bookstore.

There is no journey quite like a book tour. A pal of mine, a best-selling novelist who will remain nameless, says, "A tour is something your publisher sends you on when you've been too uppity."

You can see his point. There's nothing worse than getting up at 3:30 A.M to discover that your flight has been canceled and then driving two hours to another airport to catch a flight that will get you to the bookstore with twenty minutes to spare—that is, if there's no line at the rental car agency *and* if your GPS is working properly.

And, of course, when you arrive at the bookstore, the coordinator (who is dressed entirely in black with dyed black hair, tiny skull earrings, and black lipstick) says without taking a breath, "I never got an advanced reader's copy, so I didn't know if you were really coming, so I didn't put a notice in the paper. Could you help me move this stack of chairs so we can set up? We won't get anyone, but Corporate needs to know that we set up the chairs."

And so you say thanks and set up those chairs. Then, with ten minutes to go, a freak thunderstorm hits. Winds gust to 40 mph. You watch people pull into the bookstore's parking lot and back out again.

If this happens to you, and it probably will—soldier on. A positive attitude really makes all the difference in a tour. You just have to be open and roll with the experience. Because despite the bad beginning and low turnout, the coordinator could turn out to be a sweet gal, an avid reader, who sits in front and laughs at all your jokes. She can also tell you that you can buy Special Effects hair dye in a wide range of colors, but that the

Atomic Pink, Nuclear Red, Joyride, Cupcake Pink, and Napalm Orange will all glow in the dark.

Travel certainly enriches.

The biggest secret of touring is that you have to make it fun, for both you and everyone you meet. That's not easy—sometimes you're sick or lonely—but it's crucial to you and the survival of your book.

Tours *are* difficult. We miss our family and our own bed. We want to eat our granola with soy milk in our favorite bowl in the morning and not stand in some hotel buffet line trying to decide what has less fat: doughnuts; biscuits and gravy; or a sausage, egg, and cheese bagel.

Besides, it's unnatural to speak with strangers from 6 A.M. to 10 P.M. when you make your entire living sitting alone in a room talking to yourself. But you do it, because it's the best way to build an audience.

HOW TOURS ARE CREATED

When your book is announced in your publisher's catalog and you know you're going to tour to promote the book, part of the information included is a list of areas where the house is going to send you. Booksellers in those areas then contact their sales representatives and ask if you'll be available to come to their store. As part of their request, they provide your publisher with basic information including how much you sold last time you appeared and how much they sell of your work in general. Based on this information, the publisher will decide whether to include the store on your tour.

Touring is all about sales. Your announced tour location is based on either your past sales (if you're a repeat author) or markets that your publisher thinks will like your book. For example, Tim Dorsey writes books about Florida. When he wrote his early work, his publisher planned Florida-based tours. As Tim built his audience, the scope of his tours widened, but he still spends a great deal of time in Florida where his fan base is.

If you were born and live in Minnesota and write general fiction books, your tour will more than likely be based out of that state.

If you don't live in New York City, Los Angeles, Seattle, Miami, or San Francisco and you don't write about those places, your publisher may be reluctant to send you to those cities because they are very difficult markets to break in to. There's so much competition for events that authors who don't have a fan base there, or aren't connected to the community, will have a very difficult time garnering an audience. Even if an organization or bookstore invites you, your publisher may be reluctant unless it's clear that you can sell at least fifty to one hundred books—and then, that's still a very small amount considering how expensive it is to travel and stay in those cities.

If your publisher doesn't want you to travel somewhere, that doesn't mean you can't go. It just means that you have to schedule the event so it won't conflict with the obligations that your publisher has made for you—and you'll have to pay for it yourself.

If you do discover that you want to pay to travel to an event, you need to make the most of your money. If you go on your own, ask your publicist if she can set up some media events (like TV or radio), send information to the press, and contact other bookstores in the area so that you can do drop-in signings or other events that are in nearby, but not conflicting, markets.

GENERAL CONSIDERATIONS REGARDING TOURS

If your publisher isn't paying for a tour, or is only paying for part of one, you can still tour—*if* you think it's worth it—but you have to really think it's worth it.

If you're an unknown, you probably won't garner a huge crowd (unless there's a built-in crowd like at a university event). But don't get discouraged; you build an audience. It takes a while. The point of all tours is for you to meet booksellers and form personal relationships with them, get to know staffs, and have an adventure with whatever number of readers do show up.

While on tour, you're sort of a literary Fuller Brush salesman on a journey of true self-enlightenment: like Siddhartha without the Buddha thing.

If you hate the idea of *selling* your book, you're not alone. There are many blogs on the Internet devoted to writers' tour stories. Just search "book tour horror stories" and you'll find quite a few.

But it does get better. Gradually. Eventually. It has to.

Tours and public appearances are an important part of a writer's life because they give you a chance to connect with your "sales force"— the booksellers, reviewers, librarians, bloggers, journalists, and readers. These people are your audience, your friends, and your co-conspirators. You can learn as much from them as they learn from you.

Monetary Considerations

It costs a great deal to tour, so when a bookstore says that it forgot to do the publicity or couldn't get books from the distributor, it's not just distressing—it's costly.

Flying to a location, renting a car, staying in a hotel, and buying meals costs anywhere from $700 to $1,600 depending on the site. Driving to an overnight reading is cheaper, but you still have to pay for gas, wear and tear on the car, a hotel room, and food. A nearby event can run about $200, if you have to spend the night. A driving tour of five overnight stops typically runs about $1,200. Much of this expense is tax-deductible, but still it represents a very large out-of-pocket expense.

Most publishers are not sending authors on tour because they don't see the financial gain in general. But for the author, it's about building your brand. So, you'll need to figure out what you can comfortably afford to do. When someone contacts you about a date, it's always good to be clear about money. Tell them if you have to pay for it, or part of it. Ask if they have a special rate with a nearby hotel.

In general, if the publisher pays for any tour event, it will usually be just for hotel, car rental, flight, and maybe your meals, but sometimes meals are not covered. If you can drive your own car, they may pay you mileage. Or not. Again, this is up to the publisher.

A literary escort is an interesting expense to add to the equation. For a set fee, this person does a lot of work that a publicist would do, such as calling media and arranging for stores to get your book so that you can sign copies of them. She will also pick you up at the airport, drive you around to bookstores for drop-by signings, and take you to your readings. Most charge by the day plus mileage and can run anywhere from $250 to $1,000, depending on your needs and the city.

Most services are very good. Some are even great. In San Francisco, one service brings a basket of treats to keep your energy level up. However, hiring a service is not a sure way to make your tour stop successful because the quality of these services varies greatly from city to city. It's best to ask your publisher for recommendations.

BOOK FAIRS AND FESTIVALS

Book fairs and festivals give you a lot of exposure to readers, but they can be very expensive and very disappointing—if you let them. Some festivals will pay for hotels and travel, some can't. Some don't pay for anything at all and expect you to engage in a wide variety of activities including private cocktail parties for the board and donors, lectures at local schools, and writing workshops (for which they charge but provide you no compensation for teaching).

There are no standards, unfortunately. How you're treated and what you can expect depends on the professionalism of that year's hosting committee. Since writers need to meet readers, organizers hope that you'll be willing to pay your way to have the ability to do that. And you are, but all these events add up quickly, so you should be choosy and evaluate the cost up front.

Most mystery festivals, such as Bouchercon and Thrillerfest, expect you to pay to attend and often don't confirm your program slot until close to the date. So you have to be prepared to spend $2,500 on airfare, hotel, and registration to go to Hawaii when you really don't know what level of exposure you'll have. You may discover that you'll be on the 8 A.M. Saturday panel that has forty people in attendance—and that's not going to sell enough books to cover your costs, or even cover the cost of lunch. And, unfortunately, you'll need to make your non-refundable reservations and send in the registration fees well in advance.

Whenever you're asked to appear at these events, you have to look at it as a donation of time and money because you want to support readers and reading in various communities. Do it for the adventure. Do it for fun. Do it because you want to attend anyway. Don't do it because you think you can sell a ton of books.

It's always a good idea to weigh the benefits of each request because each will be different. And some events may even hurt book sales.

Recently, a large festival had everyone sign a legal document that bound the writers not to appear anywhere else in the surrounding area for thirty days. For those of us on a book tour, this was a difficult request because we only had a month to make an impact with our books. If we blacked out our home market for one event, or blacked out a strong market area, we could lose a lot of sales. And since there were four hundred authors signing at this event over the course of three days, it was easy for a writer's audience not to find him.

The real problem with festivals and fairs is that many readers, while they will come to your session, really come to see the headliners and buy books from them. Unless you already have an audience, you usually don't sell a lot at the event itself. But sales do happen. If you appear with a headliner, you have a better chance to sell. And you'll often find that your Amazon numbers go down after a festival. People may not pay $23 for someone they don't know well, but the online price of $15 seems fair.

Are festivals and fairs worth doing? In many cases, they are good experiences. Some places treat you very well, and the organizers are great fun. You can meet other authors and may expand your exposure to readers. You can also stop by local bookstores and sign stock. And, if you check the attendee lists for friends and business contacts, you can spend time with people you need and want to see.

But before you agree to go, talk to others. Even if your publisher is not sending you, it's best to ask your publicist what experience other authors have had with each festival, and if she thinks the exposure is worth it.

PERSONAL CONSIDERATIONS

This is a tough one. While travel can be great fun, and is certainly necessary for a writer's growth, it can also make you horribly homesick. You really need to try to determine how long you are able to stay away from your loved ones. And, if you work, just how much time can you really get away from your job?

Time Management

If you teach, you can sometimes arrange your schedule so that you can get away after a Wednesday morning class. This works out well since many successful book signings take place later in the week. You can fly out on a Wednesday afternoon (reading your students' homework on the plane), rent a car, drive to several engagements, and then fly back on Sunday night. It's exhausting, but it can be done for a limited time.

Endurance

Are you tough enough to tour? A tour is fun for about two weeks. After that, it becomes a serious undertaking that demands stamina, good humor, and a strong sense of self-esteem. It's often like you're a contestant on *Survivor*, except that you're alone and you can't get voted off the island, even if you want to.

BASIC PLANNING CONSIDERATIONS

It's important to build your tour in such a way that you don't need to be some sort of lonesome road warrior. Try to limit your appearances to cities and towns where you know you have an audience. This doesn't necessarily mean places that you've been before, but places that express interest in having you come out. Cold calling never helps in this situation. Some bookstores will agree to your event just to get you off the phone.

Make sure you check out any request thoroughly; the Internet is great for that. It's always good to know if a bookstore has had events before and who they've had. If they just sponsor local authors, you may have a really difficult time getting an audience.

Enlist Readers as Tour Directors

Post a blog on your Web site and send out an e-mail blast asking readers if they'd like you to come to their town. I know that sounds simple, maybe even simple-minded, but if you're going to spend six months out of a year on the road, you want to go where there will be people who will make an effort to come to see you and get their friends out, too. It takes a lot less stamina to travel when you have readers there who are willing to serve as your hosts.

An added plus is that many times readers will actually contact the bookstore and pitch your work. So, even if the store can't fit you in their schedule, they are aware of you, know you have an audience, and may be more willing to stock your book.

Contact Potential Audience Members

Check your Web site's tracker, like Google Analytics, to see if you have any visitors from the area you'll be traveling to, or nearby. It's really important to make sure you have some readership in the city you're traveling to. Social media tools including Twitter, Facebook, Good Reads, MySpace, and LinkedIn can help define and build your fan base and give you a good idea of where you should be spending your energy. If you're not savvy about social networking, or don't have the time, you can always hire a college student for a few hours a week to coordinate your Internet image. It's worth it. All these tools are quite sophisticated and really help you market your work throughout the country.

Tour Survival Tips

Just before I left for my first tour, Tom Robbins gave me some sage advice. "Don't drink too much, Google every city you're going to and find restaurants where you can get a good meal, and never go anywhere without hand sanitizer."

Here's a list of more tips I've picked up along the way:

1. Never stand when you can sit.

2. Never miss out on an opportunity to go to the bathroom or do your laundry.

3. Resist the urge to stay out late with pals. Nap when you can before the event, or, at the very least, lie down with a cool cloth over your eyes.

4. If you can book your own tour, do it. If you do it right, you can get better deals for your publisher, a more manageable schedule, and begin to build relationships with bookstores.

5. Manage your stock signings. This type of signing is where you just "drop in" (as it's sometimes called) and sign. No event. There usually is not an audience or a set time. Sometimes, bookstores will announce the fact that you're signing stock and let their customers know when you're supposed to stop by, but that's fairly rare. Always ask how many copies each store has. Most tour organizers and publicists have no sense of geography and you really don't want to drive two hours to sign five books.

6. Plan your meals. Know exactly where you are getting dinner and when before you leave for an event. Never miss a meal. Never think you will pick up something somewhere afterwards. Events can run late or just be exhausting, and without a plan, you won't eat. Buy a sandwich before the event and bring it in your bag if you have to. Cookies and fries for dinner will quickly take their toll, even if you eat that way at home. The extra stress of travel can make you sick without balanced meals. Eat your fruits and vegetables. Stay hydrated. You can always go back to your evil ways when you get back home.

7. Don't eat anything you get from anyone (except the bookstore staff). I know that sounds cynical, but most people in the public eye make this a rule. You really want to stay safe.

8. Use the vacation message feature on your e-mail. You'll answer the ones you want to anyway, but you really don't need to put in another day's work after giving a reading. Most requests can wait a day or two.

9. Your escort is neither your date nor your new friend. She is paid to take you around in a safe and efficient manner. There is no need to feed this person or accept the stress of listening to the problems she has with her loved ones/other authors/ boss, unless you want to. If you want to, fine. But it's also okay to be the client and set up boundaries. Be professional and well mannered but don't be afraid to say, "I'm exhausted." She shouldn't take offense at your lack of desire to chat.

10. Be sure to build in time to rest and work. Learn to sleep on planes if you can. Travel by train on the East Coast—you can write on trains, stations are usually in the heart of town (no expensive cab rides to and from the airport), and the lack of security makes it less stressful and easier to pack for.

11. Don't drive. If a hotel offers a shuttle service, stay there. I find these services work great; all you do is call when you're ready to get picked up. It's very stress-free, and the less you have to drive in a strange city, the happier you'll be. While GPS is a great tool, it's not all that accurate, and it gets easily confused in some cities. Better to leave the driving to the locals.

12. Don't get into cars with people you don't know. While it is cheaper to let a volunteer drive you around, it also can be dangerous. Not everyone is a safe, or sober, driver, and often they are too busy talking to you, trying to make you feel welcome, to pay close attention to the road. Most writers, myself included, have many stories about near misses. The Pulitzer Prize-winning journalist David Halberstam was killed when a volunteer went through a red light and was broadsided. You just never know. So, try to stay within walking distance of your event or let a cab or hotel shuttle take you around.

13. Take time to be a tourist. You do need to make an effort to have some fun. Besides, you can learn something about an area that you may be able to use in a story.

14. Try to stay in the same hotel chain, preferably one with breakfast included. The beds are usually the same, so it feels like you're sleeping in your "own" bed and you get a better night's sleep. Most breakfast buffets offer an array of choices including yogurt, fruit, and low-fat milk. Some also offer a "to-go" breakfast bag with fruit, a muffin, granola bars, and water. After I eat breakfast, I always take a breakfast bag, too, so that I know I'll have something to drink and eat when lunch rolls around.

15. Get receipts for everything, even gifts. I usually bring a large envelope marked with the name of the tour city (or cities) and date and then stuff everything inside. You can sort it all out when you get home. Don't forget to get a receipt when you fill the rental car with gas and tolls, too. It all adds up.

AN ALTERNATIVE TO TOURING IN BOOKSTORES

If you feel that you would like to give touring a try but your publisher is unwilling to tour you, or you might not be able to foot the bill yourself without a guaranteed audience, you might explore the idea of house parties. Kelly Corrigan, the first-time author of *The Middle Place* (Voice/Hyperion Books), traveled around the country doing readings in people's homes. She'd lived in many places in America and made many friends, so they donated their houses and some refreshments, and Corrigan spent evening after evening reading from her memoir about her and her father's struggles with cancer. Each party lasted about two hours and books were available for sale.

"For the first twelve days," she said, "my goal was to shake hands with a thousand people. I'm sure I did more than that." With a mention in *O Magazine* and a feature on *The Today Show,* Corrigan's book rose to fifteenth on the *New York Times* nonfiction best-seller list.

There are some drawbacks to this solution. First of all, you have to have a large network of reliable friends. You have to be able to trust that when you show up for the event, they are going to have an audience of at least twenty book buyers there to meet you.

Then there's the issue of stock. You may have to be willing to travel with a trunk filled with books. Depending on your publisher and the amount of money that you're willing to invest, this may not be a realistic expectation. Since authors are usually able to buy their own books from 40 to 50 percent off the cover price, some publishers do not allow authors to resell books. And you certainly are not allowed to return them. Even at half price, the investment in non-returnable stock can be staggering.

But these are problems that you can work around. The "Insatiable Critic" from *New York* magazine Gael Greene promoted her memoir *Insatiable: Tales from a Life of Delicious Excess* (Warner Books) at house parties. Each guest was told to bring a copy of her book. In an effort to make sure that no one was turned away at the door, Greene bought an extra twenty copies at a nearby store.

She sometimes did restaurant signings, too. Similar to house parties, she read while people ate. The evening was ticketed, with the price of the book included.

Besides just relying on friends, there are some other ways to create house parties, or at least events very similar to them. If you are connected to a group like a sorority, alumni association, investment club, or political organization, you may be able to enlist its help in sponsoring an event.

If you offer an event for a non-profit and are able to donate a portion of the sales, you'll not only do a good turn, but you'll also build an audience with people who will always remember your kindness. That's never a bad thing. Sometimes the publisher can provide books under the guidelines of "special sales," which, depending on the publisher, may make these books returnable. They can also find you a bookseller to help with the event. You'll need to check with your publisher's marketing department to see what's possible.

As far as the actual event goes, printed invitations sent through the post office are often nice, but e-mail works, too. It's always good if you can provide your host with a JPEG of your book cover and your pitch paragraph, so they know how to talk about the book. And it's also helpful to remind your host to make the invitation sound like this is a welcoming, fun event and not a retail experience. The phrase, "I love this book, I think you will, too" is certainly better than "my friend is a writer and needs help with sales."

Many writers directly appeal to book clubs and visit the gatherings in person. On Chris Bohjalian's Web site (chrisbohjalian.com), he has a Reading Group Center page that offers everything you need to know to discuss his work, plus the opportunity to have him meet with your book group via phone.

The page also includes a form that the book club leader fills out, which outlines what book they are planning to discuss and provides contact information that is then added to Bohjalian's mailing list. This is a great way to appeal to fans and to keep that mailing list growing so that you can send out notices for your next book when it's ready.

Whatever book party route you take, always keep a list of everyone who came. When your next book comes out, you can send a personal note to them on a postcard. And don't forget to contact the media, just as if it were a regular book signing. You just never know if a reporter might take an interest in this grassroots approach. And then you may find yourself on the front page of the Variety section.

OFFERING WORKSHOPS

Many bookstores, both large and small, are more than willing to consider offering a free workshop for their readers rather than a reading. The general public is still not used to attending readings, while most college-educated people have been to a workshop or two. So, depending on the venue, your crowd can be much larger, and they will be more interested in buying a book if you've offered them a way to meet you in manner that meets their comfort zone.

Your choices of workshop topics are endless. However, you need to consider your audience. While it may be interesting to offer quasi-academic lectures based on topics that are related to your work, such as "The History of Women Mystery Novelists," you might not gather a crowd at a general-topic bookstore unless a chapter of the mystery writer's guild Sisters in Crime meets there.

So, unless you're presenting at a specialized bookstore or university, you may want to consider presenting a generic writer's workshop of some sort. Most people are interested in writers and their lives and often want to try to get something published. You'd be surprised how many people you can get out on a Thursday night with a free "How to Be a Published Writer" workshop.

Bookstores are not the only places to offer your services. Many adult education programs and academic institutions are also looking for someone who is willing to offer instruction. Don't forget clubs and civic groups, too. As far as book sales go, you have a wide variety of options. You can bring your own stock in, call your publisher to arrange for sales, or have the coordinator call a local bookstore.

Countdown to Your Event: Things to Remember

- **Help with publicity.** At least two weeks before, post your event on your Web site and any other Web site that you feel will bring in a crowd. Social networking sites geared towards books, like GoodReads.com and BookTour.com, can often bring in a local audience. If you know anyone who lives near the event, contact them and ask if they can come and bring some friends. Warm bodies in the seats are a very good thing.

- **Do prep work.** About two weeks to ten days before the event, call and check that your book is in stock. Call again about five to seven days before just to make sure that they haven't run out.

- **Check in.** Call the store a day or two before the event to remind them that you're coming and find out of there's anything they might need. For example, if they're having problems getting books, and that sometimes does happen, you need to make some calls to your marketing department or lug a case with you.

- **Don't forget to check the time and location.** You'd be surprised how many times people change these things and forget to tell you. And don't assume your publicist has confirmed, even if you asked him to. Sometimes, that just doesn't happen. Besides, the bookstore would much rather hear from you.

- **Arrive early.** Despite the fact that you're expected fifteen minutes before the event, it's really nice to show up an hour before. An early arrival gives you a chance to get comfortable with the environment, get to know the staff (a very important thing to do if you want them to hand sell), help them craft your introduction, greet people as they arrive, and sign presales.

It's easier on the nerves, too. Nothing's worse than rushing in at the last minute and slamming through a presentation. Plus, having time for a more personal touch gives you a chance to make the event pay off beyond that night's sales numbers.

- **Bring extra books.** Whatever you do, don't forget to take a case of your books with you. Two cases, if you're driving. You never know when you will run out. If you leave books with a seller, have them order a replacement case through their sales rep and then have it shipped to you—this way you get credit on the sale.

MAKING YOUR EVENT WORK FOR YOU

The entire point of touring is to make a good impression and sell your work. Nothing's worse than giving a reading to a full house and realizing that somehow you've made them uncomfortable. Well, there is something worse—reading about it on the Internet the next day. Here are some ways to help your event be a success.

What to Wear

As far as clothes go, try not to be sloppy, but wear what makes you comfortable. You're a writer, not a CEO or model—although some cultures do expect you to look more corporate than others. Sue Grafton once told me that the Germans expect women in business suits. So, if you are going overseas, you should ask your publicist or editor about what would be culturally appropriate.

A reading is a party that celebrates the written word. Show up in a fabulous jacket or embroidered shawl thrown over a simple black travel dress and sensible shoes, in a Hawaiian print shirt, or in a turtleneck and tweed jacket—it doesn't really matter as long as it's clean and you feel comfortable wearing it. Simplicity and comfort are the key, especially since you're going to spend a lot of time on your feet and most of the airlines now charge a good deal for bags.

On the other hand, you can be *too* comfortable. One writer wore a well-used sweat suit to her reading and people kept talking about her outfit during and after the event. You want to have people paying attention to your work and not your clothes.

Keep in mind that whatever you wear, somebody is going to take a picture of you and slap it on the Internet, so you want to think about what you're wearing in terms of being photographed in it. The camera adds ten pounds, and white and bright colors make you look larger.

So keep it simple, especially if you're on the road for a while. If you can't roll it and steam it out in the bathroom, you don't want to take it. You don't want to lug a lot of stuff around with you that needs more care than you do.

Showtime

While there's probably a huge temptation to have a drink before the reading (or four, if you're not used to public speaking), it's best not to. Not so much because one drink will send you into some confused haze, but because you really don't want people to smell alcohol on your breath. That may sound old-fashioned, but you'd be surprised how conservative people around the country can be about alcohol, even if it's served at the reading. Since you're at the reading to sell books, and there's probably a martini awaiting you somewhere on the way back to the hotel, why take a chance that you're going to offend someone?

Your Performance

As soon as you're introduced, always thank people for coming and the bookstore for having you. It's only good manners.

Introduce the book by giving a quick synopsis and read for about fifteen minutes—if you're a good reader. You can start at the first chapter and then pick a snippet later in the text that is self-contained.

Don't pick something out of the center of the book and give a long introduction; you'll lose the audience. After the reading, tell a couple stories and take questions. You're out in about thirty to forty-five minutes.

If you want to read aloud from your book, you should. The key to a good performance is to read in a clear conversational tone without a lot of inflection. Some mistake giving a reading for doing a monologue. They are not the same. As reader, it's your job to deliver the text clearly. Pausing for jokes is a good idea (always wait for the laughter to die down before you continue) but other than that, just read. Don't wink. Don't make it seem jokey or ponderous. Just let the text speak for itself.

If you hate to read or know that you're not very good at it, just choose a short section that doesn't need much set up, two pages max, and read that. Or just tell a few interesting stories about the book and fill the time up with that. Take questions after about twenty minutes (it's always good to wear a watch that you take off and lay on the podium in front of you).

Whatever you do, keep your presentation to about thirty to forty-five minutes and try to be polite no matter what kind of questions are asked. Take everyone seriously. Always tell the truth, or at the very least be charming when you evade the answer.

Unruly Audience Members

No matter what happens, stay calm. Most readings will be fun and there won't be a problem; however, sometimes, the whole thing just takes a strange turn. When I toured with *In the Company of Angels,* all manner of people who believed in angels came out—including one woman who wore tinfoil under her coat and spoke to her own personal angels during the reading. Security escorted her out.

The Q&A can sometimes be the place where people will veer off into odd places. Some will want you to "get them" an agent, and when you tell them you can only give them helpful suggestions as to how to find one, they may get angry. Some may object to your work. Or some are just odd. No matter. Be polite and graciously change the subject. It will be over soon.

When it comes to security issues, most bookstore owners will calm anything that happens while you're in their store. If you're worried about someone in particular, they'll even have staff members walk you to your car, or walk you themselves. Just ask. Some writers I know take a friend with them when they travel on tour; somebody to be your "handler" makes sticky situations easier.

After the Reading

After the reading, you should be signing books. Every book should be opened to the title page, which is usually a page in the front of the book that has the title of your work and your name. When you sign, it's best to use a Sharpie brand fine point permanent marker. It makes for a bold and archival quality signature—some collectors love it. But, if they don't, they'll usually supply you with the pen of their choice.

If you have a crowd waiting for you to sign, take a tip from Starbucks. In larger markets, the coffee chain has a person go through the line to take "pre-orders" in an effort to keep customers committed to go through with the sale. If you have somebody touring with you, they should walk down the line, greet people, make a little small talk, and make sure each book is opened to the title page.

It's also good for this person to carry Post-Its. He can ask each reader if the book is to be autographed and, if so, to whom. Then ask the name to be spelled. (The more you tour, the more you will be amazed at how people spell their names these days. "Mary" can actually be spelled "Marriey.") Once the name is written out on the Post-It, the note is then attached to the title page and the book jacket flap is used as a bookmark to keep the title page accessible.

When you autograph a book, it's good to try to think of a phrase to go along with your signature that has something to do with your book. Lots of writers do this, and it's a nice tradition to uphold. You don't want to be funny or coy, just leave the reader with a good wish as a way to thank them. Daniel Wallace, author of *Big Fish*, sometimes does little quick cartoon drawings of himself.

When you sign your name, it's a good idea to create a signature style that you only use when signing books. Your book signature should never be your legal signature because you really don't want to give the general public an opportunity to learn how to forge your name. It's just not good policy.

Besides, if you have bad handwriting, you're going to want to create a signature that people can actually read. Bookstore owners warn that their customers will often not actually buy a book they had signed if they can't read the signature or inscription. They just stick it in the stacks and walk away. That's why many stores now have the customers pay for the book before you sign it for them, not after. If you make a mistake, such as getting a name wrong or writing something the person doesn't like, they'll often leave it behind, too. So, pay attention and give it the old Palmer Method of penmanship.

When you're done signing for people, and you've signed all the special orders, ask the bookstore owner if you should sign stock, or unsold books.

After the signing is finished it may be time to find that martini, but sometimes you get detained. Maybe one or two people have waited to talk to you about agents or their own book, or maybe they're just lonely. Maybe they liked you and want to buy you dinner or drinks. How you respond depends on you, but sometimes your martini can wait for an hour or two.

A book is a conversation. You begin it. Your reader has a right to want to respond. It's always rude to walk away from a conversation, especially when you started it.

Still, if you don't feel like staying, either because you really are too tired or you feel uneasy about the person, it's fine to leave. When this happens, if you have the energy, it's nice to give them a business card and tell them to send an e-mail. And if they do, you can continue the conversation online. It's a good way to build a loyal readership.

I know your mother told you this when you were growing up, but it still applies—especially when you're in the public eye—don't get into a car with a stranger.

And do not accept manuscripts from anyone—this has to be a firm rule. Thank them for thinking of you, tell them about Web sites where they can workshop it, or agents they can send it to, but do not take it. If you accept an unsolicited manuscript from someone who is not your student, and they later say that you plagiarized their work, you're not going to be able to prove otherwise. It will be their word against yours. As far-fetched as this scenario seems, it happens with such frequency that even film companies warn that they will return any manuscript unopened.

PUBLICITY

Even if you have a publicist, you'll often find that there are times when you need to get press, at the very least you need to get a listing in the events calendar, so it's important to handle the media with the respect that all overworked people deserve. Here are some basics:

1. FIND THE HOOK

You need to find the hook for your book—the one surefire thing that will interest your reader. Most of us, except for James Patterson, don't have experience in marketing or advertising, so it's sometimes difficult. But all of us do have some people skills. We are observers of the human condition, after all. Think of the hook as that opening line of a flirtatious volley: You try to size up what interests the other person and present that part of yourself in an interesting and charming light.

If Mark Haddon's *The Curious Incident of the Dog in the Night-Time* was just about an average fifteen-year-old boy trying to solve a mystery, it would have been just another book. The fact that the protagonist, Christopher Francis Boone, has a rare form of autism and he knows every prime number up to 7,057, but cannot understand human emotions—especially the failure of his parents' marriage—sets this book apart in a most compelling way. It hooks you.

Once you find the hook in your own work, use it to craft your pitch for interviews, e-mails, and public appearances. It should be one of those things you say over and over again because it connects you to the reader, and that's the one thing we really all want to do.

2. CREATE A PITCH

You may think that if you're with a publisher, and maybe even have a publicist working with you, that you will never need to write a pitch for your book. Well, that's not usually true. There may be exceptions, but most editors will ask you to come up with some sort of pitch copy (like for the back cover or catalog). You also may be asked to review and edit the press releases. Someone on the marketing staff will write the final text, but they like you to help shape what they ultimately write because you know your own work better than anyone.

It's a very interesting process to see how they shape what you send in. And, since they are often very good at what they do, they come up with turns of phrase that you can use in your own pitch.

I keep using the word "pitch," and while that is a sales term, it does fit here. Once that book is written, you are its chief salesperson. If you haven't thought about how to talk about your book, you need to. It's good practice to take a moment somewhere during edits and write a pitch for your book.

To begin, think about to whom you're pitching. Not many people these days, and certainly not people in a newsroom, have much time to spare. So you really need to create a pitch that runs about one paragraph with a great opening sentence and a strong summation. That's about all most people have time for.

The opening sentence contains the hook. It's probably the most difficult to write because it demands that you condense the intent of your book into one vivid, and yet accurate, sentence. For example, Tolstoy's *War and Peace* could be described as "A lush Russian epic revolving around the intermingled lives of five aristocratic families swept up in a perfect world destined to be destroyed."

It's not flashy, but it does get to the core of the matter. *War and Peace* is a big book, and if you only have one sentence, you have to choose your pitch wisely. Go with the family-drama angle with a side of suggested romance, because most family dramas sell well, as do romance novels, and everyone has an idea about what books like that are like. It's concrete.

While this is a marketable description of Tolstoy's book, it's also extremely limited. His masterwork is really about ideas: war, peace, love, death, and just about everything else he wanted to ruminate on during the course of 1,296 pages. But you can't say that in an opening sentence and grab the reader's attention because a book of ideas is not exactly a great selling point, although people often love a book based on ideas, or a philosophy. Look at Mitch Albom's *Tuesdays With Morrie*.

Still, with your opening sentence you have to connect with the reader on a basic level to get his attention. Then, once you hook him, you can go on and explain the philosophical subtext if you wish, although it might be better just to let people discover it when they read your book.

Keep in mind that that first sentence doesn't need to be flashy. And, if the book is not funny, you don't want to use a funny or flippant sentence to explain it like "War and peace—that pretty much sums it up." The tone should always be in keeping with the work. It should show why readers would care about this book.

Here's an example of a pitch from HarperCollins for *The Lost Memoirs of Jane Austen* by Syrie James:

> This stunning novel explores a fascinating premise—if Jane Austen's memoirs were discovered, what would they reveal?

That sentence grabs your attention completely. It's a fascinating premise, so you're interested and want to know more, and so will the media. After that opening, the pitch gives us a little more about the premise behind the book:

> Hidden in an old chest in her brother's attic, Jane Austen's memoirs are uncovered after hundreds of years, bricked up behind an old wall. Written shortly before her death, one volume was preserved immaculately, and its contents both shocked and thrilled readers. Detailing a love affair the author was apparently determined to keep secret, Jane's memoir offers readers untold insights into her mind and heart. Many rumors abound about a mysterious gentleman said to be the love of Jane's life—finally, the truth may have been found.

What's interesting about this paragraph is that it speaks about the memoirs as if they are nonfiction. This technique engages you as you read. It makes you feel that the memoirs may actually exist, even though you know they don't. Still, you connect to the idea because this paragraph makes it seem plausible.

At the end of the pitch, the writer should provide a summation of the novel that is designed to seal the deal. Here's HarperCollins':

> Syrie James creates a grand romance for Jane, seamlessly weaving together fact and fiction to present us with a tale of love and heartbreak—a tale from which all of Jane Austen's novels would stem.

The idea that this book is based on facts makes it even more compelling because it does allow for the possibility that something in this book inspired Austen's novels. And so, if you are a fan of Austen, you are surely the market for this book.

Take your own book and give this a try. After you've created the perfect pitch, you can use it to promote your book with everyone—from members of the media to your readers.

3. COMMUNICATE IN A PROFESSIONAL MANNER

Nothing drives a reporter crazier than a gimmick. Yes, it gets their attention, but it can backfire, and often does. For example, if your book is called *The Summer of Vanilla Ice Cream*, don't deliver a press release wrapped around a quart of ice cream to the newsroom of your local paper and expect the editor to chat with you. First of all, most people in the public eye make it a policy not to accept food from private individuals. Secondly, you have no idea if the reporter that you're targeting has food issues, or even likes ice cream. Finally, it's just rude to drop in on someone.

In most cases, a press release is really all you need.

If you feel strongly about sending some sort of funny give-away, keep in mind that reporters' desks are littered with promotional items that they did not ask for and do not want. In some cases, reporters can't accept them, and they're directly donated to Goodwill.

What's even worse, many view promotional tools as a sign that the thing being promoted is not that good. If it was good, the reasoning goes, why do you need a gimmick? While baseball caps and T-shirts may seem like a good idea, for the media it's a distraction and may be destined to be given or thrown away. That said, fans do love stuff and booksellers do, too. So, if you want to do some promotion, think of it more as a gift for your fans and not as a way to help your book get more attention.

And, if you do decide on some food item, keep in mind that food sent to an office as a PR tool—as with Karen Stolz's Hyperion novel *World of Pies* and all the pies they shipped to media and booksellers—is always delivered by a third-party source for later consumption. Your relationship with the press is long term; you really don't want to get it off to a poor start.

4. WHAT MEDIA OUTLETS SHOULD BE PITCHED?

To prepare for your book's launch, you or your publicist will need to send press releases to every general-interest media outlet, including the local newspapers of cities that you will be appearing in. This process takes place about four to six weeks before your event. City magazines are great to send to also, but you'll need to send to these well in advance, about the time you receive your ARCs.

If your publisher isn't doing ARCs, you can send your own excerpts of the book, just a chapter or the highlights of several chapters, with an offer to send the entire manuscript if it's desired. Don't send more than ten pages for the initial contact. And, whatever you do, make sure it's your very best stuff and that it's been completely edited so that there are no glaring errors.

If you've written a novel that is both literary and yet somewhat popular in style, it should also be sent to a cross section of national magazines that still do book reviews such as *People, The Atlantic,* and *Harper's.* Like city magazines, these also have long lead times, about three to four months.

Where to send your pitch is based on research. If you want to send to *The Oxford American,* you'll need to read their other reviews to understand what they like and visit their Web site to get a good feel for the publication. If your story is set on the Mississippi Delta, they may be willing to take a look—especially if you are from that area, or grew up on the same side of the Mason-Dixon line.

When you've done your research, and feel a magazine is a good fit, customize your pitch to their specific audience, which in the case of *Oxford* are Southerners and those interested in the South.

When you send your pitch, either by e-mail or snail mail (faxes are easily lost in a newsroom), make sure you send it to the right person. Web sites usually list who gets what and how they would like queries sent; some places only accept e-mails these days. If the media outlet doesn't have a Web site, call the publication and ask if they have a book editor. If they don't, or if you can't tell, the features editor would be a good choice.

If your novel has a specific focus, like wine, you may also want to send a pitch and an ARC to the wine columnist. Even if he can't review it, he may serve as an advocate for you.

A caution about television pitches—you need to make sure that you have the right kind of hook for their audience and don't be afraid. While many daytime news programs do feature books, television is a difficult medium for the writer who has no background in it. It's stressful, very visual, and extremely condensed. You'll have about three to five minutes to establish who you are, why people should like you, what your book is about, and why they should buy it. And, you should look good doing it. No fop sweating. So, just relax, be yourself, and stay focused. It will be over before you know it. And if it doesn't go as well and you thought it should, don't get discouraged. Television takes practice. The more television you do, the less foreign it seems, and the better you get.

5. CURRENT-EVENT PITCHES

If your novel is about a string of clerical killings in Miami, and the Boston Archdiocese is experiencing a similar tragedy, the gruesome fact is that some media outlet will probably want to talk to you about your book. The media is always looking for tie-ins to stories or trends.

You have to be very careful how you behave in a situation like this. You never want to seem as if you're capitalizing on a horrible situation, because you're not. Or, at least, you shouldn't be.

The media wants to speak to you to see if you can shed any light on a puzzling situation, or give some sense of hope. When dealing with tie-ins to tragedy, like the ancient storytellers before you, you may be asked to provide comfort and wisdom—and that's the way you should look at it.

Trend tie-ins are less fraught with professional dangers. Lisa Daily is a professional dating expert who has a syndicated daytime show that appears in many markets across the country. She's also written a novel, *Fifteen Minutes of Shame,* about a dating expert who gets dumped by her husband on national television. Of course, she's written the perfect tie-in novel for herself, and every market she was syndicated in wanted to have her on.

The first time I met Lisa was in the Cincinnati Airport. She was returning home from a several-month tour with a gigantic replica of her book cover strapped onto her rolling carry-on. It was, essentially, a billboard that she could fold up and place in the overhead compartment. Everywhere in America, people stopped and chatted with her, and those conversations helped sell books and promote her show.

If it's possible, given what you've written, you should waste no opportunity to create a tie-in to your own profession, a cultural trend, or the world at large. And, if you can rig a rolling billboard, that's always good, too.

6. PRESS CLIPS

The media often likes to see how others view your work, so always send articles that have been written about you or links to interviews. Producers especially want to know how you come off on camera or radio, so give them a list of shows you've appeared on and offer to supply tapes. Or post clippings of the shows on your Web site.

If you haven't done much media and don't have any samples, consider some of the bloggers who do literary-based podcasts. If you like their work, pitch your book. Many run wonderful Web sites and understand how to do a great interview. Plus, they're always looking for subjects. When the interview is over, you'll have a product to send to producers who need a little encouragement.

Getting media, like building an audience, is done step by step. You build a grassroots foundation with bloggers and community newspaper people and then use the materials they generate to approach larger and larger organizations.

7. NEVER DELAY

Time is always tight, so when any media organization asks you for something, make sure you send it out right away via e-mail, overnight delivery, or courier service, if in town. If they don't get your materials, they might not do your story.

If you're working with a publicist from your publishing house and you suspect that they won't have time to respond, you may be able to get their FedEx number and mail things out yourself.

8. THE INTERVIEW ITSELF

Once you land that interview, it's important to be professional. The media loves to work with somebody who has her act together because it makes their job so much easier. And when the media loves you, it shows. You relax. They relax and the interview goes well.

If you're on television or radio, know how long you're going to have and prepare accordingly. Find a passage from your book that is visceral, but not too graphic, and short. About a page will be more than enough.

If you have a print interview, it's good to send a confirmation e-mail with a headshot, press release, bio, and résumé. Things get lost easily in a newsroom, so redundancy is never a bad idea. During the interview, restate your pitch and focus on two or three key selling points in your book. Don't go off-topic, and don't think *anything* is off the record.

Be as charming as you can naturally be, or, at the very least, be agreeable. If you've had a difficult time getting to the interview or had a fight with a loved one, leave it in the rental car. Don't talk about it unless you can make it a riotously funny story that has something to do with your book. Everything you say and do should be about the book. If you're on television, say the title as much as you can. Hold a copy of it in your lap so that the audience can see the book jacket when the camera takes longer shots. Wear a jacket so that they can easily place the microphone on you and the wires can be hidden (Plus, it's cold in the studio if you're not under the lights.) Don't forget to turn off your cell phone, and don't chew gum.

And, if in the course of any kind of interview the reporter makes a mistake, correct it as soon and as graciously as possible.

Humor always helps, but not everyone is funny. So, just be polite and gracious. If you're a professional interviewee, someone will notice and be more than willing to have you come back next time around.

If you're having a certifiably bad interview, it's important to remember that most reporters aren't trying to make you look bad, they just want to get at the "truth of the matter." Unfortunately, that sometimes means that they will bring up bad reviews. So, when going into any interview situation, you should know what the critics object to in your work and try to understand if it's brought up. Just go with it. Don't get defensive. Don't say "everybody's entitled to their own opinion"—people know that and it just makes you seem childish. You can say, "I don't agree, and my mother doesn't agree either." Or anything else that makes people laugh or distracts them. You just want to try to guide the conversation back to a less uncomfortable place.

Some interviewers, however, want to make things controversial. They want you to be uncomfortable. It's not so much about you per se, it's more about pumping up ratings. Controversy usually sells books, but it's also stressful for the person in the center of the maelstrom.

It's easy to avoid the situation, however. Since the writing community is very small, you usually will know who these media people are. Ask around if you have to. It's always good to know what you're up against, so you have the chance to decide if you really want to be in that position.

Call-in shows are the strangest of all animals. You can get great listener questions, but sometimes an old flame calls just to make you crazy—which makes for great radio for the show and a huge mortification for you.

Given all this, you should *still* do radio whenever anyone asks.

New York City talk show host Long John Nebel often began his interviews with indignant statements such as, "How could you write what you wrote? That's scandalous."

He would then use the word "scandalous" a few times, and even provide a page number where the most offending passages could be found. Pretty soon hundreds of books were sold because everybody wanted to read something scandalous.

There really *is* no such thing as bad press.

9. THE FOLLOW-UP

Never forget to thank your interviewer. Send an old-fashioned snail mail thank you or an e-mail. The choice is yours. While you're there, if you have an extra copy of the book, it's always nice to sign one over to them. Or just sign it so that they can give it as a gift.

If you're doing electronic media, always ask if it's podcast, or if there's a link to the broadcast which you can link on your Web site. All media love cross-promotion.

Try to keep in touch. Writers are always working on the next thing. As soon as you get a publication date, it's always good to try to reconnect with a friendly note.

10. DON'T BE A PEST

Everyone says that persistence is an admirable trait, but there's a fine line between giving it one more try and stalking a reporter. If they say "no," take that for their answer. You're trying to build a relationship with the media, so you have to respect their desires. Send a "thank you, maybe next time" note to people you feel will be important to you.

And, if a reporter covers your book and hates it, don't argue with it. Bad reviews are part of the territory. Sure, you could humiliate them for writing about your protagonist as a man when it was a woman, but that never gets you anywhere. At least you had ink, which is more than a lot of writers can say.

Remember, as long as you get your name out there, you can sell books. *Kirkus Reviews* is famed for giving rather unforgiving reviews, but that never stops publicists from being overjoyed if they can piece one nearly praiseful sentence together. So be a good sport about whatever happens in the media.

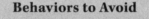

Behaviors to Avoid

- **Don't cold call the media: They hate that.** Just send your press release and they will call you if they are interested. If you find that you do need to call, drop them an e-mail and ask when would be a good time for "a quick question," and keep it quick.

- **Don't call and ask if they received your information.** Unless you have a relationship with the person already, that's usually very annoying. If they did request a reader's copy and you want to make sure that they actually got it, it's fine to send an e-mail, but don't pick up the phone.

- **Don't repackage your pitch over and over again with hopes of wearing the media down.** If they didn't like it the first time, they are not going to like it the fourth time and will probably hate you a little, too.

- **Don't flirt.** It sends mixed messages and you don't want to do that. Remember, this is a long-term relationship. Like any good friendship, it should be based on mutual respect.

11. CREATE PROFESSIONAL
PROMOTIONAL MATERIALS

If you have to write your own press release, remember that the best are short, pithy, and fun. One page will do. Bullets and boldface do help, but use them sparingly. Begin with the title of your book, the publisher, date of release, and price. Add your pitch. Then give a paragraph about yourself. Slap in a photo and a copy of your cover. Mail it. It's about that easy.

Make sure your résumé is up to date, as well as your Web site. Web sites are the number one way people learn about you, so it's always good to include the address on your business cards, press releases, and any place you have contact with the public, such as your e-mail. Of course, that means you have to update your site and make sure it's working. Nothing is more frustrating to a reporter than to click on a link that doesn't work or to be given out-of-date information. If you really don't want to work on your site, enlist your teenager or hire a local college student for a few hours a week.

12. LYING

Don't even think about it. And, don't ever entertain the idea of stretching the truth. Or hyping it. The world is very small these days, and information is at most people's fingertips. Look at how many memoirists have been exposed as liars, and how it's hurt their careers. So, even though the temptation is great, honesty will get you further with the media in the long run.

SELF-PUBLISHING

Here's a fact that people often forget—*A Christmas Carol* was self-published. In 1843, Charles Dickens was a famous novelist who had fallen from grace. His audience had abandoned him and the critics had turned on him. Debt-ridden and looking at the end of his career, he didn't panic. Instead he sat down and wrote a small book about what was considered by the Puritan-influenced society to be an unfavorable holiday. It took him six weeks. His publisher rejected it, but Dickens believed in it. And so he scraped together all the money he could to print *A Christmas Carol*, and it was a huge success.

Publishers aren't always right.

But you can see their viewpoint. Books need to make money—that's just an annoying fact of life. Dickens was not selling at all. And he'd chosen to write about Christmas, which was a holiday that no one really celebrated at the time. This book had no obvious market, and, even in 1843, for a publisher to take a risk on a manuscript, it must have an obvious audience.

When an editor goes to buy a book, he must be able to read a manuscript and say three things: "I love it. I want it. This is perfect for the thirty-five to fifty-five female market (or whatever market it's perfect for)." And then the amount of the advance will be based on how many books he thinks they can sell.

But, if editors read your manuscript and can only say, "I love it and I want it," but they know that the book will be difficult to sell to a larger market, you may have to be like Charles Dickens and consider self-publishing. So, how do you know if it's a route that's right for you?

> **1. Your book has a small audience.** For example, if you're written a young adult novel whose target market is adopted Korean teens, you may want to publish the book on your own.

There just won't be that large of an audience nationwide; however there certainly is a market. Area histories and community cookbooks are also of limited interest to larger publishers but are valuable texts that should be printed and often do very well on a local level.

2. **You know your audience, and you know it's large, but you can't convince a publisher that it's out there.** Certain books are just too difficult for traditional publishing houses to market—they defy description. And so publishers pass on them. *The Celestine Prophecy,* a landmark New Age book, was turned down by every publisher James Redfield shopped it to. Luckily, he had the passion to market it himself, and eventually it became an international cottage industry with millions of copies sold worldwide and was translated into thirty-four languages.

3. **You see self-publishing as a stepping-stone to a traditional career.** Mystery novelists Steven Thayer (Viking) and M.J. Rose (Ballantine Books), along with fantasy author Sherrilyn Kenyon (St. Martin's Paperbacks), all went from being self-published to getting picked up by major presses. The only way a writer can really make this transition is if he can clearly demonstrate that there *is* a large audience for what he is doing, and then find a publishing executive willing to listen.

4. **You want to be a published author just for the fun of it.** You love to write and aren't really trying to make money at it. A self-published writer once told me she didn't want to make any money, saying, "It's a good way to meet people." There really are some people who just like being an author, and don't care to make a living at it. Or, don't need to. They love to talk about books, and they are having a great time doing that.

If you find that you fit into one of these categories, and you want to self-publish, you need to keep in mind that this is not an undertaking that can be entered into lightly. Printing, distributing, and marketing a book is an expensive and stressful process. In order to be happy with this choice, you really must understand why your book is not being published commercially and identify a specific market for it—even if it's a small market. And, you have to understand that it's been a long time since 1843.

These days there's a stigma on self-published books. It's easing up a bit, but in many circles, the sentiment is still rabid. Some traditionally published authors, book festivals, larger booksellers, and even readers will not deal with self-published authors at all. "That's not self-publishing, that's self-*printing*," they say. And, unfortunately, even if self-published authors get picked up by major presses, some people still won't allow that their books may be good.

Self-publishing is a difficult road for a writer. You can't do it solely because you think it will be a quick and easy way to get your work out into the hands of readers. Unfortunately, some of the self-published people who are not very happy with their choice were too impatient to follow the traditional routes and are now disappointed that sales are not going as well as they thought they would.

I certainly understand the need to want to see quicker results. In an optimal situation, with traditional publishing it's about two to three years from writing the first page to promoting the book in the stores. When you self-publish, you can have that down to six months or a year—but then the real work begins.

And it *is* real work.

If you market your own book, it's a difficult task. Most authors don't have the same resources, experience, or savvy to market the way a publisher can. And they certainly don't have the same access. A book reviewer once told me that she wouldn't review any self-published books.

"They don't even edit these things, and they expect me to read them?" she said. "I don't care if I miss the next great unsung writer. I just don't have time to wade through all this stuff."

So that's what you're up against. Still, if you like people, like marketing, and have no expectations of getting rich overnight—doing it yourself is an adventure, and with the right attitude, selling your book can be great fun.

Once it's in print, you can take it to book fairs, reading festivals, farmer's markets, community events, flea markets—anywhere you think the audience for your work is. Many bookstores, including Borders and Barnes & Noble, also have days where they invite non-traditionally published authors to come in and sign. It takes a lot of time to make these opportunities happen, but you can do it. And you can enjoy it.

Just keep in mind that attitude is everything. There's no need to be ashamed to be self-published. If you have a book you believe in, then you should be proud of it. I won't deny that there is a prejudice, but if you're professional about your work, you can overcome it.

TIPS FOR SELF-PUBLISHING

If you decide to publish your own book, you'll want to approach the process with an open mind, but not an open pocketbook. Here are some tips to help make your decision a successful one.

- First, and foremost, make sure your book is edited. Even though most books have typos, you have to hold yourself to a higher standard to keep your readership.

- There are many options for publishing your work. Explore all venues, including e-books. You want to find the right format to get your work to your audience in an efficient, appropriate, and inexpensive manner.

- Some subsidy presses charge writers a fee to edit, design, and print their work—and then retain the rights to that work. That sort of situation should be avoided. When a writer pays to have a book published, she should retain the rights to the book.

- Always check out the publisher. If there is a lack of information on the Web site, including no telephone number, or if the listed number provides only a recorded message, be very careful about proceeding.

- If the publisher makes promises that seem too good to be true, they are. Run.

- If the publisher tells you how easy the marketing process is, again, run.

- If the publisher promises you national media, including television and radio, laugh. Then run.

Don't worry. There really are good publishers out there for you to work with. You can find them through ads in magazines or meet them at book fairs. Don't get impatient. Just remind yourself that your work deserves an opportunity to be read, and if you work hard enough, you can bring the readers to you.

LITERARY ESTATE PLANNING

No one ever likes to think about a will, but writers need to figure out who has say over their work after they're gone. You never know when something you write will suddenly become a "hot property." F. Scott Fitzgerald was long dead when Brad Pitt and Cate Blanchett appeared in the film adaptation of his short story "The Curious Case of Benjamin Button."

If that happens to you, you need to think about who will be able to strike the right deal for your family. Your agent, if he's still alive? A fellow writer? What happens if your last manuscript is accepted after your death and your estate hasn't gone through probate? And what if everyone in your family has passed? Who would you like to see make decisions for your work, or benefit from a rediscovery of it?

All these things need to be sorted out. Too many writers leave their families trying to figure out whom the best publisher for their final work is or how to respond to inquiries from the film industry. It's very stressful for people who don't know anything about the business and have no idea what your literary last wishes would be.

Since intellectual property is such a specialized field, and many family lawyers have no idea how to deal with that element of an estate, Minneapolis attorney Ferdinand Peters, who deals with intellectual properties, researched the issue and has come up with a solution that he feels will work for writers. The following is not legal advice, but should be seen as a possible framework that you and your attorney can consider. He writes:

> Although it is quite helpful to authors/writers/creative people who have literary assets to create a simple will that includes them, it just puts these wonderful people down a potentially dangerous path. Don't get me wrong on this—I think that when it comes to "no will" or "a will," I would almost always

pick the latter. But a will that is weak or super-generic just might produce a mistaken feeling of confidence in a person who executes it, since it most likely could be found to be not enforceable under almost any law anywhere.

Here is what I propose—why wait for a will to kick in when you can avoid having a judge scrutinizing a potentially flawed/unenforceable holographic will, when you can right now, no waiting required, execute a revocable trust naming yourself as trustee during your lifetime, with successor trustees named, etc., etc.—this is also called a "living trust." If you execute such a trust, and put all your property into it, except possibly, joint tenancy/joint account assets, then you don't have to go to probate when you die to have your will figured out.

Here's an example of what a living trust agreement looks like.

REVOCABLE LIVING TRUST AGREEMENT FOR AN INDIVIDUAL

[Note: This creates a trust for the lifetime use of (e.g., a single person) as Grantor with both the Grantor and a Third Party as Co-Trustees. Upon the death of the individual, property in the trust goes to any person specified in the trust.]

REVOCABLE LIVING TRUST AGREEMENT

This Revocable Living Trust Agreement is made this (day) day of (month), (year), between (name), of (address), City of (city), State of (state), herein referred to as Grantor, and (name), of (address), City of (city), State of (state), herein referred to as co-trustees.

Whereas, grantor is now the owner of the property described in Exhibit A attached hereto and made a part hereof, and Whereas, grantor desires to make provision for the care and management of such property, and the collection of the income there from, and the disposition of both such income and such property in the manner herein provided:

Now, therefore, for the reasons set forth above, and in consideration of the mutual covenants set forth herein, grantor and trustees agree as follows: 1. Transfer of Property: Grantor, in consideration of the acceptance by trustee of the trust herein created, hereby conveys, transfers, assigns, and delivers to trustees, their successors in trust and assigns, the property described in Exhibit A attached hereto and made a part hereof, by this reference, which property, together with all other property that may from time to time be held by trustees hereunder, is herein referred to as Trust Estate. Grantor, and any other persons shall have the right at any time to add property acceptable to trustees to this trust and such property, when received and accepted by trustees, shall become part of the trust estate. 2. Disposition of Income and Principal: Trustees shall care for and manage the trust estate and collect the income derived therefrom, and, after the payment of all taxes and assessments thereon and all charges incident to the management thereof, dispose of the net income therefrom and corpus thereof, as follows: During the lifetime of grantor the trustees may pay income of the trust estate and such portions of the principal as the grantor from time to time may direct to the grantor, or otherwise as he/she directs during his/her life. After the death of the grantor the successor trustee shall distribute the trust estate to the following beneficiary or beneficiaries who shall survive me: (names and addresses)

_____

_____

_____

The share of any beneficiary who shall be under the age of (age) years shall not be paid to such beneficiary but shall instead be held in trust to apply to his/her use all the income thereof, and also such amounts of the principal, even to the extent of all, as the trustee deems necessary or suitable for the support, welfare, and education of such beneficiary; and when he/she attains the age of (age) years, to pay him/her the remaining principal, if any. If any beneficiary for whom a share is held in trust should die before having received all the principal thereof, then upon his/her death the remaining principal shall be paid to his/her then living child or children, equally if more than one, and in default thereof, to the then living descendants of the grantor. Notwithstanding anything herein to the contrary, the trusts hereunder shall terminate not later than twenty-one (21) years after the death of the last beneficiary name herein. 3. Revocation and Amendment: The grantor may, by signed instrument delivered to the trustee, revoke the trusts hereunder, in whole or in part, or amend this Agreement from time to time in any manner. 4. Successor Trustees: In the event of the death or incapacity of both trustees, I hereby nominate and appoint as successor trustee (name) and (address). In the event the successor trustee does not serve, I appoint whomever shall at the time be the first designated beneficiary hereunder. The trustees and their successors shall serve without bond. 5. Trustees' Acceptance: This trust has been accepted by trustees and will be administered in the State of (state) and its validity, construction, and all rights thereunder shall be governed by the laws of that state. In Witness Whereof, grantors and trustees have executed this Agreement on the date above written. _____ Grantor

Co-Trustee _____ Witness 1

Co-Trustee _____ Witness 1

Witness 2 Sworn to and subscribed before me this (day) day of (month), (year). My commission expires: _____

Notary Public _____ Date Exhibit A (Separate Page) (Listing of property included in this agreement)

All of the intellectual property rights of Trustor/Settlor currently in existence and hereinafter created, including but not limited to, all copyrights, trademarks, and literary works.

APPENDIX A:
The Jargon: Words and Phrases You Need to Know

Like every industry, publishing is filled with jargon, and everybody expects you to know it. It's maddening. I've compiled a list of the most frequently used words and phrases to help you navigate corporate-speak. Keep in mind that this list does not contain legal advice: It just defines the terminology so that you can understand your agent, lawyer, or editor a little better.

Advance: The "advance against sales," this money is supposed to tide you over until the royalty checks start arriving. It can be given out in thirds, with a third upon signing, a third upon the timely completion of the work, and a third upon publication. It can also be divided into halves with the first half paid upon signing and the final half paid upon completion. Sometimes, if the book is complete, a house may opt to pay upon acceptance.

Advance reading copy (ARC): See *Bound galley*.

All rights: If you grant all rights to a publisher, it is free to reprint your material or to sell it elsewhere without paying any additional money to you. All rights means just that—you've granted away all your rights, including film, anthology, and electronic. It's never a good idea.

Auction: When your book is offered to several publishers at once and all are interested in buying it. In most auctions the, highest bidder usually wins. However, in a book auction authors often get a chance to speak with their potential editor(s) before the deal is done. If they aren't comfortable with the sale to that person, they can opt to go with another.

Author's alterations (or AAs): Changes made at the page-proof stage that are not corrections from the copyedited manuscript (printer's errors, or PEs), which the author can be charged for.

Author questionnaire: A very long and very important document for the marketing of your book. You'll be asked to provide a list of media contacts, personal contacts (people who could blurb your book), and your suggestions as to what the selling points of your book are. You need to take as much time completing this document as possible because the more information you give your publisher, the better job they can do to promote your work.

Big-box: A chain store that looks like a big box and is generally more than 50,000 square feet. Along with groceries and televisions, they usually offer books at a reduced price and do a large amount of volume. Prime examples are Costco, Wal-Mart, BJ's, and Sam's Club. A big-box is often called a supercenter, superstore, or megacenter.

BISAC subject codes: BISAC (Book Industry Standards and Communications) has a series of standard categories that are used to categorize books.

Bleed: An image that is intended to extend beyond the trim marks of a page. When an image is to be extended to the edge of the page, it should be about 1/8" of the edge so that when the pages are trimmed any small variations in the trim will not be noticeable.

Blurbs: Quotes given about your work by other authors. Blurbs are used to help readers understand your work through the eyes of their favorite writers. It's the writer's job to find someone whose audience is similar to his own to provide a blurb. A blurb usually comes from writers who are friends, teachers, or colleagues that you work with, meet at events and have become friendly with, or share an agent or editor with. Most writers will not blurb books for people they have not met unless asked by their agent or a mutual friend. Books usually have three blurbs.

BookScan: This service by The Nielsen Company (a provider of audience measurement services, such as television ratings) claims to be able to track the number of books sold in America. They say they can "capture" through scanning about 70 percent of hardcover sales. In theory if you've sold 10,000 books according to BookScan, then you've actually sold about 30 percent more than that number. That's why some authors will buy a single use/single title pass to check their sales—but that's not really such a good idea. BookScan does not report books from small publishers, self-published books, or books sold at independent booksellers. Their numbers are only culled from chains like Barnes & Noble, Amazon.com, and big-box stores like Costco, but not Wal-Mart. If you really feel you need to know how your book is doing, you should have your agent call your editor.

Bound galley: Otherwise known as an advance reading copy, or ARC, galleys are your uncorrected page proofs bound together so that they can be sent to reviewers, booksellers, and media outlets. An ARC can give you good insight into how much money your publisher is planning to spend on your campaign. If your ARC looks a lot like a paperback, with a full color cover, it says your publisher is expecting the book to do well. If it's bound with a plain cover, then the expectations are modest. Since these are your uncorrected proofs, there will be mistakes in them. Everyone knows that; ARCs are sent out just to give everyone a general idea about the book. Most reviewers know to check text against the published version, but still mistakes are made—you can't let them get to you.

CMYK (Cyan, Magenta, Yellow, and Black): The four colors used to create full-color prints. When combined they allow you to create the entire color spectrum.

Commercial house: A for-profit publisher.

Copyeditor: Your editor and agent may not be able to read your entire book before it's published, or even afterwards—that's where the copyeditor comes in. It's the copyeditor's job to not only read and edit your grammar, but also to fact check and iron out some of the logic and form issues. Many copyeditors are freelancers and not on staff. If you have any question about the edit, you have to go though your editor, or her assistant, to approach the copyeditor.

Copyright: Holding a copyright for a work means that you own it and have the ability to grant publication rights, or the right to copy, to a publishing entity. This includes hardcover, paperback, audio, and possibly translation. What you grant to your publisher varies, as some agents like to hold back translation and audio rights to sell on their own, but everything will be defined in the contract.

For more about the law and your rights, visit the Web site for the U.S. Copyright Office (copyright.gov). You may also look for information from the Authors Guild, the National Writers Union, or a local chapter of Volunteer Lawyers for the Arts.

Course adoption: A book, although not a textbook, that is a required text in a college course.

Creative Commons: A Web-based service that provides free tools that allow authors to mark their creative work with the reuse restrictions that they see fit. You can use this service to change your copyright terms from "All Rights Reserved" to "Some Rights Reserved," and be quite specific as to what types of rights the user can have.

Dingbat: Ornamental elements that define a break in the text.

DPI (Dots per Inch): The measure of image resolution; the higher the number, the sharper the image. You need at least a 300 DPI for any photo to be published properly.

Drop-in (or drop-by): Also known as a "stock signing." When you drive to a bookstore on a pre-arranged day just to sign stock. There is no event. The signed books will then be labeled and placed on the shelves for sale.

Electronic rights: The right to allow others to publish electronic versions of your work, like e-books. The Authors Guild argues that writers should be compensated for the electronic reproduction of their work, just as they are compensated for print reproduction.

Exclusive rights: The exclusive right to publish your work (like a story) for a set period of time (like a year) without it appearing elsewhere (like an anthology or another magazine).

First North American serial rights: The right to be the first publisher of your work one time in North America. You still have the right to sell first serial rights to the same work in places other than North America, such as First British Rights or First Australian Rights, unless you sold All Rights.

First rights: The right to be first to publish your work. You can only sell first rights once.

Foreword: Introductory matter not written by the author.

Foul matter: Material no longer necessary for the publisher to keep on file, such as the copyedited manuscript and the first pass pages.

French flaps: Extensions of the cover of a paperback that fold back inside the book and hold extra copy. They look like the book jacket on a hardcover.

Frontlist: The season's new books.

Front matter: Everything before the first chapter: the half-title page (a page that includes only the title of the book), the title page (title, author's name, etc.; this is where you sign when you do readings), copyright page, dedication, foreword, preface, and table of contents.

Full-color: When you print using Cyan, Magenta, Yellow and Black, also known as CMYK, to achieve all colors in the spectrum.

Grayscale: Any photo or image made up of varying tones of black and white. They will be converted to grayscale when added to your page.

Gutter: The white space that separates the type on facing pages of a book.

Headbands: Ribbons found at the top and bottom of hardcover books designed to be used as bookmarks.

Hook: The angle or element of your book that will interest the reader.

Image resolution: The detail of a photo based on the amount of pixels in its image. When people talk about the resolution of a photo, let's say your author's photo, they'll either refer to the number of pixels per square inch (ppi) or the number of dots per square inch (dpi). The terms are basically interchangeable.

Imprint: A publishing division with its own list of titles within a major publishing house. The list often mirrors those found in smaller presses; they are usually more niche, literary, or esoteric than commercial. Most imprints have their own staffs.

Internet rights: The right to publish your work on the Internet—and that's all. Any anthology or CD culled from this publication must be negotiated.

Jobber: A giant book wholesaler.

LTD: Life to date. Sales numbers of your book from the moment it hit the shelves until now.

Marketing department: Responsible for ads buys and the "packaging" of you and your book. They work closely with the sales department. If you have any sales questions, such as numbers or concerns about books not being at events, your agent (or you) will speak to a representative from marketing, although she may go through your editor first, as a matter of courtesy.

Mass-market books: Paperbacks printed to be sold in drugstores, big-box stores, airports, and supermarkets. They're less expensive than trade paperbacks.

Monograph: A book, usually scholarly, on a single subject or limited aspect of a subject. Many dissertations have been reworked and sold as monographs.

Option clause: The publisher's right of first refusal on an author's next book. If the publisher passes, you can take it somewhere else. Some contracts allow the publisher to match the new offer, if they wish.

Orphan: The first line of a paragraph left sitting by itself at the bottom of a page.

Out of print: When the publisher decides to no longer print your book. Many small presses will not declare books out of print but let them go out of stock, which means the same thing if they don't reprint.

Perfect bound: When pages are glued to the spine; the binding for paperbacks.

Permissions: Any piece of proprietary work (including lyrics, poetry, artwork, and text) that needs the owner to allow for reprint. Under Fair Use law, you are able to quote a work without requesting the author's permission. However, U.S. copyright law doesn't set forth specific word lengths under its rule of fair use. The standard industry guideline is about 100 words from a short work (short story, essay, article), and 300 words from a book-length work. With poems and song lyrics, only a line or two can be quoted before permission is required.

PMS: Pantone Matching System. A color system used by all designers, in addition to marketing and PR people, to chose the colors they need for all printed matters, including your book jacket.

Pre-emptive offer: A publisher's bid that keeps a project from going to auction.

Proofreading symbols and abbreviations: These are a series of marks that will grace your manuscript, telling you what changes need to be made. You'll be expected to know these and to respond to inquiries using them. The most frequently used are:

Symbols:

$\overset{\wedge}{,}$	insert a comma
$\overset{,}{\vee}$	apostrophe or single quotation mark
$\wedge$	insert something
$\overset{\text{``}}{\vee}\ \overset{\text{''}}{\vee}$	use double quotation marks
$\odot$	use a period here
⸺ᱝ⸺	delete
$\sim$	transpose elements
$\overset{\frown}{\smile}$	close up this space
$\overset{\#}{\wedge}$	space needed here
¶	begin new paragraph
No¶	no paragraph

Abbreviations (these are usually found in the margin with an arrow pointing to the issue in question):

Ab	faulty abbreviation
Agr	subject/verb or pronoun/antecedent
Awk	awkward expression or construction
Cap	faulty capitalization
CS	comma splice
DICT	faulty diction
Dgl	dangling construction
- ed	problem with final -ed
Frag	fragment
||	problem in parallel form
P/A	pronoun/antecedent agreement
Pron	problem with pronoun
Rep	unnecessary repetition
R-O	run-on sentence

Sp	spelling error
- s	problem with final -s
STET	let it stand or "Go back to my original wording" (used if a proposed edit is inaccurate)
S/V	subject/verb agreement
T	verb tense problem
Wdy	wordy
WW	wrong word

Provisional contract: A contract based on a proposal that contracts the author to the publisher but doesn't commit them to the author.

Publicist: This is the person assigned to help you respond to appearance requests (booking the date, hotel, and travel if you want them to) and setting up interviews.

Publication date: Also known as the "pub date," when your books should all be shipped from the warehouse and arrive in the stores. Your book will be available to the media for review about six to eight weeks before this time, but the book will be embargoed (not sold) until this date.

Published well: The publisher has promoted you in every way possible from having sent review copies, placed ads, and worked hard to sell the book into stores. The result should be a bestseller.

Pulp: If your book has not sold a certain amount, it will be "pulped" or shredded.

Public domain: If a work is in the public domain, it can be used in total without getting the author's permission. There are two ways to know if it's available. If it was created before 1978, it will come into public domain twenty-eight years after it was first published, unless the copyright was renewed, in which case it will then be available seventy-five years after it was first published. For works created in 1978 or after, the copyright is in force for the life of the author plus fifty years.

Reading line: A descriptive subtitle that isn't an official subtitle, but does appear on the book jacket.

Remainder: Books that remain after too large a print run. The ones that are not shredded are sold at a large discount.

RGB (Red, Green, Blue): These three colors represent the entire color spectrum. Digital images that you scan or that you take with a digital camera will be in RGB color mode and need to be converted to CMYK when you go to print.

Sales department: These are the people you will never speak to, but they're your cheerleaders. Your editor will pitch them your work, and if your book engages them, they will really work on selling it to booksellers. They love books and want you to succeed. However, they are very busy and really don't have the time, or energy, to engage with every author on a personal level. An unwritten rule is that the writer is never to talk to the sales force unless a representative from the sales team calls the writer.

Sample chapter: When your agent presents a book proposal, a sample chapter is part of the submission. It should provide a sense of the entire work and be highly polished.

Short discount: While most commercial books are discounted 40 to 50 percent, scholarly books come with a "short" discount (more like 20 percent), so a bookseller has less incentive to sell them. There's not a lot of profit in these books and so general bookstores often don't carry them.

Signatures: When printing hardcover books, pages are bundled together in groups of thirty-two that are folded and sewn into the binding. These are known as signatures.

Slush pile: The pile where unagented manuscripts are placed to read by editorial assistants. The editors themselves usually read agented manuscripts first.

Stock: Books that sit on the shelves waiting to be sold. Often, when you do a reading, you'll sign stock for the bookstore. Signed books sell better than unsigned copies.

Style sheet: A list that's sent along with the copyedited manuscript, which includes words and phrases that have been changed for consistency. For example, if your editor changed the word "dumpster" to "Dumpster."

Subsidiary rights: The right of a publisher to use your work in a format other than its own hardcover or paperback editions including film, foreign, audio, and electronic rights. This can also include book-club reprint editions, anthologies, or textbooks, and first or second serial rights.

Track: The sales record of an author's previous books. This is how they decide what books to order.

Trade: As in the "bookselling trade." Trade books go into all bookstores; textbooks and academic (short discount) books do not.

Trim size: The size of your final book after it is printed, bound, and trimmed. A trim size of 6"x9" means the printed book will be 6 inches wide and 9 inches tall.

Vanity press: Any press that you pay to have your book published.

Warranty: It's your word that you are who you say you are, that you have written the work, and that everything you say in it is correct.

Widow: The last line of a paragraph left alone at the top of a page.

Work-for-hire: If someone pays you to write something, and it is agreed that you are writing it for them and without any further claim on the work, then that is a "work-for-hire" situation. It's like selling a car—it's no longer yours. The publisher will be the legal owner of the work. This is usually not the case with existing works and so this stipulation should not be agreed to on a completed project unless you've consulted with a lawyer.

Worldwide rights: The right to publish English-language versions of your book in all countries. This is not the same as translation rights. This means that the publisher has a branch in Canada and wants the option to print your book there, too.

APPENDIX B:
Books to Keep You Going

The following are books that are useful, inspiring, and worth keeping close by.

- *On Writing* by Stephen King. A wonderfully entertaining and informative look at one writer's journey.

- *Bird by Bird: Some Instructions on Writing and Life* by Anne Lamott. The classic meditation on the profession and life in general.

- *The Artist's Way: A Spiritual Path to Higher Creativity* [10th Anniversary Edition] by Julia Cameron. A great book that helps you shake up how you think about work and life.

- *Zen in the Art of Writing: Releasing the Creative Genius Within You* by Ray Bradbury. A wild series of essays that are wise ("You must stay drunk on writing so reality cannot destroy you") and inspirational in a way that only this master of science fiction can be.

- *Ernest Hemingway on Writing* edited by Larry Phillips. An interesting group of thoughts on work culled from Hemingway's writing and letters.

- *On Becoming a Novelist* by John Gardner. A seminal work about craft and morality.

- *The Faith of a Writer: Life, Craft, Art* by Joyce Carol Oates. An inspirational guide by a modern master of craft.

- *The Spooky Art: Some Thoughts on Writing* by Norman Mailer. A practical look at the life and business by one of the most memorable writers in history.

- *Mortification: Writers' Stories of Their Public Shame* edited by Robin Robertson. Funny, endearing, and somehow comforting, this collection of essays written by a wide variety of writers including Margaret Atwood, Billy Collins, Patrick McCabe, and Rick Moody will not only give you great insight into the business, but also the humanity (and humility) one needs to succeed.

INDEX